PENGUIN BOOKS

FOR CRYING OUT LOUD!

For Crying Out Loud!

The World According to Clarkson
Volume Three

JEREMY CLARKSON

PENGUIN BOOKS

PENGUIN BOOKS

Published by the Penguin Group
Penguin Books Ltd, 80 Strand, London WC2R ORL, England
Penguin Group (USA) Inc., 375 Hudson Street, New York, New York 10014, USA
Penguin Group (Canada), 90 Eglinton Avenue East, Suite 700, Toronto, Ontario, Canada M4P 2Y3
(a division of Pearson Penguin Canada Inc.)
Penguin Ireland, 25 St Stephen's Green, Dublin 2, Ireland (a division of Penguin Books Ltd)
Penguin Group (Australia), 250 Camberwell Road, Camberwell, Victoria 3124, Australia
(a division of Pearson Australia Group Pty Ltd)
Penguin Books India Pvt Ltd, 11 Community Centre,
Panchsheel Park, New Delhi – 110 017, India
Penguin Group (NZ), 67 Apollo Drive, Rosedale, North Shore 0632, New Zealand
(a division of Pearson New Zealand Ltd)
Penguin Books (South Africa) (Pty) Ltd, 24 Sturdee Avenue,
Rosebank, Johannesburg 2196, South Africa

Penguin Books Ltd, Registered Offices: 80 Strand, London WC2R ORL, England

www.penguin.com

First published by Michael Joseph 2008
Published in Penguin Books 2009
7

Copyright © Jeremy Clarkson, 2008
All rights reserved

The moral right of the author has been asserted

Typeset by Rowland Phototypesetting Ltd, Bury St Edmunds, Suffolk
Printed in England by Clays Ltd, St Ives plc

ISBN: 978-0-141-03812-4

www.greenpenguin.co.uk

Mixed Sources
Product group from well-managed
forests and other controlled sources
www.fsc.org Cert no. SA-COC 1592
© 1996 Forest Stewardship Council

Penguin Books is committed to a sustainable future
for our business, our readers and our planet.
The book in your hands is made from paper
certified by the Forest Stewardship Council.

This is dedicated with gratitude to the Green Movement, the Americans and the Health and Safety Executive for giving me so much to write about.

The contents of this book first appeared in Jeremy Clarkson's *Sunday Times* column. Read more about the world according to Clarkson every week in the *Sunday Times*

Contents

Mother knows all the best games

Can we be honest for a moment. You didn't have a good Christmas, did you? Your turkey was too dry, your kids spent all day glued to their internets, and you didn't bother watching the Big Christmas Film because you've owned it for years on DVD.

What you should have had to liven things up was my mother. She arrived at my house with a steely resolve that the Christmas holidays would be exactly like the Christmas holidays she enjoyed when she was a child. Only without the diphtheria or the bombing raids.

My mother does not like American television shows because she 'can't understand what they're on about'. She doesn't like PlayStations either because they rot your brain. And she really doesn't like internets because they never work.

What she likes are parlour games. And so, because you don't argue with my mother, that's what we played.

The kids, initially, were alarmed. They think anything that doesn't run on electricity is sinister and a little bit frightening.

So the idea of standing up in front of the family and acting out a book or a film erred somewhere between pointlessness and witchcraft.

Strangely, however, they seemed to like it. Mind you, playing with a seven-year-old is hard, since everything she acted out had six words and involved a lot of scampering up and down the dining room, on all fours, barking. Usually, the answer was that famously dog-free movie with four words in the title, *Pirates of the Caribbean*.

My mother, on the other hand, could only act out books and films from the 1940s, but this didn't seem to curb the kids' massive enthusiasm. They even want to watch *The Way to the Stars* now, on the basis my mother made it sound like Vice City.

I loathe charades but even when I tried to bring a halt to proceedings by doing *The Beastly Beatitudes of Balthazar B*, they cheered me on with roars of encouragement. Other books I used to try to ruin the day were *Versailles: the View from Sweden*, which is nearly impossible to act out and even harder to guess. And when that failed, Frank McLynn's completely uncharadable *1759*.

Eventually, with my mother still chuntering on about Trevor Howard's impeccable and unAmerican diction, and the seven-year-old still under the table barking, and me trying to act out *If*, mercifully, we decided to play something else.

Not Monopoly. Dear God in heaven. Please spare me from that. I'm due in Norway on Thursday and if we break out the world's most boring board game, I'd still be cruising down the Angel Islington in my ship. Happily, it turned out that in my mother's world Monopoly is far too modern and that in her day you made your own entertainment.

So out came the pens and paper. I can't be bothered to explain the rules of the game she chose, but in essence you have to think of countries, or girls' names or things you find in space that begin with a certain letter. It sounds terrible compared with watching *The Simpsons* or shooting an LA prostitute in the face, but you know what, the kids loved this even more than charades.

The seven-year-old was so keen she developed a sudden and hitherto unnoticed ability to write. I'm not kidding. We pay £5 million a term to have someone teach her. She has a nanny. And we spend endless hours trying to get her nose out of *Pirates of the Caribbean* and into a book, but to no avail. She has never, once, written anything down that could pass for a word.

But that day she wrote until her pen ran dry, and wailed like a banshee when it was time for bed.

With the kids tucked up, I did what any sane man would do and reached for the television remote. But my mother had other plans. So we put a tablecloth over the jigsaw she'd been doing and played cards.

What a buzz. It was a blizzard of smoke, wine, trumps and tension. There's no television show, no internet site and certainly no PlayStation game that provides you with the same thrill as sitting there, a bit drunk, in a room full of lies, with a fist full of rubbish. A game of cards, it seems to me, provides everything you could possibly want out of life. It's as exciting as any drama and as convivial as any dinner party. It's also fun, free, environmentally friendly and something you can do as a family.

What's more, having discovered that my seven-year-old can write, I also discovered the next day during a game of Blob! that she can perform complicated mental arithmetic. She's claimed for 12 straight months that she can't count but she can sure as hell count cards. I swear to God that in the three days of Christmas she learnt more than in the last three years of school.

There's more, too, because I also swear to God that we had more fun as a family than could have been possible if we'd powered up the Roboraptor and turned on our internets.

So, today, while you are stabbing away at buttons on your PlayStation, wondering why you keep being kicked to death, or watching a film that you've seen a million times before, only without advertisements, might I suggest you flip the trip switch on your fuse box, light a fire and break out the playing cards, the pens and the paper.

Just avoid the charades.

Because that's just nature's way of explaining why you never made it as an actor.

Sunday 1 January 2006

On your marks for a village Olympics

While watching the absolutely breathtaking New Year's Eve firework display in London I finally formed an opinion on the question of Britain hosting the Olympic Games.

I should explain at the outset that I don't much like athletics. Running is fine when you are late for a train, or when you are nine, but the concept of running in a circle for nothing but glory seems a bit medieval if you ask me.

Speaking of which, the javelin. In the olden days when men ate bison and Mr Smith had not yet met Mr Wesson, I should imagine that a chap with an ability to chuck a spear over a great distance would end up with many wives. But now, I don't really get off on watching a gigantic Pole lobbing a stick.

It's the same with the hammer. When some enormous Uzbek hurls it into row G of the stadium's upper circle, do we think he is the best hammer thrower in the world? Or the best hammer thrower among those who've dedicated the past four years of their lives to throwing hammers? With the best will in the world, that's not a terribly big accolade.

No matter. The Olympic Games are like Richard and Judy. Whether you like them or not, they exist and they are popular. The question that's been vexing me these past few months is whether I should be pleased they're coming to London.

I think Lord Sir Pope Archbishop Earl Duke King Seb Coe should be richly rewarded for having secured a British win. He was employed to beat the French and by wearing a beige suit and talking about multi-ethnicity he did just that. Good on him.

Now, though, the staging of the event will be handed over to those who built the dome, run the National Health Service, operate Britain's asylum system, manage the roads, set up the Child Support Agency, invaded Iraq, guard Britain's European Union rebate and protect the nation's foxes.

So if we spool forward to the summer of 2012, to the opening ceremony of the London Games, what are we likely to find? A perfect ethnic blend of London school-children prancing about in the nearly finished stadium wearing hard hats and protective goggles lest they are exposed in some way to the Olympic flame. But no swimming pool because health and safety thought it was a 'drowning hazard'.

That's then, though. What's worrying me most of all are the next six years as we struggle under the global spotlight to get the infrastructure built.

To me, good design and cost are the only consider-ations. But I'm not in charge, health and safety will be. And they're going to spend every waking moment fight-ing with those who want all the seating to face east, to keep the Muslims happy, those who have found a rare slug in Newham and would prefer the village to be built elsewhere and those who want all the electricity to come from the wind and the waves, because of global bloody warming.

All Olympic Games since Los Angeles in 1984 have either made a profit or broken even. But I bet Britain shatters that record. Because unlike the Americans and the Australians, and especially the Greeks, we're obsessed with save the whale, feed the poor, green ideology. And we've got it into our heads that even on a construction site no one need ever be injured.

And if people are prepared to waste our money on hi-vi jackets and organic prayer mats, then think how much they'll be prepared to waste quenching the greed of those who live and work on the proposed site.

Already I've heard businessmen say the compensation they're being offered to move their hopeless company somewhere else is nowhere near enough. They can smell the money and know that all that stands between them and a retirement home in Spain is a bunch of woolly-headed liberals who couldn't balance the books at a village tombola.

So, what's to be done to avoid this cataclysmically expensive fiasco? Well, we could hand the whole job over to the French. Or the army. But since, on balance, I want the Olympics to come here, how's this for a plan? We take the Olympics back to its roots and host the whole thing at my kids' school. No, really, I was walking across the playing fields the other day and found myself wondering what more the Olympic bods might need.

At the annual school sports day they can simultaneously stage six sprint races, four games of hockey and several swimming events in the full-sized pool. There's even a nearby river for Matthew Pinsent. Work needed to make this an Olympic venue would involve nothing more than an enlargement of the long-jump sandpits. And I know a local builder who could do that, with no danger to his workforce, and no impact on global warming, for about £250.

I'm not really kidding here. If you log onto Google Earth, you will find that despite the best efforts of John Prescott to build houses on every school sports pitch in the land, the south-east of England is still littered with a mass of sports facilities. There are enough swimming pools in Surrey alone to keep Mark Spitz going for 40 years.

This, then, is my vision: not to host the safest, least offensive, most globally cooling Games of all time. But the smallest. And then we could spend the savings we make – about £5 billion – on the most important part of the Olympic ceremony. The fireworks.

Sunday 8 January 2006

We're all going on a celebrity holiday

We learnt last weekend that the government in Sardinia is planning to impose punishing wealth taxes on billionaire visitors who come to the island in their enormous gin palaces or their onyx aeroplanes. I'm sure this went down well with those of a *Guardian* disposition.

In essence, those whose boats are more than a mile long will be hit where it hurts most, in the wallet. And second homes within 200 yards of the coast will attract a special council tax that will cause the owners to go cross-eyed.

And the excitement doesn't stop there because, get this, the leader of the government, Robino Di Hood, says the money raised – and it could be £550 million a year – will be spent on baby foxes and mending the ozone layer.

Of course, delicious though the scheme might sound in eco-socialist circles, I doubt very much the super-rich will pay up. Sardinia is a pretty little place for sure, but there are many other pretty little places they can go to instead. So they will. And losing them will kill Sardinia off as a tourist destination more quickly than news of some poorly chickens.

Let me explain. A friend of mine returned recently from a break in Jamaica. 'So how was it?' I asked, expecting to hear about the food, the hotel, the beach and how many times he'd had his arms cut off by crack-fuelled Yardies.

But no. Instead he told me he'd seen Helen Fielding, Laura Bush and the entire Eastwood family – with the disappointing exception of grandaddy Clint.

This is now how we judge holiday locations. Not on what we see, but on who we see.

And on that basis, Reykjavik knocks Jamaica into a cocked hat because last year, on a family holiday in the land of fire and ice, I trumped Helen Fielding and Laura Bush with Dame Kiri Tiki NikiWara and then trumped the Eastwood family by seeing Clint himself, checking in while I was checking out.

News of this enthused another friend so much that he went to Iceland for a winter holiday and returned to say that yes, the nightlife was very jolly and the volcanoes very active, but that the highlight had been sharing a ride in the hotel's lift with Quentin Tarantino.

This is what always made Sardinia such a tempting destination. Forget the emerald waters or sandy beaches. It was the chance you might catch a glimpse of Princess Caroline and Roman Abramovich raving it up in one of the Aga Khan's bars.

That's why Sardinia has always been better than Corsica. Yes, the French island is more visually stunning than its Italian neighbour, and historically way more interesting as well. But it has always been let down by the quality of the celebs.

On numerous holidays there, the only people I've ever clocked are Zoe Ball, Mick Hucknall and Jeremy Paxman.

Mind you, that's better than Dubai. On my last visit I found myself sharing a hotel with Chris Tarrant, Grant Bovey and Anthea Turner. It was like being stuck in a warm and fuzzy ITV daytime chat show. All I needed to complete the saccharine picture of harmlessness and syrup was television's Richard Hammond.

Barbados is a fine case study here. It's one of the most populated countries on earth, the terrain is fairly non-mountainous and many people with tattoos holiday in the south. So why go? Well, obviously, there are direct flights and many fine restaurants, but it's who you see in those restaurants that empties Cheshire so comprehensively.

At somewhere like the Cliff, it's possible to spot Gary Lineker, Laurence Llewelyn-Bowen and Ulrika Jonsson on the same night. That's a triumvirate to make anyone's holiday complete. Think about it: confirmation that your taste in food and islands coincides perfectly with the doyens of football, home improvement and er, being Swedish.

And I'm not being snobbish either. I know plenty of cool and trendy media people who go on holiday to Tuscany every year in the desperate hope that while they're shopping in San Gimignano for some fair-trade, organic pesto-flavoured, nuclear-free South African peace crisps, they might bump into John Mortimer.

The celeb syndrome now affects pretty well everyone and pretty well every lifestyle choice we make.

I mean, are you going to spend £1,100 on the egg-yellow alligator-skin diary featured in last week's Style supplement? Not likely. Unless of course Gwyneth Paltrow is papped with one while out shopping. Then you'll happily trade your children's health to get one.

It's why people will wait 200 years for a table in the Ivy. It's why people are salivating at the prospect of sending their children to Marlborough. A fine school, of course, made so much finer these days by the attendance of Eugenie York.

It's why the village of Barnsley in Gloucestershire has become so expensive. Yes, it sounds a bit whippetish for sure, but having Kirsty Young, the Five newsreader, as a regular in the local pub makes you out to be a player.

If, however, you find all this too ghastly and you'd rather eat your own nose than share a holiday hotel with Jade Goody and Nick Knowles, then don't despair.

Try Sardinia. Because, if this tax plan comes to fruition, it'll be full of no one at all.

Sunday 15 January 2006

The worst word in the language

Wog. Spastic. Queer. Nigger. Dwarf. Cripple. Fatty. Gimp. Paki. Mick. Mong. Poof. Coon. Gyppo. You can't really use these words any more and yet, strangely, it is perfectly acceptable for those in the travel and hotel industries to pepper their conversation with the word beverage.

There are several twee and unnecessary words in the English language. Tasty. Meal. Cuisine. Nourishing. And the biblically awful 'gift'. I also have a biological aversion to the use of 'home' instead of 'house'. So if you were to ask me round to 'your home for a nourishing bowl of pasta' I would almost certainly be sick on you.

But the worst word. The worst noise. The screech of Flo-Jo's fingernails down the biggest blackboard in the world, the squeak of polystyrene on polystyrene, the cry of a baby when you're hung-over, is 'beverage'.

Apparently, they used to have 'bever' days at Eton when extra beer was brought in for the boys. And this almost certainly comes from some obscure Latin expression that only Boris Johnson would understand.

Therein lies the problem. People who work on planes and in hotels have got it into their heads that the word beverage, with its Eton and Latin overtones, is somehow posh and therefore the right word to use when addressing a customer.

Now look. The customer in question is almost certainly a businessman, and the sort of businessmen who take scheduled planes around Europe and stay in business hotels are fairly low down the pecking order. You think they turn their phones on the instant the plane has landed because the Tokyo stock exchange is struggling to manage without them. No. The reason they turn them on so damn fast is to find out if they've been sacked.

Honestly, you don't need to treat them like you're on the set of *Upstairs Downstairs*. They do not spend their afternoons cutting the crusts off cucumber sandwiches. And they do not say grace before dinner. They're called Steve and Dave and you know what they're doing on their laptops in the departure lounge? Organising a backward hedge merger with GEC? 'Fraid not. They're looking at some Hooters Swimsuit pictures from the internet.

For crying out loud, I'm middle class. I went to a school most people would call posh. But if I came home and said to my wife that I wanted a beverage, or asked her to pass the condiments, she'd punch me.

When I travel, I don't need to be treated like Hyacinth Bucket. I want you to understand I speak like you do and that I'll understand perfectly if you say there's a kettle in my room. You don't have to say there are 'tea- and coffee-making facilities'.

And please, can you stop saying 'at all' after every question. Can I take your coat at all? Would you care for lunch at all? Or, this week, on a flight back from Scandinavia, 'Another beverage for yourself at all, sir?' What's the matter with saying 'Another drink?' And what's with all the reflexive pronoun abuse?

I've written about this before but it's getting worse. Reflexive pronouns are used when the subject and the object of a sentence are the same person or thing. Like 'I dress myself'. You cannot therefore say 'please contact myself'. Because it makes you look like an imbecile.

If you send a letter to a client saying 'my team and me look forward to meeting with yourself next Wednesday', be prepared for some disappointment. Because if I were the client I'd come to your office all right. Then I'd stand on your desk and relieve myself.

I'm not a grammar freak − I can eat, shoot and then take it or leave it − but when someone says 'myself' instead of 'me' I find it more offensive than if they'd said 'spastic wog'.

Before embarking on a sentence, work out first of all what's the shortest way of saying it, not the longest. There seems to be a general sense that using more words than is strictly necessary is somehow polite. That's almost certainly why, on another flight the other day, I was offered some 'bread items'.

We see this most conspicuously in the catering industry, where I am regularly offered a 'choice of both Cheddar and Brie'. No, wait. I've forgotten the pointless adjectives. I should have said a 'choice of both flavoursome Cheddar and creamy Brie'.

'Are you ready to order at all, yourself, sir?' 'Yes, I'll have the hearty winter-warming soup and the nourishing bowl of pasta, topped with the delicious dew-picked tomatoes, thanks. And to follow, if yourself can manage it, a plate of gag-inducing, nostril-assaulting, bacteria-laced Stilton.'

It's all rubbish. Why is a bowl of pasta more appealing than a plate of pasta? And why not simply say pasta? Because don't worry, I'll presume it'll come on some form of crockery, in the same way that I'll presume, if you put a kettle in my room, that you might have put some coffee granules in there as well.

I'll leave you with the best example I know of this nonsense. It was a rack of papers in a hotel foyer over which there was a sign: 'Newspapers for your reading pleasure'.

All they had left was the *Guardian*. So it wasn't even technically correct.

Sunday 22 January 2006

McEton, a clever English franchise

Following Tony Blair's attempts to rebrand the entire nation, we're now told that London is no longer home to the Queen, some beefeaters and 10,000 chatty cabbies who know where they're going. It is instead a vibrant multicultural city where you can hear 600 different languages on even the shortest trip to the shops.

Talk like this, we're told, is what won Britain the Olympics but, that aside, I find myself wondering what it will do for the country's balance of payments.

Tourists do not come here for our weather, or the quality of our provincial cooking. Nor are they attracted by the exceptional value of our hotels, or our beaches, or Birmingham. I've never met an American or a Japanese person who has said: 'I want to come to Britain so I can buy an Arabic newspaper from a Bengali store where the cashier speaks Polish.'

What most foreigners like about Britain is not multiculturalism or tolerance or any of that new Labour nonsense. No, what they like is our history. Shakespeare. Blenheim Palace. Soldiers in preposterous hats who don't move. Yes, they may go and see some dead dogs in a modern art gallery but that's only because they've spent the morning on the top of a sightseeing bus and they're freezing.

Do they, for instance, go back home with baseball

caps worn by modern British policemen? Or a plastic incarnation of the traditional *Dixon of Dock Green* helmet? Which gets more visitors: Anne Hathaway's cottage or Benjamin Zephaniah's birthplace?

Then there's British Airways. When the staff wore blazers and the planes were finished in grey and royal blue, captains were beating foreigners off the ramp with big sticks. When they went all ethnic with those jazzy tailfins, the whole thing went tits up.

Any British business is well advised to use pomp, tradition, tea and history in all global marketing campaigns. So we arrive neatly at the doors of a British institution that is steeped in nothing but history and tradition. Our public schools.

There are those, of an Islington persuasion, who think they are nothing more than a hotbed of outdated values, cruelty, inequality, drugs, bullying and buggery. Not so. When I was at Repton in the 1970s we did not wear tails and we hardly ever set fire to anyone. In fact, my house looked a bit like London today. There were kids from Iran, Japan, Trinidad and even Ethiopia.

Sent by parents who wanted them to have a traditional British education, most had only a rudimentary grasp of English. And yet there they were, going through the complications of puberty, thousands of miles from home, unable to communicate with teachers, matrons or even the woman in the village shop.

I felt rather sorry for them – not so sorry that I didn't steal all their biscuits, obviously – but I did feel that the downside of being sent so far away for an education far outweighed the perceived upside, that is, that you could go back to Ethiopia knowing the Latin for 'What ho'.

Now, though, Repton has come up with a brilliant idea. They've moved the mountain to Muhammad. They're keeping the old place in Derbyshire to cater for the children of Cheshire businessmen, and they're opening a sister school in Dubai.

As a money-spinning venture this is up there with the iPod. I mean, Dubai is full of Indians who will understand cricket, and Arabs who have the funds to make the desert green. It's also full of expats who'll thank God they don't have to pay the fees and 12 airfares every year. A big-name British public school in the Middle East. It's a stroke of genius. And not just for local parents but also for Britain's trade deficit.

Imagine how well Eton would go down in Los Angeles, or Harrow in Tokyo. Imagine the earning potential these schools would have; offer to put little American kids in bowlers, boaters and busbies and parents would be queueing round the block to have little Hank thrown by a mortar-boarded master into a chilly swimming pool.

Of course, in America you'd have to change the word for fagging, and in Japan I can see some complications with the traditional Remembrance Day service.

In fact, to make it really work you'd have to study the history of Harry Ramsden's. A traditional fish and chip shop, near Leeds, it was bought and then floated on the stock exchange by a former boss at KFC who wanted to make it a national dining experience. And all he needed for that was the brand. So the beef dripping in which the chips were cooked was replaced with blended vegetable oil, and the harbour-fresh fish with frozen fillets.

Now there are 170 Harry Ramsden's and I don't see why there shouldn't be 170 Etons. And before you wonder where they're going to find enough quality British staff to run a global business this big, may I point you in the direction of the Excalibur hotel in Las Vegas. Billed as a medieval hotel with turrets and legend it is, of course, just a big plastic skyscraper full of American bell-boys in *Little Lord Fauntleroy* shorts. Horrid? Absolutely, but the place is always packed.

Repton has shown the way. But if Eton were to pick up on the idea and open a chain of, say, Eton Harry Potter Experiences, it would earn Britain more than Lloyd's of London and Mrs Queen put together.

Sunday 29 January 2006

Rock school sees off drone school

William Shakespeare has probably done more to damage the cultural worth of Britain than anyone else in the whole of human history. After endlessly having to study his plays on the school curriculum, generations of children have ventured into adulthood convinced that all literature is coma-inducingly dreary. I don't blame them. Portia's speech about the 'gentle rain' is in no way as stimulating as 10 minutes on Grand Theft Auto.

I believe that Shakespeare, along with Milton, Donne and Chaucer, has a place in modern Britain. And that place is deep in the bowels of the British Library, where he can be studied by hardcore language students.

Right now, my 11-year-old daughter has a voracious appetite for books. She devours Jacqueline Wilson and reads *The No. 1 Ladies' Detective Agency* endlessly. But I can guarantee this craving will be snuffed out the moment she's introduced to *Twelfth Night*.

There's a lot of political posturing about the future of education right now, all of which seems to miss the point: that at school, children should be encouraged to study books that make reading fun.

And it's the same story with religion. Because I was forced into chapel every Sunday, and made to read the Bible, which is even more excruciating than *Paradise Lost*, I emerged from the chrysalis of puberty filled with a sometimes overwhelming desire to set fire to the Arch-bishop of Canterbury.

But music is my biggest bugbear. You see, I have no regrets about being a literary dunderhead and an atheist, but I have huge sadness that I can play the piano, but only in the same way that a dog can tie shoelaces.

There's a photographer I know. He's Welsh and drunk most of the time, but once, in the foyer of the Hotel Nacional in Havana, he sat down and played, with both hands and all the twiddly bits, some Billy Joel songs.

I couldn't believe it. This miserable Welshman had a hitherto unseen ability to bring hope and happiness to that bleak and hopeless place; he had the skill to bring them the sounds of America, the sounds of freedom. And he'd chosen to assault them with Billy bloody Joel. The bastardo.

But the women loved it. In fact, there's nothing more a woman likes than a man who can play a musical instru-ment. If you can bash out a double-handed rendition of 'O Little Town of Bethlehem' you are virtually indis-tinguishable in the eyes of womankind to Jon Bon Jovi. As a result, my Welsh friend spent most of that night being ridden round his bedroom by a Cuban teenager in a cowboy hat.

But at school they never say, 'Listen, boy, if you can master *Air on a G String*, you'll spend your entire adult life removing Angelina Jolie's.' And even if they did, you'd still struggle because the ditties they make you learn are so turgid.

The acoustic equivalent of a Shakespearean sonnet. Musical Chaucer.

So why are children not given that week's chart hits to learn? This is music they can identify with more readily than 'The Happy Farmer' or something written by a precocious Russian when he was five, 200 years ago.

If you give a child an Airfix model of a kitchen table, he won't enjoy the finished result. If, on the other hand, you give him a model of HMS *Hood*, he will.

And then he'll want to move on to bigger and better things.

When I was 10, I was made to learn songs that sounded awful on the first pass and even worse when I'd mastered them. And I can't help wondering how much more fun it would all have been if I'd spent my music lessons making siren noises while playing 'Blockbuster' by Sweet.

Had this happened, I would have progressed through T Rex, through Genesis and on to Billy Joel. And then it would have been me being ridden round the hotel in Cuba.

Of course, a lot of modern songs are riddled with sharps and flats, which make them hard for a child to grasp, but mostly it would take even the most half-witted music teacher only five minutes to convert them so you only need hit the white notes.

Take 'Ode to Joy' as an example. In my music book there's an F sharp which, from memory, means it's in G major. But in my daughter's music book, it's in C major so there are no sharps or flats at all. It's therefore easier to learn, easier to play and sounds exactly the same.

Except, of course, she has no interest in Beethoven. She wants to play 'Clocks' by Coldplay and 'Behind Blue Eyes' by the Who. She wants to end up with HMS *Hood*, not a kitchen table.

And without wishing to be selfish, as a parent, so do I. Trying to force our children to do their piano practice is like trying to force a gorilla into a dinner jacket. They have no stomach for it, and frankly neither do I, because in even a fairly large house there's no hiding place from the cacophony when they begin.

The insistence of a road drill when you're hung-over is a bad sound, but it's preferable to the noise of a nine-year-old learning a song that wouldn't be any good even if it were played properly.

I therefore have an idea. Can someone, please, bring out a song book called *Tunes Your Dad Likes in C Major*? And can Ruth Kelly stop worrying about grammar schools and put it on the curriculum?

Sunday 5 February 2006

Flogging absolute rubbish is a gift

I didn't have much to do last Thursday so I went on a day trip to St Nazaire to look at the Second World War U-boat pens.

Ooh they're big. And clever. Above the roof there's a corrugated concrete awning designed to break up bombs before they hit the structure itself, and channel the blast horizontally away from the precious submarines.

This system could even repel the blast from an RAF Tallboy. When dropped from 20,000 feet these supersonic 5-ton bombs could displace a million cubic feet of earth, creating a crater 80 feet deep and 100 feet across.

And yet when one hit the roof of the St Nazaire sub pens all anyone inside heard was no louder than the discreet cough of an embarrassed butler.

Later the Americans peppered the roof with battleship shells dropped from B-17s.

But that didn't work either. In fact, at the end of the war the only thing left standing in St Nazaire was the target.

They're still there today and you'd expect, as I did, that inside Madame Tussaud's would have run amok, with lots of waxwork Germans toiling over wooden torpedoes and millions of schoolchildren on guided tours of a real U-boat. But no. All I found was lots of graffiti and, in one pen, half a dozen upended shopping trolleys.

Still, in another there was a gift shop which I assumed would be full of Airfix U-boat kits, copies of *Das Boot*, an underwater oven glove perhaps, or maybe the very Enigma decoding machine captured by Jon Bon Jovi.

But no. All they had in the window was several trolls in traditional Breton costume – which was in no way relevant, since St Nazaire is not actually in Brittany – while inside there were plates made into clocks, lighthouses made into table lamps, place mats featuring scenes of France I wasn't in, and most incongruously of all a rack of T-shirts bearing the slogan 'Leprechaun's Corner', which is a pub in Dublin.

It's almost as though the owners had deliberately stocked the shop with anything they could lay their hands on just so long as it had nothing to do with the war.

Which seems a bit daft since I'm willing to bet that no one has ever said, 'I fancy a Breton troll for my mantelpiece so I'll go to those U-boat pens in St Nazaire to see if there's a gift shop there which can help.'

This would be like going to Windsor Castle to buy a holographic keyring of the Grand Canyon. But that said, I'm constantly amazed at the inability of gift shop proprietors in the world's tourist hot spots to sell anything that anyone might remotely want to buy.

There's always a glass dolphin, perfectly crafted, with the name of the place you're in stencilled onto the base. Now if there was just one on the shelves and if it was a bit rough and ready, then yes, you might be fooled into thinking it had been made, by hand, in a cave, by a local man in traditional national costume.

But since you're in an airport terminal and there are

2,000 of them in there, and they're all the same, and they say 'Made in China' on the bottom, and you saw exactly the same thing in San Francisco last year, only with 'California' etched onto the base, then you're not going to be fooled.

Scandinavian gift shops are big on selling smoked salmon so you can go home with a taste of the north. But they are sold pre-sliced in hermetically sealed bags, and you just know that no wizened old trawlerman has access to the sort of packaging machine which can do this. If you want industrialised smoked salmon in a plastic bag, you'll wait till you get home and call Jethro Tull.

Another gift shop favourite is the intricate 4-foot galleon, complete with real canvas sails, half a mile of cotton rigging and cocktail-stick delicate masts.

Great. But how are you supposed to get something like that home?

If you're setting up a gift shop for tourists here's a hint. Sell stuff that airport baggage handlers can't break. And more importantly, ensure that your stock reflects your surroundings in some way. Accept that visitors to a Second World War submarine pen are not necessarily going to want an Eiffel Tower snow shaker.

Well, I did, but that's because at home I have what I call the 'Cupboard of Shit'.

It's a glass-front Georgian cabinet in which I keep all of the useless rubbish I've found in gift shops over the years. Pride of place goes to a foot-long alabaster model of the Last Supper in which all the disciples are wearing different-coloured glitter capes.

But then I'm also proud of my Chinese-made plastic

New York fireman figurine, complete with a moustache and a wounded mate on his shoulder. Movingly, this exquisite piece is called 'Red Hats of Courage'.

I understand, of course, that the townspeople of St Nazaire might not want to cash in on the horrors of the U-boat war, or the British commando raid that wrecked the port in 1942, or the American landings there in 1917, or the loss in the Loire estuary of the troopship *Lancastria* and 4,000 souls in 1940.

I suppose we should respect them for that. But something relevant would have been nice. A model, perhaps, of a crowd of people in stripy jumpers with their hands held high, eating cheese.

Sunday 12 February 2006

My kingdom for a horse hitman

If a newspaper columnist wants to live an easy life, then it's sensible to steer clear of certain issues. Laying into Jesus is right out. And it's probably not a good idea to say the poor should have their shoes confiscated. But the greatest taboo – the biggest landmine of the lot – is the touchy subject of horses.

I once wrote a column suggesting that nobody should be allowed to keep a pet unless their garden is big enough to exercise it. Under no circumstances, I argued, should you be allowed to put your animal in a lorry and drive it on the public road at 4 mph.

This went down badly. It turned out that there are 3 million horsists in Britain and each one of them wrote to me, hoping that I would die soon. So I made a mental note to skirt round equine issues in future.

Sadly, though, there are now 3 million and one horsists in Britain because my wife has just bought a brace of the damn things. I don't know how much they cost but since they were imported from Iceland, I'm guessing it was quite a lot.

Not as much, however, as they're now costing the National Health Service. The first to fall off was my nine-year-old son. He'd seen his sister trotting round the paddock and, being a boy, figured he could do it too.

Sadly, I wasn't around to stop him so I've only heard from the ambulancemen what happened exactly.

The next casualty was our nanny, who disproved the theory that when you fall off a horse you should get straight back on again. Because having done that she promptly fell off a second time. We had to mash her food for a while but she's better now.

So what about my wife? Well, as I write she's skiing in Davos.

Except she's not because 24 hours before she was due to go she came off the nag, spraining her wrist and turning one of her legs into something the size, shape and texture of a baobab tree. So actually she's in Davos, drinking.

Apparently, the accident was quite spectacular. On a quiet road, just outside David Cameron's house incidentally, she took the tumble with such force that she was incapable of moving. And had to ring the nanny who, as a result of her fall, could only limp to the scene of the accident.

Needless to say, the horse, with its walnut-sized brain, had been spooked by the incident and had run off. Neither of the girls was in a fit state to catch it, which meant a ton of (very expensive) muscle was gallivanting around the road network, as deadly and as unpredictable as a leather-backed Scud missile.

After it was returned by a sympathetic neighbour, I offered to get a gun and put the bloody thing out of my misery. But no. The accident was not the horse's fault, apparently. And nor will my wife take the blame, because she's been riding since she was an embryo and hunting since foetus-hood.

What happened was that the horse skidded on the tarmac. I see. An Icelandic horse, capable of maintaining significant speed over lava fields and sheet ice, couldn't stay upright on asphalt. Of course. Stands to reason.

So now all the female members of the Clarkson household are busy joining internet campaigns to get every road in the land resurfaced with special horse-grip tarmac.

This, it seems to me, is the problem with horse ownership. You can't have one half-heartedly. Every morning you must go and clear its crap from the stables, and then you must spend the afternoon combing it and plaiting its tail and feeding it tasty apples. And then each night, as you get into bed, each bruise and aching joint serves as a painful reminder of that day's accident. Horses take over your life as completely as paralysis. You can think of nothing else.

And this gives the horse fraternity a sense that the whole world revolves around their pets too. That's why the hunting crowd are so vociferous.

Because for them it's not a pastime. It's an all-consuming life. And it's why my wife wants all roads resurfaced.

More than that, she comes back every day white with apoplexy with something a 'motorist' has just done. Not slowing down. Not moving over enough. Not coming by. Not turning the radio down. This from a woman who refuses to drive any car with less than 350 brake horsepower.

Of course, we're told often and loudly that roads were originally intended for horses, and that's true.

In the same way that the royal family was originally

intended to govern. But times move on. The horse was replaced by the car and became a toy. And now it should be allowed on the roads, in the same way that the Queen is allowed into parliament. Briefly, and by invitation only.

I've always said that if a boy comes to take my daughters out on a motorbike I shall drop a match in the petrol tank. And that if he buys another I shall do it again. But in the past month I've learnt that four legs are infinitely more dangerous than two wheels. So if he turns up on a horse I shall shoot him, and it.

In the meantime I have to content myself with the behaviour of my donkeys. All they do, all day, is run up to their new, bigger field-mates and kick them.

Sunday 19 February 2006

Where all the TV viewers went

You probably haven't seen Davina McCall's new chat show, which airs at prime time on BBC1. And that's a pity because I think it's rather good.

Throughout television history most chat-show hosts have been men. And this is a problem because men feel duty-bound to compete.

If the guest fires a .22 joke into the ether, a chap has to come back with something heavier and better. Male conversation is gladiatorial, argumentative, spiky and designed most of all to be funny.

I asked the editor of GQ magazine last weekend if he liked my new jacket. 'No,' he replied in a frenzied high-pitched squeak. 'It makes you look like a ★★★★.' Can you imagine a woman saying that?

As a result, modern, zingy chat shows hosted by men tend to be all about the host.

It's their duty to compensate for the dull guests and spar with the good ones. The only man who doesn't do this is Michael Parkinson. Which is probably why he's been around since 1912.

Davina doesn't compete either. And because she doesn't play the big 'I am' we learnt a lot about her guest last week: Martin Shaw. And what we learnt most of all is that he's rather dull. Some of his answers were so boring, in fact, that my children, with a great deal of harrumphing, got up and left the room. And this brings me to the point of my column this morning.

When I was a child I did my homework and then watched television until it was time for bed. You may say, 'Aha, but television was so much better back then', but trust me on this, it wasn't. It was grainy, lumpen, dull, black, white, infantile and all anyone could ever win was a pencil.

Even so, when I first started to appear on television in the early 1990s, people were still watching in huge numbers. I once made a rather porridgy show for BBC2 that attracted 7 million viewers. Nowadays you could only do that if you screened Angelina Jolie having lesbian sex with that new weathergirl on ITV.

Television viewing figures are in freefall. Morecambe and Wise used to pull in 25 million viewers. Now a show is judged to be a ratings success if it gets five or six. And it's not that people are watching stuff from way down the satellite listings. The figures show they're not watching at all. So what are they doing instead?

Well, we know a lot of women are in chat rooms starting affairs with old schoolfriends, and a lot of men are on MSN pretending to be 12-year-old schoolgirls.

I also know a lot are on eBay because I recently dumped a load of household waste into the online auction house and there was a global frenzy to snap up the lot. Next week I'm selling one of my bogeys and I bet I get a quid for it.

Then you have podcasts. Just last week I read about an anonymous woman called Faceless who makes a daily broadcast over the internet, telling her fans via a voice scrambler what she's been up to. I've listened and, in a nutshell, it's nothing.

She gets up, tries not to eat too much, has boyfriend problems, and says 'like' a lot. And people are downloading this rubbish. There are others who go out on the streets to make their own shows using the cameras on their mobile phones. Mostly, this involves punching anyone they come across and pushing complete strangers off their bicycles.

One of the issues that my children have with normal terrestrial television is that they can't watch what they want, when they want to watch it. 'What do you mean *Doctor Who* is on Saturday at seven? I want to watch it now.'

So off they toddle to bid for bogeys and make happy-slapping movies with each other on my phone. My youngest said the other day she 'hates' the BBC. Because so far as she's concerned, it's just 'people talking'.

I know this frightens the living daylights out of television people. They worry that they are playing gramophone records in a digital world, that they're wearing a Jane Austen-style bonnet to a club. And they're scared stiff that all their fancy graphics and micro-soundbites can only delay their inevitable demise. But I'm not so sure.

It's said that soon we'll be able to watch shows on our mobile phones, but why would you want to do that? Why watch something that's cheaply made for a small audience on a 1-inch screen when you have David Attenborough on a 42-inch plasma at home? There's only one reason why you would.

Because you can.

Certainly, eBay is interesting only because it's new. When it's been around for a while, people will realise that they didn't buy Bill Oddie's used underpants because that's what they wanted. They bought them only because they could.

I can prove this. Last year, *Top Gear* was Britain's most downloaded television show. Which means there are thousands of people out there who'd rather fiddle about with their newfangled broadband connections than sit down and watch the damn thing on television. Or record it on Sky Plus.

That would suggest we're a nation of idiots. But since we're not, I think we're just going through a phase where pushing someone off a bicycle is more fun than watching television. It won't last. Davina will.

Sunday 26 February 2006

It takes immense skill to waste time

A report last week found that *The Very Hungry Caterpillar* is now the number one bedtime story for Britain's children. But the findings also revealed that one in three parents do not read anything at all to their kids at night.

Experts say this is because grown-ups are now far too busy earning money for their metered water and their speeding fines to have much left over for the cultural needs of their young.

I'm not so sure, because last week I sat next to a thirtysomething chap at the barber's who'd come inside, not for a haircut, but to have his hands manicured. He didn't appear to be homosexual.

In fact, because he talked at some length about his forthcoming family skiing holiday, we can presume he has young kids.

So what's his excuse for not reading them a bedtime story? 'Sorry, Octavia, there's no *Hungry Caterpillar* for you tonight because Daddy spent half the day having his fingernails oiled.'

How un-busy do you have to be to think, 'It's four in the afternoon on a Thursday, so I know: I'll pop to the hairdresser's and spend an hour or so having exotic creams rubbed into my thumbs'?

And it gets worse because on the barber's shelves there were a million badger-hair shaving brushes. Who buys them? How empty does your life need to be before you think, 'No, I won't use a disposable razor and some foam from a can. If I use a brush, and whip up some lather of my own, I can make this shaving malarkey last for hours'?

Later, in Jermyn Street, which for those of you in Arbroath is a street in London where you can buy tailored shirts and shoes made from the soft underbelly of a grey seal, I saw a prosperous-looking man in a baker's shop agonising over what sort of plumped-up, crusty, almond-infused loaf he should buy. Plainly, he wasn't on a tight schedule.

Then we have a friend of mine who flew all the way to Siena to buy a selection of silk contrada flags that were then used as a lining in his next bespoke suit.

Everywhere you look these days you see people paying a fortune to waste time. It's almost as though our lives are now so wealthy and so healthy that to inject a bit of worry and angst we trouble ourselves with the scent of the soap in the guest bedroom, or the breed of sheep from which our clothes are made.

There's a shop near my flat in London that sells nothing but hand-knitted super-soft golfing jumpers. What moron gave the owner a loan for that?

What did it say in the business plan, for heaven's sake? 'Yes. The rent is expensive in Notting Hill, but I believe there are enough people who will drive right across town, park, come into my shop, buy a £200 jumper and then go all the way home again.'

I would have told her to get lost. But someone didn't and because the shop is still there after six months I can only presume she was right. There are enough people out there who are prepared to devote an entire afternoon to buying a jumper.

It's not just London either. While perusing the Google Earth website the other day – it was more fun than reading the kids a bedtime story – I zoomed in on the house where I grew up. Now this is Doncaster. A town that we were told would wither and die when the mines closed.

I don't think so, because the spy in the sky reveals that the parkland at the bottom of the garden has been converted into an 18-hole golf course.

So even there, among the out-of-work miners, there are people who have so much spare time in their lives they will spend half of it playing what's essentially an expensive game of marbles. Doubtless in the £200 jumper they drove all the way to Notting Hill to buy.

There are now 2,500 golf courses in Britain covering half a million acres. That means golf takes up slightly less space in the nation than Carmarthenshire. And with 1.2 million registered players, is about seven times more popular.

And shooting. Way back when the Tories were in power the only people who blasted away at pheasants were the idle rich and the blue bloods. Not any more. Now, for four months of the year, every wood in the land is full of people stomping about in the rain.

Today there are so many people with so much spare time on their hands that 569,000 own a shotgun certificate. And their hobby is now such big business it has created 40,000 jobs.

Then you have people who spend their free time doing surveys. One lot last week said they'd watched 168 hours of prime-time television and that gay and lesbian people were only featured for 38 minutes. How can your lives be so empty that you think this is a worthwhile use of the most precious resource you have: time?

And what about the people who decided to find out why so many parents were not reading their children a bedtime story. And then came up with the wrong answer.

It has nothing to do with a lack of time, or a hectic schedule. And everything to do with the fact that *The Very Hungry Caterpillar* is the dullest and most stupid book in the history of literature.

Sunday 5 March 2006

An Oscar-winning village hall bash

So, you've read all about the post-Oscar parties that were held in Los Angeles last week and now you fancy bringing some of that glitz, glamour and sophistication to a bash of your own.

Well, happily, the internet and the gossip magazines are awash with ideas. Obviously, you won't be able to emulate Elton John, who for his do imported thousands of roses and adorned them all with hot-pink Swarovski crystals.

And nor will you have the clout of George Clooney, who peppered his party with people like Mick Jagger, Rachel Weisz and Madonna.

Still, there's plenty of advice on what music to play, what clothes to wear, what sort of linen to use and how best to stuff a sugar snap pea with cheese made from the breast milk of a mongoose. Frankly, though, if you want to throw a party, I have a much better idea . . .

A couple of weeks ago an old friend hired a village hall in the hellhole that is Surrey and booked a Led Zeppelin tribute band to come and play.

Did I want to go? Honestly? No. I'd rather have walked through Tehran in a Star of David T-shirt.

It got worse. Our party would be all male and if there's one thing I simply cannot abide it's single-sex gatherings. What's the point? The top five worst experiences of my life have all been stag nights. All that speedboat, snooker cue, business deal, BMW, golf, 'whoa, look at the tits on that' chest-beating nonsense.

Yes, the men in question would all be old friends, people I hadn't seen much since leaving London 10 years ago. But if you're going to play catch-up, why do it in a village hall while being assaulted by four blokes who think they're Led Zep? And get this, the tickets were £15. Exactly £5 more than I paid once to see the real Led Zep.

Still, I went, and it was fantastic, precisely because no one had tried to stuff sugar snap peas with cheese. It was just a group of middle-aged people in a room who, for one night only, could pretend they were 18 again.

It wasn't easy. For instance, when I was 18 I was very good at carrying up to eight pints from the bar to where my friends were sitting.

But I seem to have lost the knack. Three glasses had me so stumped I had to make two journeys. And when I was 18 I could stand for more than 10 minutes at a time without getting backache.

Another indication of old age came when I went to the lavatory, where I overhead one chap saying to another: 'Sorry I had to land in your field the other day.' How Surrey is that?

Also, at 1970s gigs the audience provided their own eerie light by holding cigarette lighters aloft in the ballads. Not there they didn't. The light came instead from a million shiny bald patches. Viewed from the back the audience really did seem to be a big flat reflective disco ball.

Sadly, with no hair to let down any more, the audience

had tried to dress down instead. This meant Boxing Day corduroy and quilted sleeveless Puffa jackets teamed with training shoes. It wasn't a good look. But then looking good wasn't the point.

At most middle-aged parties the hosts try to be sophisticated and grown-up. But why? We have to be responsible when we're at work, and mature when we're at home with the children. Surely, on a night out, we shouldn't be quaffing cheesy peas. We should be getting drunk and shouting.

In Surrey that night we parked on someone's lawn, drank gallons of beer from plastic glasses, never spoke about schools and listened to music that wasn't dinner party Dido or background Bacharach.

This brings me on to the band.

If you closed your eyes you really could imagine that it was Plant and Page up there. And if you opened them again the illusion didn't really go away. Wigs and lots of denim did create an illusion that they were the real deal. The lead singer even seemed to have a length of authentic hosepipe down his trousers.

Although, after the gig was over, the reality came flooding back. Because the man who was Robert Plant gave me a lift to the local pub in what was undoubtedly a Renault Scenic.

Being Surrey, of course, the pub had been bistrofied. It was also spinning round quite a lot. And then the next thing I knew I was in a bed, it was 8.30 in the morning and there was a Kalahari thunderstorm in my head. And some major tectonic shifting as well.

We moan about hangovers as we grow old. We

complain that when you're 40 rather than 14 they're so much more difficult to shift. But a hangover is simply a reminder that you had a good time. You should learn to embrace it.

I certainly embraced mine. Along with the lavatory bowl, and all the soft furnishings in my house, for several days afterwards. It had been a very good party.

And here's the thing. You can do it too, for nothing. Why waste a fortune on linen and roses? Why try to be like Elton John or George Clooney when you can rent a village hall, hire a £1,500-a-night tribute band and then flog a hundred tickets at £15 a pop?

No one will feel very glamorous. They'll feel something so much better. Young.

Sunday 12 March 2006

The secret life of handbags

Every week a new survey of some kind tells us how much time we waste sitting in traffic jams or watching television or waiting for automated call centres in Bombay to quote us happy.

Recently, I was told that over a lifetime the average man wastes 394 days sitting on the lavatory. That's 56 weeks, wailed the report despairingly, though I can't imagine why. They're the happiest and most peaceful 56 weeks of a chap's life. I love being on the lavatory more than I love being on holiday, and I certainly don't consider it time wasted.

And anyway, 56 weeks is nothing compared with the amount of time I really do waste, standing outside the front door in the freezing cold waiting for my wife to find the keys in her handbag.

And then there are the aeons I waste waiting for her to answer her mobile phone.

Normally, it rings for 48 hours before she finds it nestling at the bottom of her bag, underneath a receipt for something she bought in 1972.

These days, if I suspect her phone might be in her bag I write a letter instead.

It's quicker.

The American army think they have a tough time trying to find Osama Bin Laden, who is holed out in a cave somewhere in the mountains of Afghanistan. But really they should thank their lucky stars he didn't choose to hide out in my wife's handbag.

God, I've just thought of something. Maybe he did. Maybe he's in there now, with his AK-47 and his video recorder. Maybe he's using the mobile she lost two years ago to supply Al-Jazeera with news.

I read last week that women in Britain spend £350 million a year on handbags and that there's one particular brand that has a year-long waiting list even though it costs £7,000. You wouldn't want to dance round one of those at a disco.

What's more, it's said that on average women have up to 40 handbags each. To find out why, I spoke to our children's nanny, who reckons she has about 25. Apparently, it has something to do with the seasons.

She claims she couldn't use her favourite bag in the summer because it's made out of some cow and 'would look all wrong'.

So what then? Should a summer bag be made out of cuckoos? Or dragonflies? Or Freddie Flintoff?

The idea that a handbag has something to do with style was backed up by a spokesman for Jimmy Choo, who said that if you have good shoes and a good bag you will look right.

Rubbish. If you are fat and you have only one tooth there's no handbag in the world that will mask the problem, unless you wear it over your head. And I don't recommend that because if you put your head in a handbag it would take two years to find it again.

On average, we're told, the contents of a woman's

bag are worth £550. That sounds about right. Fifty-five thousand things worth one pence each. My wife, however, claims that the contents of hers are worth 'over £3,000'. Not including cash. Or, presumably, the VAT due back on all the receipts in there.

So what does she have, then, that could possibly be worth three grand? Well, there's an iPod and the aforementioned phone. And a bag full of make-up that probably cost a hundred quid or so. But we're still £2,000 light.

So, though I know it's poor form, I've just been to the kitchen for a look and here's how it breaks down. Down below the crust, in the asthenosphere, we find a pair of spectacles that she doesn't need and three − that is not a misprint − three pairs of sunglasses. Which seems excessively optimistic, frankly.

Why, I asked later, do you have a pair of spectacles in your handbag when your eyes are fine? 'Well, I might need them at some point,' she said. So does that mean there's a Stannah stairlift in there as well, and some incontinence pads?

Below the eyewear, in the upper mantle, there is some chewing gum, which she never eats, coins for countries that don't exist any more and pills for things that cleared up 15 years ago. I did not dare to go further than this, into the inner core, for fear of finding the bones of Shergar. Or a secret pocket being used by Al-Qaeda.

But there was something I noted. You know the ivory-billed woodpecker that ornithologists believe became extinct 50 years ago? Well, let me tell you. It didn't.

I genuinely don't understand this need to carry everything you've ever owned around with you at all times.

No, really, when you're out and about you don't need to have cough medicine for children who have already grown up and finished university. And if you don't believe me, ask a man.

When I go out I take keys for the house, keys for the car, a telephone, a couple of credit cards, some money, two packs of cigarettes, a lighter and a packet of mints. And even when I'm wearing jeans and a T-shirt, which is always, I cope just fine.

Then there's my wallet. I never leave this at home, principally because it contains the single most important thing a man can have about his person: endless pages torn from newspapers and magazines. Something to read, in other words, when I'm supposedly 'wasting time' on the lavatory.

Sunday 19 March 2006

Bad-hair days on the local news

There seems to be a consensus that locally run businesses and organisations are better than multinationals and super-states.

We regularly reject the European Union in favour of quaint old Westminster, and we love the idea of local councils even though they're run by people who are a) incapable of getting a proper job, and b) mad.

All last week there was much brouhaha about plans to shrink the number of police forces in England and Wales from 43 to about 20.

This worries us. We don't want Dixon of Dock Green to be replaced with the FBI.

Then, of course, there is the high street. We loathe supermarkets even though they are convenient and sell good, clean food at low, low prices. Yet we love local shops despite the fact that they're preposterously expensive and all their vegetables are shrivelled-up weeds covered in mud.

For me, though, the worst example of parish thinking is to be found on the television every night. Local news.

I want to make it plain at the outset that I do not blame the people who run these journalistic outposts. They operate on a tiny budget that means they can only respond to fires, and idiotic press releases written by lunatics in high-visibility jackets.

Everyone interviewed on local news programmes is in a hi-vi. Just last week I watched some people clearing litter from a beach near where I don't live and all of them were resplendent in Day-Glo over-clothing. Why?

Other givens on local news are that all reporters, when covering a flood, will stand in it. And that when there's a helicopter involved, they'll stand under it so they have to shout.

Then there are the pick'n'mix stories. There's always someone laying garage flowers by the side of a busy dual carriageway. Then you'll have something about the environment, a pointless vox pop, a cute animal, possibly on a skateboard, a broken baby incubator, and someone who's just emerged from a not terribly important crisis and needs counselling.

In local news, counselling is the pay-off for pretty well every single story.

Local hospital closes down. Staff are offered counselling. Dog falls off skateboard. Owners are offered counselling. Child excluded from school. Stupid, fat parents in hi-vi jackets are offered counselling.

Then you have the slightly plump woman, with a charity T-shirt hastily pulled on over her normal clothes, who's organised a fund-raising fancy-dress fun run for the hospital that saved her husband's life after a car crash/bout of cancer/fire.

That's interesting, for the poor chap's immediate family. But it's of no consequence at all when it's happened in Southampton and you don't live there.

This is the big problem for local news teams. Unlike a local newspaper that only covers events within 10 miles, local television is nothing of the sort. Only last night, for instance, my local news programme brought details of a football match in Milton Keynes and exciting footage of a small heath fire in Dorset that injured no one and damaged no property.

I might have raised an eyebrow if I lived in one of the houses saved by what politically correct local news reporters always call 'firefighters' rather than 'firemen'. But I don't. I'm only watching because some budget-minded television executive has decided Chipping Norton, Milton Keynes and Dorset are all the same place.

So, why, you may be wondering do I tune in if these programmes make me so angry? Well, I love them. I love the gear-graunching mistakes. Last night, for instance, our local girl referred to Steve Redgrave as 'Sir Redgrave'. And I love the way some reporters really do think they're Jeremy Paxman, bludgeoning some dimwit councillor in a hi-vi jacket into issuing an apology for the cracked paving stone that caused the dog to fall off its skateboard.

But what I love most of all is the hair. The anchor's barnet is always worth a giggle, but when it cuts to the chap in the field I'm like a Smash robot, rolling around in the sitting room, with barely enough breath to summon the children to come and have a look. How does it get like that? Do they take a picture of John Kerry to the barber's? And what is it cut with? A spade?

Local hair is one of the main reasons why all the tear-jerking, bereaved-parent stories on local news go so wrong. They love someone in tears on local news.

They've seen it on *Trinny and Susannah*. They've seen it on *The Apprentice* and they know it is a ratings winner.

They also know it means they have a chance to sign off with a line about counselling.

But they can never quite pull it off. The reporter does everything right. He puts on his special 'caring' voice. The cameraman tightens for a Big Close Up when the family photo album is produced. But the parent in question won't cry because . . . well, you can't when the chap with the microphone has a dead horse on his bonce.

That's why they're always taken outside, into the cold, for the cutaways and the wides. Because the chill and some grit will get the tear ducts going and then: bang. They have the money shot.

They can go back to the studio for a couple of quick puns, a spot of off-autocue flirting with the weathergirl and then hand you back to Huw Edwards for some proper news about Iraq.

Sunday 26 March 2006

The lost people of outer Britain

As Gordon Brown droned through yet another dreary budget the other day, I was in the Yorkshire Dales, watching a hill farmer bump across the heather and snow in his old Land Rover.

Was he listening to the chancellor, I wondered. And if so, what would he make of those plans to impose a new higher rate of tax on people who drive four-wheel-drive cars, such as his old Defender.

It's a hard, brutal life up there on the roof of England, especially at this time of year when the lambs are coming. Three times a night those hardy old souls have to drag themselves out of their warm beds to stomp about on the moors with half their arm up a sheep's backside.

I watched them from my hotel room, their million-candle-power torches piercing the night like Second World War searchlights.

And for what?

A fat lamb these days is worth no more than £50. And now they have to rear five simply to tax their Land Rover. Just because someone from the bigoted metropolitan elite is waging a class war with the yummy mummies of Wandsworth.

Up there in the Dales most people think Leyburn is a long way away, Leeds is Hong Kong and London may as well be on the moon. So when they listen to the radio and the television, they must wonder what on earth everyone is on about.

What is meant, for instance, by immigration? If you look on the census form for the nearest town – Hawes – you will find that 99.6 per cent of the population is 'white' and just 0.4 per cent 'non-Christian'. I presume this blip has something to do with the local Indian restaurant.

Mostly, a dalesman's idea of exotic food is a bit of blueberry in his Wensleydale, and a foreign language is Geordie. God knows who does the plumbing.

Then you have crime. They must hear on the radio stories of gang rape and 16-year-old girls being shot in the face, and they must wonder if they've somehow tuned in to a station from Andromeda.

In a break from filming I was sitting on a bench in the middle of Thwaite (population 29) when into the village trundled the mobile library. That in itself was quaint enough. But it was nothing compared with what happened next. Because from out of the passenger door stepped a community support policewoman.

Now let's not forget, shall we, that I'm not talking here about the 1940s, or some remote Scottish island. I'm talking about a twenty-first-century village just a couple of hundred miles from London . . . where the police patrol their patch in mobile libraries.

Car chases would be interesting. Especially if the villains head for West Stonesdale. Sadly, the library can't follow on that road because it doesn't have a good enough turning circle for the hairpin bends.

But we're getting ahead of ourselves. We're assuming there are villains to chase.

'Well, there are,' said the (very pretty) policewoman. Oh yeah, I retorted with a southern sneer. 'And how many people with ASBOs are there within thirty miles of where we're standing now?'

Wrong question. 'Aha,' said the policeperson, 'we do have a woman in Wensleydale with an ASBO.' Right. And what had she done? Knifed a bouncer in a late-night brawl? Nicked a car? No, wailed Miss Dales Constable. 'She hit her brother with a stick of rhubarb.'

I am not making this up. And nor is she. I've checked and a woman called Margaret Porter was indeed given an ASBO for throwing three sticks of rhubarb at her brother.

Other crimes? Well, someone had his quad bike stolen last year, but now that Kojak could roll into town at any time in her diesel-powered library that sort of thing has stopped.

Speeding? Difficult to say, because the policewoman set up a dot-matrix site the other day but it didn't work. She's taken it to the fire station to see if they can figure out what's wrong. And if they work it out, they'll doubtless get a local coal merchant to run it back to the police station.

You get my point. We accept ID cards and traffic cameras because we know there are Albanian people-traffickers in our midst. So why are they accepted in Thwaite, where the most offensive weapon is a vegetable?

There's more too. I listened to Jonathan Ross talking about some obscure shop on Marylebone High Street. I knew what he was on about. You probably knew what he was on about. But I'd bet my left ear that the hill farmers of West Stonesdale, who can no longer read library books, had absolutely no idea at all.

Likewise the news. We hear, every day, about the chronic water shortage and how we must all stop cleaning our teeth. But up north the reservoirs are overflowing, the brooks are babbling and the concept of a water shortage is as daft as the concept of a diplomatic row over parking tickets.

Last week I suggested that local news programmes on the television are a waste of time. And that national news is much better. But the news we get is not national.

It's centred on London, which is home to just an eighth of the country's population. This, if I lived in the Dales, would be very annoying.

Nearly as annoying, in fact, as being made to pay an extra £45 a year to tax my Land Rover because someone in Chelsea recently bought a Hummer.

Sunday 2 April 2006

Cut me in on the hedge fund, boys

I have no idea what a hedge fund is, but after a day trip to Mustique last week I think I need to plant one.

At first I couldn't quite work out whether this privately owned island in the Caribbean is heaven on earth or a small piece of hell. Certainly, it's the first country I've ever been to which is completed mowed, from end to end, in nice neat strips. Honestly, I've been to dirtier, messier nuclear laboratories.

It seems sanitised somehow, but then I thought, what's wrong with that? A lot of very rich people have come here and built a world where there is no crime, no disease and no unpleasant working-class people on the beaches. Not unless they're in an apron and they're toiling over a barbecue, roasting yams.

After a day drinking wine, and swimming in the preposterously turquoise sea, going back to Barbados felt like going back to Birmingham. As our little plane took off from the freshly mowed airfield, I looked back and thought: 'No. Mustique is more than all right. It's living, breathing proof that the resurrection's a load of nonsense.'

Because if Jesus really had come back from the dead, he'd still be alive today.

And if he were still alive, it's sensible to assume he'd be living in the best place on earth. So he'd be in Mustique. And he wasn't.

Of course, some of the 90 or so houses that sit like big wedding cakes on the newly mowned hillsides belong to high-profile stars such as Mick Jagger, Tommy Hilfiger and Stewart Copeland – the second of only two policemen on the island.

But the vast majority belong, it seems, to hedge-fund managers.

Now I can describe these people to you very easily. They are all quite young, and they all appear to be super-fit. None smokes. Few drink. All have swept-back hair and dazzling teeth, and all, you imagine, would quite like to murder someone, to see what it's like. You're thinking Bret Easton Ellis. So am I.

They are also lip-slobberingly rich. There are estimated to be 9,000 funds worldwide which, between them, have assets of $1,500 billion. So they're not really hedges at all. They're bloody great leylandii.

What's more, a whopping 78 per cent of all the hedges in Europe are grown and nurtured in London. That's $255 billion. And that's great, but before we get too excited, we must first of all try to work out what a hedge fund is.

According to a friend in the City, they're brilliant because whether the stock market goes up or down, you still make pots of money. Great. Sounds like my kind of gambling. But what are they exactly?

'Ah well,' she said. 'You rent shares from someone who has a lot of them and then you sell what you've rented.' Now this, so far as I can tell, is actually called 'theft'. Small wonder they've all got houses on Mustique. They're all burglars.

'No,' said my friend, 'because you always pay back the person you've rented them from, plus interest.' I see, so you rent some shares, sell them, and then give the profit (if you've made any) to the person from whom you did the renting. That seems like a lot of effort and risk for no gain at all.

My friend became exasperated and told me to stop thinking so literally because the money never actually exists. 'It's like a house of straw, then?' I asked. 'No,' she tutted. 'It's like a house of straw that's a hologram. It isn't there.'

On the worldwide internet, a hedge fund is described thus: 'A fund, usually used by wealthy individuals and institutions, which is allowed to use aggressive strategies that are unavailable to mutual funds, including selling short, leverage, programme trading, swaps, arbitrage, and derivatives.'

Gibberish. And galling, too, because I'm not a stupid man. I'm able to grasp the most complicated concepts, especially if it means I can walk away from the table six years later with £100 billion in my back pocket, a Gulfstream V and a house on Mustique. But this hedge-fund business was eluding me.

One thing I did note was that hedge funds are not regulated like normal share dealings. I'm not surprised. How could a flat-footed policeman possibly be expected to investigate a house of straw that doesn't exist?

And there's something else. While hedge funds operate outside the law, don't exist, and always make money whether the market rises or falls, 85 per cent fail. How's that possible? That would be like losing money at the races whether your horse came in first, third or in a big tube of Evo-Stick.

To find out, I turned to a publication called *Money Week* which, in a lengthy and indescribably boring article, explained why hedges are starting to crumble. There are many reasons, apparently, none of which I could understand. But all of which are wrong.

I've given it a moment's thought and I know exactly why the business is in trouble. It's obvious. In order to function, hedge funds need wealthy investors.

But as my recent trip to Mustique demonstrated, all the world's richest people these days are hedge-fund managers. This, then, has become a business that can only invest in itself.

Soon these guys are going to have to forget about the super-rich and chase down those who are simply well off. That'd be me, and that's great. Lend me your house on Mustique for two weeks next Easter, and we'll talk.

Sunday 23 April 2006

Flying with the baby from hell

Memo to the nation's religious leaders. When delivering a sermon, here's an idea: try to make it relevant or interesting in some way.

I bring this up because last week on Radio 2's *Pause for Thought* a Buddhist was trying to tell us to think of others and not just ourselves.

Now there are many examples he could have used here. There's the parable of the good Samaritan, which has worked well for thousands of years. Or there's the parable of the John Prescott, an inarticulate fat man who was steered through life by his pant compass and his class hatred and ended up lost in a tabloid world of hate and 'Two Shags' ridicule.

But no. The story we got was about a 'wicked man' whose only good deed on earth was not treading on a spider. So when he died, the spider lowered a sliver of thread into hell so he could climb out.

With me so far? Unfortunately, lots of people also used the thread to get out and it snapped and they were all killed.

So what's the good Buddhist trying to say here? That if you let others share your good fortune, everyone will die? That the wicked man wasn't wicked after all? Or that he'd written the sermon after sniffing several pints of glue?

Whatever, the story was rubbish, so this morning I'm

going to see if I can do better with my own sermon on selfishness. It's called the parable of the British Airways Flight to Barbados.

There was a wicked man who had agreed to go on a golfing holiday with his boss.

Plainly, this had not gone down well with his wife, who had demanded that she come too, and their children, one of whom was a baby.

Now British Airways does not allow you to smoke while on board, or carry knitting needles or have sexual intercourse with other passengers.

You are also not allowed to board if you have shoes with explosive soles or if you've had one too many tinctures in the departure lounge. And if you make any sort of joke, about anything at all, in earshot of the stewardesses, you will be tied to your seat as though it was 1420, and you were in the stocks.

But you are allowed, welcomed even, into the club-class section of the plane even if you are accompanied by what is essentially a huge lung covered only in a light veneer of skin.

I want to make it absolutely plain at this point that I never took any of my children on a long-haul flight until they were old enough to grasp the concept of reason. It is simply not fair to impose your screaming child on other people, people who have paid thousands of pounds for a flat bed and therefore the promise of some sleep.

There's talk at the moment of introducing planes with standing room for economy-class passengers. Imagine the sort of seat you get in a bus shelter and you'll grasp the idea. Fine. So why not soundproofed overhead lockers into which babies can be placed? Or how about flights where under-twos are banned? I'm digressing.

The family at the centre of this morning's parable were seated in club class, between me and another columnist on the *Sunday Times*, Christa D'Souza. I said I wanted to write about them. Christa said she wanted to kill them.

The crying began before the Triple Seven was airborne, and built to a climax as we reached the cruise. And this was the longest climax in the history of sound. It went on, at Krakatoan volume, without hesitation, until we began the descent eight hours later. At which point, thanks to a change in pressure on the lung's tiny earholes, the noise reached new and terrifying heights. I honestly thought the plane's windows might break.

And what do you suppose the mother did to calm her infant? Feed it some warm milk? Read it a nice soothing story? Nope. She turned her seat into a bed, puffed up her pillow, and pretended to go to sleep.

I know full well she wasn't actually asleep for three reasons. First, it would have been impossible. Second, no mother can sleep through the cries of her own child, and third, every time I went to see Christa I made a point of trailing a rolled-up newspaper over the silly woman's head.

So why was she pretending? Aha. That's easy. I know exactly what she said to her husband as they left home that morning. 'If you're going to play golf while we're on holiday, you can be childminder on the plane. I spend all day with those bloody kids. I'm doing nothing.'

This is almost certainly why the lung was so agitated. Because the person it knows and loves was apparently dead, while it was being jiggled around by a strange man it had never seen before. Because he leaves for work at six in the morning, doesn't get back till 10 and is away all weekend playing golf.

And that's why he was put in charge of the children, and that's why the flight was ruined for several hundred people. Who then had to spend a fortnight in the Caribbean, terrified that the lung would be on their night flight back to Britain.

It wasn't. And this is the point of my sermon. I do not know what happened to it.

But if there really is a God, I like to think it was eaten by a shark.

Sunday 30 April 2006

With the gypsies in junk heaven

Back in February I told you about my Cupboard of Shit. It's a glass-fronted Georgian cabinet in which we house quite the most startling collection of pointless, tasteless rubbish it's possible to conceive.

A particular favourite of mine is the plastic figurine of a New York fireman carrying his wounded buddy through what appears to be a half-eaten tomato sandwich. But it is, in fact, supposed to be the ruined remains of the World Trade Center.

Then there's the Corsican shepherd with the melted face, the endless array of stupid creatures made from shells, a particularly horrible snow shaker and a Jesus on a rope.

British seaside gift shops are a fine hunting ground for all this stuff but even better are retail establishments within 400 yards of anything to do with the Catholic church. You should see my alabaster Last Supper in which all the disciples are wearing coats made from different-coloured glitter.

Anyway, out of the blue, I found a whole new seam to mine in my relentless quest for horror: Stow-on-the-Wold.

Those of you who have read A. A. Gill's book on the English will know that he described this Cotswold hill town as unquestionably the worst place in the world. And a lot of the locals have failed to understand why he feels like this.

It's simple. Adrian doesn't know one end of the Cotswolds from a nasty dose of cot death. He was simply aiming his poisoned quill at the town where I live. And missed.

The fact is that Stow is a wonderful place. For 364 days of the year. And then for 24 glorious hours in May it becomes the biggest campsite in the world for . . . er, I'm not sure what we're supposed to call them now.

Travellers seems wrong since they all live in houses in Dartford in Kent. I know pikey's a no-no. Er, gypsies? Is that okay?

It's easy to remember when this is on because all of a sudden the shutters come down on the normal shops and everyone within 40 miles suddenly loses all their five-bar gates. And their lawnmowers.

Oh, and every grass verge in the region is suddenly bedecked with a million chromed caravans. One of which, I couldn't help noticing, had been fitted with a wheel clamp. Who did they think was going to nick it? The Duke of Marlborough?

Anyway, the fair. Primarily, it's a place where you can buy and sell horses, some of which go for £40,000. A bauble compared to some of the Range Rovers I saw. But as is the way with these things, there are a number of stalls where you can buy canaries for £3,000, 30-year-old Ford Transits for £1,800, and terriers. I don't know how much they cost because while I was in the middle of finding out, one of them leapt six feet off the ground and tried to eat my head.

You can also buy caravans, of course, and five-bar gates, and lawnmowers. But no heather, surprisingly, or pegs, or tarmac.

As soon as I walked into the field I was assaulted by a 10-year-old kid. I reckoned that he would want to talk about *Top Gear* or some obscure Ferrari. But no. He had seen my Breitling from 700 yards away and liked it very much. Then he was joined by another kid who had noted I had the new B&O phone. Pretty soon, I figured, I'd have neither.

The people here were simply incredible. All the women appeared to have stepped straight off the stage at Stringfellows. Except that they all had double-decker pushchairs full of half a million babies. And all the men had necks like birthday cakes and forearms thicker than my upper thigh.

Aren't they all just so lovely, said the girl I went with. Well, yes, here, when they're prising a terrier off your head, I agree, they are lovely in a salt-of-the-earth sort of way. But when it's 3 a.m. and you come downstairs in a nightie to find one of them in your sitting room helping himself to your television set, then no: lovely isn't a word that springs to mind.

One thing. They were all spectacularly good-looking. I'm afraid I know very little about the origins of these people; I recall that they originated in India but they don't look Indian to me. They look like gods. With beer bellies and pushchairs. If you can imagine such a thing.

The trinkets they were selling, though, were not good-looking at all. They were absolutely hideous. Within minutes I had found at least 30 items that would fit nicely into my cupboard. But I have strict rules.

I'm only allowed to buy one thing per venue or day.

At first I was tempted by a rose bowl made from etched cut glass. And that was just the start. Some of the cut faces were brown, some were finished in 'hand-painted' enamel and some in gold leaf.

I can't begin to describe the foulness of the thing. But it was £50 so I moved on.

I finally settled on a £25 pot horse. Painted by . . . well, I have no idea. By a team of primary-school children, I think. It stands a foot tall and has golden ears and Romany scenes on its flanks. It is extraordinarily terrible and made me very happy.

Sunday 14 May 2006

Listen to me, I'm the drought buster

After two unusually dry winters Britain is no longer classified by the world's climatologists as 'unbelievably wet and miserable'. We are now listed as 'soggy and horrid' and, as a result, I've had a letter from my local water company telling me not to clean my teeth or wipe my bottom.

There is a chilling warning too. If I persist with my personal hygiene, they will ban me from topping up the swimming pool.

Of course, everyone is now running around saying that instead of sending out threatening letters, the water companies should spend some of their profits fixing the leaks.

Why? The whole point of a company is to make money, not to spend every single penny it has digging up every single road in the country to repair a system that is 150 years old and completely knackered.

Even more annoying are the swivel-eyed loonies who have blamed the water shortage on people who eat meat. They argue that thanks to climate change, south-east Britain has less rainfall per head than Sudan. So what? Monte Carlo probably has less rainfall per head than the moon. It just means that a lot of people live in Monaco, not that the Monegasques have to walk to a standpipe every morning with buckets on their heads and flies in their eyes.

On top of all this you have those who say that the

hosepipe ban is not the fault of climate change or the water companies but is all down to John Prescott and his insane plan to house everyone from eastern Europe, Africa and South America in a starter home on the outskirts of Canterbury. 'That's why there's a water shortage,' they say. 'It's all being stolen by Somalian rapists.'

Of course, normally, I would leap at the chance to pour scorn all over Two Shags but I'm afraid I don't subscribe to this ridiculous blame culture. And so, instead of sitting around with a dirty bottom and scuzzy teeth, pointing an accusing finger at anyone and everyone, I have been working out what might be done.

The fact of the matter is that from 1760 Britain's rainfall patterns have been up and down like a pair of whore's drawers. We have a handful of very wet years and then a handful of dry ones. And we've always managed just fine.

What has changed recently is that Mr Prescott has moved south. I've moved south.

Everyone's moved south. Ever wondered why you never hear about anything going on in Scunthorpe these days? It's because the entire population now lives in Guildford. And what are all these émigrés doing?

Well, mostly they're standing in dried-up lake beds wondering where all the water has gone.

What's urgently needed in the south-east are more reservoirs. And that's a problem.

In the north when you build a reservoir you lose, at worst, three small villages and a couple of bats. But wherever you build such a thing in the south-east would mean drowning something a bit more substantial. Like Marlow, for example. Or Windsor Castle.

What's to be done? Well, if we head back up north we find Kielder Water, one of the largest man-made lakes in Europe. It was first mooted in the 1960s, when everyone felt that heavy industry in the north-east would need more and more water to stay competitive. But it was opened in 1976, at pretty well the precise moment when the last of the region's heavy industry closed down.

I'm sure there are people there now, still working out who was to blame for this mistake. I'm not. I'm wondering how it might be possible to get some of those 44 billion gallons of water to my toothbrush.

How hard can it be? An idea, first mooted in the *Sunday Times* seven years ago, suggested that the water could be scooped into massive plastic bags and then floated down the North Sea. This idea was tested in Greece and then forgotten. I'm guessing because plastic bags full of water when put in the sea will, er, sink.

No, the only sensible way to move water from the north to the south is in pipes, and please don't tell me this can't be done. If we can get gas from Siberia to the back of my Aga, without a single leak at any point on the journey, then, I'm pretty certain, we can get water from Tyne and Wear to my lavatory bowl.

Doubtless you are all thinking that the cost and disruption of such a pipeline would far outweigh the benefits. But who says it has to go by land? Why not run it offshore down the east coast?

You wouldn't even need any energy-sapping pumps because the base of the dam at Kielder Water is 460 feet higher than central London. It would be downhill all the way. Complicated? I don't think so. Brunel could probably have designed and built such a thing in about a week.

I have another idea. In places like Dubai, where the rainfall is even lower than ours, they build desalination plants and get their water from the sea. Why can we not do this? At the very least, drinking sea water will help to keep the sea levels down.

Unfortunately, none of these ideas will ever come to fruition because everyone is far too busy blaming everyone else. You can take the consequences if you want to and end up in the Middle Ages.

Me? I'm going to spend the summer washing my bottom with Evian and topping up my swimming pool with gin.

Sunday 21 May 2006

Trust me, work is more fun than fun

Last week David Cameron suggested we should think less about money and more about the quality of life. And immediately every socialist in the land started running around shaking his fist, saying it's all right for some with their big houses and their floppy hair. But that some people have to work to have money for pigeons and whippets.

Of course, that's true. But I don't think Mr Cameron was addressing the nation's factory workers, who already have a good life. They clock off at 5.30 on the dot and are in the Dog and Communist 10 seconds later.

I think he was talking to the middle classes, who work and work and work and never have time to play Monopoly or Swingball with their children. And I bet his ideas had some appeal.

Staying at home all day, tending the garden, never missing a school play and rearing geese all sounds lovely. Especially if you're a provincial GP who's just spent the morning lancing boils and playing with the varicose veins of the town's pensioners.

Certainly, there are days when I think of jacking it all in. Last night, for instance, I was driving round a sodden airfield in Surrey in a Vauxhall Vectra while my son was third soldier from the back in *Beowolf*. I should have been there.

And what's more, I could have been there. Thanks to the kindness of those who bought my book last year I probably do have enough now to stop working.

Of course, there would have to be some sacrifices. I wouldn't be able to afford a car, for instance, and we'd have to move to a much smaller house. And there'd be no more holidays, or birthday presents for the children. And we'd have to eat lawn clippings. But the biggest loss of all would be my job.

This is the point I think Mr Cameron missed. Yes, for five minutes a day the idea of living the *Railway Children* dream with my kids in pinny dresses waving at trains all day long sounds great.

But for the rest of the day I love what I do.

Of course, there are times when I have to drive a Vauxhall and it's raining. But there are times when I drive a Ferrari and it's not. And best of all there are times like right now when the house is quiet and I'm tucked away in my little office writing. This is not a chore. It's called work, but there's nowhere I'd rather be.

And come on, be honest, it's the same for you. Yes, the provincial GP may not like having to examine an endless parade of sagging, ageing flesh, but who knows, the next person through the door may be Kate Moss.

Furthermore, deep down, a doctor must feel pretty good when, after a seven-minute appointment, he makes someone better. He could not replace that contentment if he were at home arranging flowers.

Take Saturdays as a prime example. This is the day when I hide away in the office, writing the following week's *Top Gear* show. Sure, I could be playing Cluedo with the kids. But they like to watch MTV more, and if I watch MTV with them I become very agitated, which causes a row.

For family harmony, then, the best place I can be when they're watching MTV is in the office. They like this too, because when I'm in the office I'm earning money that they can spend on PlayStation games, and that improves their quality of life hugely.

Also, if we have money, they can go to school in a car, which is more comfortable and much safer than going on an ox cart. And, I suppose, if I'm honest I didn't really want to be at *Beowolf* last night. It is a very dull play when performed by professionals. Give it to a bunch of 10-year-olds, and you know what? I'd rather drive a Vauxhall Vectra in the rain.

Then there's the question of marital happiness. At present, I come home late, fall asleep on the sofa and dribble slightly until bedtime. My wife is very happy with this arrangement. Whereas she'd be very mad if I were here all day trying to be helpful.

It is a known fact that men, when bored, cannot last for more than 15 minutes without imagining that DIY is an instinctive ability like mating and eating: that being a male means we simply must be good with an electric sander. Men must never be bored while at home, then; otherwise the whole house will fall down.

Furthermore, we need the buzz we get from working; the juice. When I read out the script I've written for *Top Gear* and the production team sit there yawning, I have 12 hours to write a new one.

And that's a roller-coaster thrill. I love it. I love the

pressure. And I fear there wouldn't be any if I spent my days waving at trains and growing cabbages.

The simple fact of the matter is that, for the vast majority of the time, the vast majority of the people like and enjoy their jobs.

So stick at it. Unless you're Tony Blair, that is. You are allowed to go home and spend more time with your family, because that way we'll get David Cameron, who promises he'll do the same.

And that, a country with no leader, would improve the quality of all our lives immeasurably.

Sunday 28 May 2006

Pot-Porritt wants me eliminated

For many years I've poked fun at environmentalists, fondly imagining that my opposition to their nonsense was about as ineffectual as Denmark's opposition to American policy in the Middle East.

Oh sure, the eco-people sprang out of the bushes from time to time to plant a custard pie in my face, in the same way that a 16-stone man might leap out of bed at night and swat a particularly annoying bluebottle.

And yes, when I make jokes about gassing badgers, funny little men with curious downloading habits go onto the internet and put my name and address in their To Be Killed folders. But despite this, I've always felt like a bit of beef dripping in a big vat of tofu.

No, really. The eco-ists have the ear of the prime minister, the leader of the opposition, the whole of the BBC, most of the country's newspapers, every single university campus and nearly every government in the world. Whereas I have the ear of the Ford Capri Owners Club. Which is comprised of half a dozen men in Dennis Waterman-style leather bomber jackets.

Last week, however, it transpired that I may be more of a nuisance than I imagined. Jonathon Pot-Porritt, the former director of Friends of the Earth, who now heads the government's UK Sustainable Development Commission, says he can't get his message across because everyone's too busy watching me driving round corners too quickly on *Top Gear*.

He called me a bigoted petrolhead and said that anyone who shuts me up should be given a knighthood.

Now I've seen *Goodfellas*, and as a result I know that 'shutting someone up' is Martin Scorsese-speak for having someone killed. Crikey. A man in the government wants me dead. And it's not like they haven't done this kind of thing before . . .

So I'd just like to say, if my body is found in a wood at some point in the not too distant future, it wasn't suicide. Tell Lord Hutton that Swampy Porritt did it.

I should be worried, I suppose, but mostly I'm rather flattered. For years I've felt like King Canute sitting on the beach, watching helplessly as the tide of eco-offal rolls inexorably towards the shore. But now Mr Pot-Porritt has come out of nowhere to say that I really do have the power to hold back his plans to make trains out of cardboard and create electricity by composting Tories.

I should explain at this point that Pot-Porritt and I have history. I once interviewed him on a television show, and out of common courtesy the producer edited the slot to ensure we both scored an equal number of points. In fact, Porritt made a tit of himself, trying to argue that cars were responsible for the then floods in Uckfield, East Sussex.

Unfortunately, my mother-in-law lived in Uckfield and I knew full well that the waterlogged high street had nothing whatsoever to do with global warming, and everything to do with the way the local flood plain had been buried under a million tons of Prescott-approved housing.

Porritt stammered a lot and was forced to agree. But he said the heavy rain was all our fault. In much the same way that he now says the drought is all our fault.

And what's more, he even has Sir David Attenborough on side these days.

Now my respect for The Attenborough as a broadcaster is boundless. He could tell me that I was a giant panda and I'd believe him. He could come on the television and say koala bears can fill in tax forms and I'd stroke my chin appreciatively.

But when he comes on the television to say Sienna Miller's Range Rover has broken the Gulf Stream and overheated a guillemot, well, I'm sorry, but I just nod off.

Because finger-wagging environmentalism, even from the God of the electric fish tank, is catastrophically boring.

No, honestly. Being told to give up polythene to prevent something that might not happen is like being told to give up drink because it might damage your liver.

Yeah, but, when you're at a party having a nice time, really who gives a damn?

I can prove this. Because last weekend the BBC ran a save-the-planet quiz show on BBC1 against *Top Gear* on BBC2. And guess what? More people watched the planet being savaged than watched a load of weird beards trying to save it.

I offer a piece of advice, then, to Mr Pot-Porritt this morning. Try living like I do. Don't drop litter. Recycle whatever can be recycled, without talking about it. Grow your own vegetables. Eat meat. Use whatever means of transport is the most convenient. And when you wake to find the sun is shining, call some friends round for a barbecue and be happy.

Don't worry about the topsoil and the coral reefs. Remember that in 1900 we lived for an average of 49 years and that now we live to an average of 78. Remember, too, that we have reduced poverty more in the past 50 years than we did in the preceding 500. And rejoice at the news that all the waste generated by the United States in the whole of the twenty-first century – all of it – will fit in a landfill site just 18 miles across.

You will enjoy your short time here on earth so much more, and what's more, if you stop telling us what to do all the time, so will we.

Sunday 4 June 2006

Simon Cowell ate our strawberries

I forgot to buy a book for a flight from Edinburgh to London this week, so I stared out of the window the whole way. And two things became obvious: Britain has a great deal of water. And while nobody was looking it seems that someone has bubble-wrapped the entire countryside.

Now the fox has been sorted, 'polytunnels' are the latest must-have cause for concern in the shires. They enraged an old lady in Herefordshire so much last week that she pulled one up and tossed it aside. Not exactly suicide bombing but she seems to have got her point across.

Let me try to encapsulate the problem here. Growing strawberries under polytunnels increases the harvest window from six weeks to six months, which means we don't have to fly them over from Namibia or Chile, or wherever it is that strawberries come from normally.

Fine. But polytunnels are more of a blot on the landscape than a rambler's socks, and what's more, strawberries grown in their shadow have the same nutritional value as office furniture.

Needless to say, the supermarkets say it's all our fault because we demand year-round strawberries that look nice and feel firm, and to hell with the fact that you'd be better off eating the punnet.

Hmmm. And who exactly do the supermarkets mean when they say it's 'our fault'? We know that the working classes do not eat strawberries because they do not eat any fruit or vegetables, which is why they are all so ugly and malformed. And we know that the upper classes have no need of the supermarket strawberry because they have vegetable gardens in which they grow their own. Often, these vegetable gardens are called Lincolnshire.

So it's the middle classes who are demanding tasteless but perfectly formed strawberries, is it? I don't think so. Because the middle class is too busy poring over the olive-oil counter in Carluccio's. Thanks to Gordon and Jamie we are now educated in the ways of the culinary world.

And we therefore know that eating a supermarket strawberry is a bit like making love to the most beautiful girl in the world and finding out she's got bird flu.

Even though the 602,000 cigarettes I smoked have given my mouth the sensitivity of a smelting-plant crucible I know that the fruit and vegetables in my garden are a million billion times more tasty than the fruit and veg grown in a plastic bag in Kidderminster.

If you're going to Wimbledon this year, chances are you'll be offered strawberries grown in this manner. They're called Elsantas and I suggest a test. Drop one on the floor and it'll bounce. Which is fine if you want to play tennis with it, but it's not so good if you're planning on putting it in your mouth.

No, I'm sorry. Supermarkets buy polytunnel strawberries not because we want them, but because they are factory farmed, picked by Lithuanians, and are therefore cheap. Which means they make more money, which, of course, is fine by me.

What's to be done? Well, to cure the problem we must, I'm afraid, turn our attention to Simon Cowell. Because, you see, it's all his fault.

Simon's a lovely chap but his stack 'em high, sell 'em cheap attitude to music means that these days pop stars never last long enough to make much cash. And that means the country is being starved of super-rich rock gods. And super-rich rock gods are the only people who know how the countryside should be managed.

Farming in Britain is now pointless because the working classes only eat fat, and the middle classes want everything to come from Tuscany. That's why farmers have bubble-wrapped the countryside; it's the only way to survive when you've been bubble-wrapped yourself, by a hundred miles of red tape.

There's more too. At the moment the only respite from the mile upon mile of polythene is oilseed rape, which, I'm sure, is part of a communist European Union plot to feed the Continent's swivel-eyed eco-loony vegetarians while punishing the blue-eyed intelligentsia with hay fever.

Of course, there are still a few small copses left to break up England's yellow and plastic land, but when the metro-veg-heads in power get round to banning shooting, they'll be torn up as well to make way for more polythene. Unless we get Simon Cowell out of the music business and find a new Pink Floyd.

One of my pleasant rock-star friends recently moved from London to the Cotswolds and bought a farm. And he's now spending his children's entire inheritance on making sure the new pad looks and feels like it did in the fourteenth century. There are sheep, not because they make nice money, but because they make a nice noise in the morning. There are woods, because they look pretty, and now, in the ancient barns, traditional cheese is being hand-churned by women with big breasts. It's rock'n'roll and it's cheesy. But I like it.

I'm making a serious point here. Britain, from the air, would be a butchered place were it not for the rock stars who spend so much money keeping their bits of it nice. So if you want to get rid of polytunnels there's only one solution. Go out and buy another copy of *Dark Side of the Moon*.

Sunday 11 June 2006

The united states of total paranoia

I know Britain is full of incompetent water-board officials and stabbed Glaswegians but even so I fell on my knees this morning and kissed the ground, because I've just spent three weeks trying to work in America.

It's known as the land of the free and I'm sure it is if you get up in the morning, go to work in a petrol station, eat nothing but double-egg burgers with cheese – and take your children to little league. But if you step outside the loop, if you try to do something a bit zany, you will find that you're in a police state.

We begin at Los Angeles airport in front of an immigration official who, like all his colleagues, was selected for having no grace, no manners, no humour, no humanity and the sort of IQ normally found in farmyard animals. He scanned my form and noted there was no street number for the hotel at which I was staying.

'I'm going to need a number,' he said. 'Ooh, I'm sorry,' I said, 'I'm afraid I don't have one.'

This didn't seem to have any effect. 'I'm going to need a number,' he said again, and then again, and then again. Each time I shrugged and stammered, terrified that I might be sent to the back of the queue or, worse, into the little room with the men in Marigolds. But I simply didn't have an answer.

'I'm going to need a number,' he said again, giving the

distinct impression that he was an autobank, and that this was a conversation he was prepared to endure until one of us died. So with a great deal of bravery I decided to give him one. And the number I chose was 2,649,347.

This, it turned out, was fine. He'd been told by his superiors to get a number.

I'd given him a number. His job was done and so, just an hour or so later, I was on the streets of Los Angeles doing a piece to camera.

Except, of course, I wasn't. Technically, you need a permit to film on every street in pretty well every corner of the world. But the only countries where this rule is enforced are Vietnam, Cuba, North Korea and the United States of America.

So, seconds after breaking out the tripod, a policeman pulled up and demanded that we show him our permit. We had one that covered the city of Los Angeles . . . except the bit where we were. So we were moved on.

The next day I was moved on in Las Vegas too, because the permit I had didn't cover the part of the pavement I was standing on. Eight inches away was fine.

You need a permit to do everything in America. You even need a passport to buy a drink. But, interestingly, you don't need one if you wish to rent some guns and some bullets. I needed a 50 cal (very big) machine gun. 'No problem,' said the man at the shop. 'But could you just sign this assuring us that the movie you're making is not anti-Bush or anti-war.'

Also, you do not need a permit if you want – as I did – to transport a dead cow on the roof of your car through the Florida panhandle. That's because this is banned by a state law.

Think about that. Someone has gone to all the bother and expense of drawing up a law that means that at some point lots of people were moving dead cows about on their cars. It must have been popular. Fashionable, even.

Anyway, back to the guns. I needed them because I wished to shoot a car in the Mojave desert. But you can't do that without the say-so of the local fire chief, who turned up, with his haircut, to say that for reasons he couldn't explain, he had a red flag in his head.

You find this a lot in America. People way down the food chain are given the power to say yes or no to elaborately prepared plans, just so their bosses can't be sued. One expression that simply doesn't translate from English in these days of power without responsibility is 'Ooh, I'm sure it'll be fine'.

And, unfortunately, these people at the bottom of the food chain have no intellect at all. Reasoning with them is like reasoning with a tree. I think this is because people in the sticks have stopped marrying their cousins and are now mating with vegetables.

They certainly aren't eating them. You see them growing in fields, but all you ever find on a menu is cheese, cheese, cheese, or cheese with cheese. Except for a steak and cheese sandwich I bought in Mississippi. This was made, according to the label, from 'imitation cheese'.

Nope, I don't know what that is either but I do know that out of the main population centres, the potato people are getting fatter and dimmer by the minute.

Today the average petrol-pump attendant is capable, just, of turning on a pump when you prepay. But if you pay for two pumps to be turned on to fill two cars, you can, if you stare carefully, see wisps of smoke coming from her fat, useless, war-losing, acne-scarred, gormless turnip face.

And the awful thing is that you don't want the petrol anyway, because it'll simply get you to somewhere else, which will be worse. A point I shall prove next week, when we have a look at what happened in Alabama. And why the poor of New Orleans will sue if the donation you make isn't as big as they'd hoped for.

Sunday 2 July 2006

Arrested just for looking weird

Last week I wrote about my recent trip to America, and to be honest it didn't go down well. I don't think I've ever been on the receiving end of such a blizzard of bile. One man called me an 'imbosile'. Hundreds more suggested that it'd be better for everyone if I just stayed at home in future.

And do you know the awful thing? I haven't finished yet. Last week's column was just an introduction, an *amuse-bouche*, a scene-setter. It's this week that things really start to get going . . .

So far we've looked at the problem in America of power without responsibility.

Step out of the loop, do something unusual and you'll encounter a wall of low-paid, low-intellect workers whose sole job is to prevent their bosses from being sued. As a result, you never hear anyone say: 'Oh I'm sure it'll be all right.'

You know the Stig. The all-white racing driver we use on *Top Gear*. Well, we were filming him walking through the Mojave desert when, lo and behold, a lorry full of soldiers rocked up and arrested him. He was unusual. He wasn't fat. He must therefore be a Muslim.

It gets worse. I needed money to play a little blackjack in Vegas but because I was unable to provide the cashier with an American zip code he was unable to help.

It's the same story at the petrol pumps. Americans can punch their address into the key pad and replenish their tank. Europeans have to prove they're not terrorists before being allowed to start pumping.

I seem to recall a television advertisement in which George W. Bush himself urged us all to go over there for our holidays. But what's the point when you can't buy anything? Or do anything. Or walk across the desert in a white suit without being arrested.

The main problem, I suspect, is a complete lack of knowledge about the world. I asked people in the streets of Vegas to name two European countries. The very first woman I spoke to said: 'Oh yes. What's that one with kangaroos?'

Then you've got New Orleans, which, nearly a year after Katrina, is still utterly smashed and ruined. Now, I'm sorry, but insects can build shelter on their own.

Birds can build nests without a state handout. So why are the people of Louisiana sitting around waiting for someone else to do the repairs?

I tried to help out. I tried to give a car I'd been using to a Christian mission.

But I was threatened with legal action because the car in question was a 91 and not the 98 that had allegedly been promised. A very angry woman accused me of 'misrepresentation'.

Not everyone in America is deranged, of course. Sammy certainly isn't. Sammy was helping us out washing cars, and one night, over dinner, he explained how he'd become so badly burnt. And why, as a result, the best he could hope for out of life was washing cars for cash.

His car had exploded after it was rammed from behind by an off-duty cop. He was taken to a hospital that had no air-conditioning, in California, in the summer.

Not nice when you have third-degree burns to half your body.

And to make matters worse, there was nobody to help him go to the loo, so he either did his business where he lay – or went through untold agony by rolling over to pee on the floor.

The bill for his botched plastic surgery was half a million dollars, $15,000 of which came from the cop's insurance. This means Sammy can never get a proper job, or buy a house or find credit.

The government, he says, is waiting for him to pop up on the radar and then they'll come round to get their greenbacks back.

Of course, many Americans would say our health service is far from perfect and I'd agree. I'd agree there are lots of things wrong with Britain.

I'd also agree, having been to every single state in the US – apart from Rhode Island – that there are good things about America. The hash browns, for instance, served up by Denny's are delicious, you can turn right on a red light and er . . . well, I'm sure there's a lot more but I can't think of anything at the moment.

Among the things I don't like is the way everyone over 15 stone now moves about in a wheelchair. As a result, it takes half an hour to get through even the widest door. And I really don't like the way that every small town looks exactly the same as every other small town. Palmdale in California and Biloxi in Mississippi are nigh-on identical.

They have the same horrible restaurants. The same mall. The same interstate drone. Live in either for more than a week and you'd be stabbing your own eyes with knitting needles.

But it's the idiocracy that really gets me down. The constant coaxing you have to do to get anything done. 'No' is the default setting whether you want to change lanes on a motorway or get a drink on a Sunday. It's like trying to negotiate with a donkey. Once, I urged a cop in Pensacola, Florida, to use his common sense and let me load a van in the no-loading zone, since the airport was shut and it would make no difference. 'Sir,' he said, 'you don't need common sense when you've got laws.'

That, I think, probably says it all.

Sunday 9 July 2006

School reports are agony for parents

For most people, childhood memories are dominated by cloudless summer days and lashings of Robinson's barley water. Not mine, though. Mine are dominated by the mornings when I'd come downstairs to find my school report had arrived.

Throughout the term I'd assured my parents that I'd been working hard, and that the small fire in the chapel had been nothing to do with me. But there, in the report, was solid, irrefutable proof that I hadn't been working hard at all.

Even today, 30 years later, I can recite, verbatim, the comments from a history teacher. 'Even if, as he claims, he was unwell, his mock exam looked like it had been written by someone who was trying to be deliberately stupid. Or who was four years old.'

I can recall, too, the way my parents looked as they thumbed through page after page of abuse and home truths. And also the look of utter bewilderment when the general studies master said I'd been a 'quiet' member of the set. This might have had something to do with the fact that I hadn't been to a single one of his lessons. Because I'd been in the chapel, playing with petrol.

My father would point out calmly that I'd let the school down, the family down and that I'd let myself down. My mother would throw frying pans at me. And

I'd sit there, unable to conceive of a more horrible experience.

Well, it turns out that there is something more horrible after all. Yes, it's bad being the child in these situations, but I have now learnt that it's even worse to be the parent.

In the early years of a child's schooling, reports are fairly meaningless. You learn that your pride and joy has made a lovely paper plate without cutting her head off and that she has grown some watercress, and you swoon with joy.

But then, as common entrance approaches, everything changes. For 12 years you've known, with no question or shadow of doubt, that your child is the greatest, most brilliant and most popular human being in the whole of human history. His paper plates were magnificent and his watercress divine.

You have had visions of him, on stage, thanking the Nobel academy. But then, suddenly, along comes a report that says that, actually, he's a bit thick.

Teachers, of course, are very good at softening the blow. They use words such as 'pleasing' and 'encouraging', no matter how many members of staff he has stabbed that term. 'Johnny is becoming very adept with his knife. Perhaps he would do well if he were to think about a career in a slaughterhouse.'

My housemaster was brilliant at this. In my final report he said: 'We like Jeremy very much. When he is sent to borstal, we hope it is not too far away so that we can come to visit him from time to time.'

The trouble is that no matter how hard they try to mask the truth, you can't ignore it, in the same way that you'd find it hard to ignore a tiger if it were in your car. Praise is lost in the background clutter. You're used to it. Everyone is always nice about your kids. They have been since they were in a pram.

But criticism; that's a whole new area. That leaps off the page and hits you straight in the heart. 'Annabel needs to concentrate more,' is no different from saying 'Annabel has a face like a duck's arse'. It smarts.

Take Zidane, who was sent off while playing football for France: he was showered with sympathy when he explained that the Italian player had insulted his mother.

So why should you not headbutt your child's teacher in the chest when he writes to say that Johnny daydreams too much in Latin?

God knows, I know what it's like to get a poor review. I know how much it stings, and I'm 46. So imagine how much it must hurt when you get one aged 11.

No, really, imagine if your boss wrote a report on how you were doing at work . . . and then sent it to your children. 'Peter has made pleasing progress in mergers and acquisitions this year and we're encouraged with his efforts to stop looking up the secretaries' skirts. But he must try to avoid selling stocks too early or he won't be getting a promotion any time soon.'

My wife came downstairs the other night and asked what I thought of her new outfit. I was honest. I gave her a proper report and said it made her look mad. And was she pleased? Was she hell. As we got into the car to go out, the windows frosted over on the inside.

It's not the done thing to present others with an honest

appraisal of their performance. I know I'm useless on the tennis court but I don't like my partner to say so.

And yet that's exactly what a school report does.

The one I read this morning even went so far as to reveal the class average time for a 100-metre race, and how long, in hours, it took my daughter to cover the same distance. And the point of this is . . . what exactly? To make me feel guilty for breeding a mutant?

Well, it hasn't worked because those who can run fast are, in my experience, apes.

I can, however, end with a crumb of comfort for those of you whose children received poor reports last week. Nobody who is successful in life ever had a good one.

Sunday 16 July 2006

How to make a man of a mummy's boy

Last week, on a Radio 4 show called *The Moral Maze*, a woman said that all men are wife-beaters and warmongers, and that a boy brought up by women is bound to become a better balanced human being.

Maybe this is so. But he is also bound to spend too much time on the telephone talking about nothing in particular. What's more, he will be late for the start of all TV films and will therefore have no clue what's going on, he will read books in which nothing ever happens, he may well turn out to be a teensy bit gay, and worst of all he will grow up never having seen an F-15 fighter jet loop the loop at an air show.

He may well have seen a B-1 bomber make a full-bore, combat-power take-off, but only through the fence at Greenham Common. And that means he won't have been in the company of someone who agreed that, yes, it's much prettier and far more amazing than anything from the dreary and pointless mind of Jane Austen.

Last weekend I took my boy-child to the Royal International Air Tattoo at RAF Fairford. This is not something that would have happened if he'd been brought up by a heavily breasted feminist with greasy hair.

Sadly, we didn't quite make it in time for the Red Arrows, which meant we ended up watching their routine from the side of the road a few miles away. Strangely, it was much better.

Of course, the display is designed to look choreographed and excellent from one side of the airfield, where the audience is standing. It's designed so you go 'ooh' and 'wow' at all the carefully rehearsed passing manoeuvres.

But if you look at it from three miles away, on the other side of the airfield, it's like looking at the underside of a tapestry. It looks like a mess, like a selection of people with Parkinson's disease have climbed into their jets after getting very, very drunk. You don't go 'ooh' or 'wow'. You find yourself shouting: 'Jesus Christ. They're going to f★★★★★★ hit each other.' And diving for cover in the hedge. Or was that just me?

After that, the other team displays looked a bit weak, if I'm honest. Oh, except for the Swiss. Perhaps because they never have to train for any actual combat, their formation flying was as precise as their watches. The Jordanians weren't bad either. Sadly, the Israelis couldn't make it. They sent a note saying they were a bit busy.

I'd say the highlight of the day went to the Russians, who turned up with a Power Ranger fighter jet called the MiG-29, which can fly – and I'm not making this up – backwards and upside down at the same time. It can also stop, fall from the sky like a leaf and then tear over your head so low that it gives you a new parting at 500 mph, while making a noise so immense it very nearly undid the Duke of Kent's tie.

It was an epic spectacle, as magical as anything you've ever seen in the West End and as loud as anything you ever heard at Knebworth. And what made it even more breathtaking is that there were no wires and no special effects. What you were watching was Johnny Russian spending 15 minutes idly tearing up the laws of physics.

Next up were the Americans, who have nothing in their armoury that can even get close to the lunacy of the MiG. It was like giving Paul Daniels a white rabbit and putting him on stage after the Cirque du Soleil.

Can this have been deliberate on the part of the show's organisers? To bring the Americans on after the main event. To humiliate them a little bit. I do like to think so.

It turned out, however, that the Americans are quite capable of humiliating themselves. While the F-15 was whizzing about, a USAF staff sergeant came on the public-address system to tell us all what was going on. Unfortunately, he'd brought exactly the same script he uses back at home . . .

'You are watching with pride,' he began and was wrong immediately. I wasn't watching with pride. I was watching with a Pimm's.

The rest of his spiel was like listening to the fingernail express screeching to a halt on a blackboard the size of Alaska. The F-15, he said, has patrolled the skies for 30 years, protecting 'this great nation's way of life from the tyranny of terrorism, blah blah blah'. It was even accompanied by that swelling one-cal soft rock music that causes visitors at American air shows to rise to their feet and weep.

I looked around at the RAF bigwigs with whom I was sitting and, amazingly, none of them was openly vomiting. Mostly, they were smiling the smile you might give your boss if you've got him round for dinner and he's just made an inappropriate remark about your wife's panty line.

My boy-child wasn't. He was beaming the beam of someone for whom the meaning of life had just become clear. He spends most of his life with two sisters, a mother, a granny, a nanny and a housekeeper. Even our dogs are girls. And yet here he was watching an F-15 climb with its burners lit from ground level to 17,000 feet in 11 seconds. With his dad. And he loved it.

So here's a tip. It's the Farnborough air show this weekend. If you've got a son, go. If you haven't, go upstairs and make one.

Sunday 23 July 2006

My near-death toilet experience

When we heard recently that Syd Barrett, the reclusive former member of Pink Floyd, had died at his semi-detached home in Cambridge, many things intrigued those who remember his music. Why did he choose to live alone? Why did he shun the money? What was he doing in such a small house?

But for me only one thing was truly shocking. He had died at the age of just 60.

Now I know that if you're 17 years old, 60 is as far away as the moons of Jupiter.

But for me, living in the accelerated space–time continuum of middle age, 60 is tomorrow morning.

Scientists say the smallest measurement of time is a femtosecond. A million-billionth of a second. But when you're older than 45, the smallest measurement of time, actually, is one year. And if I live to 60, I only have 14 left. That's 5,000 days. And that's only 120,000 hours.

I think often about how I shall die and when. I find myself looking at really old people and wondering what it must feel like; to know that you've reached a point where your life expectancy is measurable in minutes. Why aren't they all running around waving their arms in the air panicking; because they must surely know that soon everything that they hold dear – everything – will be replaced by the utter blackness of eternity?

I get a lot of practice at thinking these things because in my life every lump, bump, cough, ache and pain is the onset of some terrible killer disease. I catch ebola three times a week, and back in June, having discovered a nodule of something unpleasant near my left elbow, became fairly convinced I'd become the first person in human history to catch arm cancer. A few days earlier, I had managed – just – to shake off a nasty bout of ear TB.

Of course, most of my ailments are designed so that I can lie on a sofa while my wife brings me poached eggs on toast. I've never really thought I had cancer, so I've never really known what it must be like to stare the Grim Reaper in the face and know that time's up. Last weekend, however, all that changed . . .

Now I want to make it absolutely plain before I go any further that I do not find bottoms or anything which comes out of them even remotely funny. I am not seven years old and I am not German. But there's no way of saying what I'm about to say without being lavatorial. I'm sorry for that.

What happened, you see, is that after my usual morning's number twos, I noticed that the water in the bowl was red. Which meant, of course, that I had, without feeling any pain, passed a small amount of blood. Plainly, I had prostate cancer.

I am aware of this disease. I know that it is the most common form of cancer among men and it is likely to strike when the victim nears 50. I even know what colour wristband you should wear to show you support it (blue).

I knew, too, that I needed, urgently, to check mine out and so, armed with nothing but a well-oiled finger, went ahead and violated what for 46 years has been a strictly enforced one-way street.

I shall spare you the pain and the humiliation of this hideous potholing expedition, but I feel duty-bound to explain that once I was in there, ferreting about, I realised that I didn't know what a prostate is, or what it feels like or where it is exactly.

It's much the same story with the endless requests we get from doctors to check out our testicles for early signs of cancer. I'm sure this is jolly good fun, but unless you tell us what we're looking for, how will we know when we've found it?

And skin cancer too. How can you tell the difference between a mole and a melanoma? I'm sure it's possible if you've spent seven years studying medicine, but what if you're a fork-lift truck driver? I've examined thousands of photographs of malignant skin growths and they all look like every freckle on my body.

After a bit of research on the internet I discovered that a prostate is about the size of a walnut, that it's used to make fluid in which sperm is transported and that it lives 'near' the rectum.

And eventually I did discover something in my bottom that fitted the description.

But with knowledge gleaned solely from the BBC website – which almost certainly will blame the rise in popularity for prostate cancer on either the Israelis or global warming – and with nothing to hand except a soapy index finger, I'm afraid I wasn't able to say whether whatever I'd found had cancer or was in rude good health.

The only evidence I had was the blood, and that really was enough.

I was finished. I wasn't even going to last as long as Syd Barrett.

I heard the other day that 80 per cent of patients, when told by a doctor that their tests for cancer had been positive, make a joke of some sort. Wearily, I went downstairs wondering what mine might be. Something about getting the spare room painted, perhaps . . .

And there in the kitchen was my wife. 'Morning,' she said cheerily. 'Have you been to the loo yet, because that beetroot we've been eating doesn't half make it red.'

I've never felt so happy in all my life.

Sunday 30 July 2006

When I am the Mayor of London

It seems that while I wasn't paying attention someone publicly suggested that I stand against Ken Livingstone as the official Tory candidate in the forthcoming elections to find a London mayor.

My initial reaction was predictable. Why should I give up a handsomely paid job which involves driving round corners in a selection of Ferraris and Lamborghinis so that I can earn £134,000 a year doing something I don't want to do, for a party I'm not sure about, in a city where I don't live?

However, since that initial moment of shock and awe, I've given the matter some serious thought and I've decided that, actually, I'd rather like to give it a shot. I mean, how hard can it be?

Sure, the white paper drawn up to create the post was the largest parliamentary document since the Government of India Act in 1935, but so far as I can tell, the job of running the capital is no harder than being a lift attendant.

For starters, the original white paper stated that the Greater London Authority should have up to 250 staff, at a cost of £20 million. But Uncle Ken has blasted through this and employed 630 people at a cost of £60 million. And with that lot running around, crossing the i's and dotting the t's, what's left for me to do?

On the first day I'd instruct my people to go out into

the capital and get rid of all the bus lanes. And then I'd sell off all the bendy buses to somewhere like Los Angeles, which has big enough roads to handle their vast bulk.

Then I'd go to the Ivy for lunch.

On Tuesday I'd look out of the window for a bit and marvel at how the traffic was moving freely. And then I'd go to the Caprice.

And in the afternoon I'd have a nap. Then, in the evening, I'd put the mayoral eco-car on eBay and buy a Range Rover.

Wednesday is when we record *Top Gear*, so I'd pop down to Surrey and drive round some corners in a Lamborghini. And then I'd go back to London in the Range Rover and maybe take in a show.

You think I'm joking here. But I'm not. Uncle Ken is plainly so bored that he spends his day thumbing through *The Observer's Book of Despots*, seeing which swivel-eyed lunatic he can have round for dinner that night. So far he's had Islamic cleric Dr Yusuf al-Qaradawi, who spends his free time urging people to beat up their wives and throw stones at homosexuals.

And then, of course, he played host to the Venezuelan president, Hugo Chavez, who after just six months in office has even managed to upset the Swedes. They're so cross with him they've refused to sell him any more Saabs, which must have shaken him to the core.

I'm not sure who I'd have round. Probably one of those porn stars that keep being elected to non-jobs in Italy. But, whatever, on Thursday I'd reintroduce fox-hunting to the boroughs of Islington and Hackney. You might think this provocative, encouraging men in hunting pinks to gallop around Tofu central, but it's no more offensive than Ken's obsession with 'ethnic inclusivity' in places like Kensington and Chelsea. And there'd be fewer upturned wheelie bins for the bin men to worry about.

I suppose I should have a look at the congestion charge too. I've thought about this and I've decided there'd be a charge of £50 a day for all cars, which would keep tatty rubbish out of the city, and £500 a day for bicycles.

Anyone who's too mean to buy a car is too mean to spend anything in the shops, so there's no point having them. They can go to Dunstable instead, or Bedford, and not spend anything there.

Implementing this would take, what, 15 minutes. Which means that by Friday I'd be a bit stumped for something to do. Maybe I'd call the police, who would be under my command, and tell them to catch some burglars.

Oh no, wait. I know. I'd get someone to replace the statue of that woman with no arms and legs in Trafalgar Square with a full-size bronze model of a Spitfire.

Of course, this life of leisure presumes that I'd get elected in the first place, but I can't see this presents too much of a problem. I mean, Ken has a pool of 381,790 voters on whom he can call – this being the current circulation of the *Guardian*. That means there are 5.6 million Londoners who don't want their town hall full of marketing assistants and equality advisers.

I'd therefore replace them with a team who'd look into ways of changing the Notting Hill carnival into an annual drag race for monster trucks. And I'd pass a law banning people from entering the London marathon in diving suits or chicken outfits. This kind of thing is acceptable at provincial fancy-dress parties, but if your outfit prevents you from finishing the race within six hours, don't come crying to me if you're mowed down by a stockbroker in a BMW.

In the second week I'd sell the mayoral offices to a property developer, sack the 630 staff and, after turning out the lights, sack myself. Because when you actually stop and think about it, a London authority is a tier of government we can't afford and don't need.

There. That's my manifesto. Still think I'm a good idea, Dave?

Sunday 6 August 2006

How to blow up a dead seal

Last weekend the *Sunday Times* Home section devoted a lot of space to moving to the seaside and living for the rest of your life in a chunky polo-neck sweater and yellow wellies. It all looked terribly idyllic.

But I have a cottage by the coast and let me tell you there are certain aspects of life by the sea that you might not have considered: like, for instance, what you are supposed to do when an 8-foot seal comes to the beach outside your house and dies.

No, I didn't club it. And nor had it become entangled in the £40 worth of fishing equipment that I lose in the oggin every evening. Global warming? Perhaps, but contrary to the teachings of Rolf Harris there is another, more common way for seals to die. It's called old age.

Whatever, it was dead and despite a limited knowledge about these things I knew that I had maybe two days before it would start to smell pretty bad.

'Push it into sea,' said one local. A fine plan, I'm sure, but such was the weight of the thing I think it would have been easier to push the sea onto the seal. God, it was heavy.

And worse, while trying to manhandle it through the shallows, its eyes fell out.

So now I'm standing up to my shins in water that's being stained a sort of pungent reddy brown, and all around small fish and crabs are fighting one another to eat the eyes. This is something David Attenborough doesn't show.

The gruesome, cruel, revolting side of nature.

I'm not ashamed to admit that after only a very short while I was prodigiously sick. And then the crabs start to eat that.

Happily, I recently bought a special eight-wheel-drive vehicle for just such an emergency, so I reversed this on to the beach with a view to pulling the seal above the high-water mark. Carefully, I tied a rope to its flippers, and promptly pulled them off.

Say what you like about seals, that they're cute and so on, but I can assure you they are incredibly badly made. The slightest tug or nudge causes bits of them to come away.

Anyway, after much revving and many arguments with my wife about what sort of knot would be best, we finally had the beast on dry land. But then what?

Momentarily, I considered towing it to a nearby beauty spot where people were camping illegally. A rotting seal with no eyes or feet would soon clear them away. 'No,' said another passing local, 'you should turn it into a coat.'

This raises an interesting point. You might think you're prepared for a life by the sea. You can probably paint, and arrange flowers, and make jam from kelp, but can you skin a seal? I'm willing to bet you can't. And neither can I, so I decided to burn it.

Of course, I've watched Ray Mears many times and I know that it's easy to light a fire with nothing but patience and some dry wood. But this is the Isle of Man and I'd like to see him find some dry wood here. It all falls into two categories: damp or sodden.

I collected as much of it as I could, along with half a ton of litter that's always easy to find on a beach, and made what would pass for a Viking funeral pyre . . . and then went to the garage to buy a couple of gallons of diesel.

Not since the wreckers were operating round these parts has the Isle of Man seen such an enormous blaze. All day it spat and crackled and I went to bed that night pleased that I'd found an appropriate and dignified way for the seal to be dealt with.

But it didn't work. The seal emerged with nothing more than a lightly singed coat.

So I built an even bigger fire. This one was going to make the conflagration in Hemel Hempstead look like the pilot light in your boiler. I bought diesel, petrol, meths, engine oil, kindling and even a light sprinkling of gunpowder. Then I lit a match and knew immediately I'd overdone it. The pile didn't catch fire. It exploded.

The savagery was incredible. It looked like Beirut out there. Nothing within 50 yards was as it had been. Except the seal. It remained in one piece, only now it had a small gash in its stomach through which its intestines were poking. These smelt terrible.

I therefore rented, for the not inconsiderable sum of £175 a day, a bulldozer so that I could dig a grave for the lightly singed, mildly split corpse.

This is an expense you might not have considered when thinking about moving to the seaside.

Have you ever tried digging a grave on a shingle beach?

It can't be done. Shingle is the geological equivalent of the Hydra. You scoop 10 stones out of the way and immediately 10 grow back to fill the cavity.

By the time my 24-hour bulldozer rental period was up, the hole was just about big enough for Willie Carson. But not a big dead grey seal, so I'm afraid there's no happy ending. It's still out there, making the whole postcode smell like Cambodia's killing fields.

I thought that a life by the sea would be relaxing. I thought it'd be nice to work here.

And it is, although I must say this is the first newspaper column I've written while wearing a gas mask.

Sunday 13 August 2006

The Royals, a soap made in heaven

So, Prince Harry has been photographed in a nightclub squeezing the ample right breast of a pretty young blonde. Good. I wish he'd gone further, caught a spot of syphilis, and then driven home in a bright red Ferrari at 150 mph.

For years people have argued about whether or not we should have a royal family, and that if we should, what kind of role it should play in today's world.

Should it be old and stuffy, a moth-eaten metaphor for the Britain that once was? Or should it have a more meaningful role than opening hospices and asking visiting dignitaries from Bongo Bongo land if they've come far?

And if it does have a more meaningful role, what should it be? I mean, how can you move something along when it has the millstone of history around its neck?

You can't, so how's this for a brilliant idea I've just had? You simply cut those irksome ties with the past and move the royal family into the most modern arena of them all . . .

We have a craving for soap opera in this country. *Coronation Farm* and *EastEnders* are watched by millions of people every night. We can't, it seems, get enough of who said what to whom, and what the ramifications of that might be. Other people's lives.

Other people's trivia. We lap it up.

And now we're drinking from the saucer of *Big Brother*

as well, which when you think about it is just another soap opera only with no storyline, no plot and no actors. Just a lot of very clever editing to make these dreary non-people look interesting.

And boy, does it work. So desperate are we to keep abreast of their fortunes that even today, several years after she left the *Big Brother* house, Jade Goody, who is part woman and part scientific blunder, is still unable to go to the gym or pop to the shops without being papped.

Is there room for more? More *Love Island*? More *I'm in a Jungle*?

More soap. More bit-part nobodies to feed the insatiable hunger of the British red-topped tabloids and the legions of readers?

Yes, of course there is, and so, ladies and gentlemen, I give you . . . *The Royal Family*. We turn the whole damn shooting match into a reality soap opera, stripped across the week's TV schedules with late-night updates and a big publicity machine to feed the morning papers.

At present the cost of the royal family to each taxpayer in Britain is 60p a year.

That looks like bad value when all the key players ever do is open stuff and talk to vegetables. But 60p a year for a five-times-a-week soap opera. That would be the best-value television in the world.

We already have the cast of characters. There's Miss Ellie, in the shape of the Queen. Quiet. Dignified. And always in charge. Then you've got Wills as JR, Harry as Bobby, and Charles, who had no equivalent in *Dallas* but only because they never thought to include an eco-mentalist uncle who talks to his food and gets cross with buildings.

Of course, we'd also need a Cliff Barnes. A bit of a joke. A bit of a loser.

Someone with a real and genuine grudge against the Windsors. And I know just the man: Mohamed al-Fayed, whose son died in a car smash in Paris with the eco-mentalist uncle's first wife. Jesus. What scriptwriter could have come up with a plot line as good as that?

We even have a modern-day interpretation of Pam in the increasingly gorgeous shape of Zara Phillips. She'd pop up from time to time in dresses with lower and lower necklines, on the arm of her boyfriend, who plays rugby for his country.

Do you see what I'm getting at here? That the story's already been written. That the characters are already in place. So no clever editing is necessary. That we have the house – several houses actually – and best of all that the family, with the possible exception of Philip, and maybe Anne, would leap at the chance to have their currently rather silly lives given some meaning and purpose.

I'm not joking. Being born into a 'soap opera' is no more stupid really than being born into a 'royal family'. And I do think that at a stroke it would make Queen Victoria, and the Queen Vic for that matter, look hopelessly out of date.

We wouldn't ask them to do anything different to what they do already. But instead of being shocked when Harry drives his small hatchback through Wiltshire at 60 mph, we'd be dismayed that he wasn't doing twice that, in a Lamborghini.

And when he leans over to fiddle with the bosoms of a blonde, we won't wonder what the country's coming to. We'll hope that shortly after the picture was taken, and under the glare of the watching cameras, he slipped into his Hermann Goering outfit, bent her over the DJ's deck and gave her a damn good seeing-to.

Why not? At the moment everyone is screaming for contestants on *Big Brother* to make jiggy-jiggy, so why would it be any different for Harry and Wills, and the delectable Zara?

Will they oblige? Well, that's just the point. That's the fizz. Because we just don't know. Of course, we could employ scriptwriters, but no matter how good they might be they'd never come up with what the royal family manages all by itself.

Sunday 20 August 2006

I'm calling time on silly watches

After many years of faithful service, my watch has gone wrong. It just chooses random moments of the day to display meaningless times which, speaking as the world's most punctual person, is a nuisance. Especially as I shall now have to go to a shop and buy a replacement.

Yes, I know I could send it to the menders but, because I really am the most punctual person in the world, what am I supposed to do while it's away? Use the moon? For me, going around without a watch is worse than going around without my trousers.

Of course, I have a back-up. My wife bought it for me many years ago with her last salary cheque and it's very beautiful. But, sadly, my eyes are now so old and weary that I can't read the face properly. Which means I turned up to meet an old friend one hour late last week. And that, in my book, is ruder than turning up and vomiting on him.

It also brings me on to the biggest problem I've found in my quest to find a new timepiece. There's a world of choice out there but everything is unbelievably expensive and fitted with a whole host of features that no one could possibly ever need.

I have flown an F-15 fighter and at no point in the 90-minute sortie did I think: 'Damn. I wish my watch had an altimeter because then I could see how far from the ground I am.' All planes have such a device on the dashboard.

Similarly, when I was diving off those wall reefs in the Maldives I didn't at any time think: 'Ooh. I must check my watch to see how far below the surface I have gone.' Thoughtfully, God fitted my head with sinuses, which do that job very well already.

You might think, then, that my demands are simple. I don't want my new watch to open bottles. I don't want it to double up as a laser or a garrotte. I just want something that tells the time, not in Bangkok or Los Angeles, but here, now, clearly, robustly and with no fuss. The end.

But it isn't the end. You see, in recent months someone has decided that the watch says something about the man. And that having the right timepiece is just as important as having the right hair, or the right names for your children, or the right car.

Over dinner the other night someone leant across to a perfect stranger on the other side of the table and said: 'Is that a Monte Carlo?' It was, apparently, and pretty soon everyone there was cooing and nodding appreciatively. Except me. I had no idea what a Monte Carlo was.

Then we have James May, my television colleague, who has a collection of watches.

Yes, a collection. But despite this he has just spent thousands of pounds on a watch made by IWC. Now I know roughly what he earns and therefore I know what percentage of his income he's just blown on this watch and I think, medically speaking, he may be mad.

It turns out, however, that his IWC, in the big scheme

of things, is actually quite cheap. There are watches out there that cost tens or hundreds of thousands of pounds. And I can't see why.

Except, of course, I can. Timex can sell you a reliable watch that has a back light for the hard of seeing, a compass, a stopwatch and a tool for restarting stricken nuclear submarines, all for £29.99. And that's because the badge says Timex.

Which is another way of saying that you have no style, no sense of cool and that you may drive a Hyundai.

To justify the enormous prices charged these days, watchmakers all have idiotic names, like Gilchrist & Soames, and they all claim to make timepieces for fighter pilots and space-shuttle commanders and people who parachute from atomic bombs into power boats for a living. What's more, all of them claim to have been doing this, in sheds in remote Swiss villages, for the last six thousand years.

How many craftsmen are there in the mountains, I wonder? Millions, by the sound of it.

Breitling even bangs on about how it made the instruments for various historically important planes. So what? The Swiss also stored a lot of historically important gold teeth. It means nothing when I'm lying in bed trying to work out whether it's the middle of the night or time to get up.

Whatever, these watch companies give you all this active-lifestyle guff and show you pictures of Swiss pensioners in brown store coats painstakingly assembling the inner workings with tweezers, and then they try to flog you something that is more complicated than a slide rule and is made from uranium. Or which is bigger and heavier than Fort Knox and would look stupid on even Puff Diddly.

I think I've found an answer, though. There's a watch called the Bell & Ross BR 01-92 which, according to the blurb, is made in Switzerland from German parts by a company that supplies the American military and is used regularly by people who make a living by being fired from the gun turrets of Abrams M1 tanks while riding burning jet skis.

Who cares? What I like is that it's very simple and has big numbers, but what I don't know is whether it's reliable and whether people laugh at you because of it at dinner parties. Anyone got one? Anyone know?

Sunday 27 August 2006

Amazing what you can dig up in Africa

Not that long ago a chap from the town where I live took his metal detector for a walk in some local fields and found a hoard of coins, one of which revealed the existence of a Roman emperor who was not mentioned in any of the history books.

It all sounds jolly exciting, but I suspect that for every man who finds gold at the end of his garden there are about a million who devote their lives to the search for buried treasure and end up with a collection of old Coke cans and the gearbox from a 1957 Massey Ferguson.

That'd be like devoting your whole life to DIY and never once erecting a single usable shelf.

Nevertheless, last week I joined an archaeological search party on the Makgadikgadi saltpans in Botswana. And guess what? Within just four hours we'd unearthed an early Iron Age burial ground. That's like taking up alchemy and making gold on your first attempt.

Our guide, quivery with excitement, stepped from his quad bike and told us in a hushed whisper, as though he might disturb the scene with sound waves, that we must go lightly in case we trod on what might turn out to be an important artifact.

Pretty soon he was on his hands and knees piecing together what had plainly been a rather badly made bushman vase, and my children were bringing him beads fashioned from bits of ostrich shell.

'Oh my God,' he wailed. 'Do you know what these are? These beads! They're the dawn of art. They're the first example anywhere of early hominids decorating themselves. You can draw a direct line from these beads to the Renaissance.'

Well, I looked at one as hard as I could, but so far as I could tell it was a small piece of ostrich shell with a hole in the middle. Not exactly *Indiana Jones and the Temple of Doom*. I've seen better in Ratners.

Then he found some fossilised wood and I honestly thought he was going to burst.

'Do you know what this is?' he wailed excitedly. 'It's only the third piece of fossilised wood ever found out here!'

Well, I examined all the angles and couldn't see why this was important in any way. If it was just a piece of wood, then so what? This tells us that many years ago there were trees. I sort of knew that. And if it had once been part of, say, a chair, then what does that tell us? That Iron Age man had a grasp of carpentry? Well, he would.

I should explain at this point that many years ago some archaeologists dug a huge hole in my school's grounds, claiming they'd discovered the most important Viking site ever. Every day they went in there with their toothbrushes and their nail files, and every night I'd leap in there in my cowboy boots, because the whole site was strictly out of bounds. This meant it was a tremendous place to have an undisturbed cigarette. Archaeology, then, has never really floated my boat.

And what's more, it turns out I'm not very good at it. I wandered about with my hands in my pockets failing to see anything even remotely man-made. Perhaps, being tall, my eyes are too far from the ground, but whatever, in the whole day I didn't unearth a damn thing.

My seven-year-old daughter, on the other hand, turned out to be quite an expert.

Having found several beads and some potted shrapnel, she uncovered what turned out to be a human leg bone. Quite how our guide worked this one out I have no idea, because to me it just looked like a long thin stone.

And quite why it mattered I don't know either. Over the years many people have died, so it stands to reason that there are many bones out there. Finding one in the ground is like finding a star in the night sky or an idiot in local politics.

It's the same deal with pots. People have always made them. And people have always dropped them on the floor. So finding the pieces today is of no moment.

I watch *Time Team* on television occasionally and every time one of those earnest young men pops out of his hole with a bit of crockery I just want to say: 'Oh why don't you just go to the pub.' Archaeology, as we all know, is simply a tool that enables very stupid people to get into university. Fuse it with media studies and you end up with Tony Robinson.

Desperate to enliven my morning of walking around with my hands in my pockets, I planted my iPod under the crust of the salt and then called over my family to show them what I'd found.

'Look,' I exclaimed to the assembled group. 'These

Iron Age Johnnies were more advanced than we thought.'

It fell rather flat, if I'm honest. The rest of my family were genuinely captivated by our find and the history it represented.

They didn't think it even slightly odd that our guide logged the location on his portable GPS system, saying he'd return as soon as possible with a team of experts from America.

Can you believe that? That people are prepared to fly halfway round the world to poke about in the ground looking for pots, for no financial gain.

No, really. They will simply donate their finds to a museum so they can be looked at by daytrippers who are only in there because outside it's raining.

Sunday 10 September 2006

If you're homeless find a hedgerow

Last week the government announced the latest figures showing the number of homeless people in Britain. And they don't make any sense.

No, really. The report says that from April to June of this year 19,430 households applied to their local councils and were accepted as being homeless. I don't understand. How can you be a 'householder' and be homeless?

To find out I turned to Shelter, the housing charity, which says there are 130,000 homeless children in Britain. No there aren't. I travel a great deal, often to the north, and I've never once seen a homeless child.

The only homeless people I ever see are rather frightening-looking Scottish men who prowl the streets of Soho with their angry dogs begging for money. 'Eat the dog. Then we'll talk,' is what I always say.

I don't want to belittle homelessness. I understand that it must be very scary to find yourself with no friends, no family and nowhere to stay. I think often about how terrible that moment must be when you realise, for the first time, that you really have no bed that night. It sends a shudder down my spine.

Think about it. Slipping into a pair of cardboard pyjamas and being serenaded to sleep by passing trains, knowing that the price you pay for a mug of soup is a half-hour lecture on God's infinite wisdom.

In fact, it's because I care so much about homeless people that I have some advice for anyone whose life has gone so far down the crapper that he's only reading this newspaper because he's sleeping in it. And here it is. Move out of London and into the countryside.

If you hole up for the night in a shop doorway in London, those street-cleaner men will come along and squirt you with powerful jets of icy water.

And then, when you're all soggy and cold, you'll be moved on to another doorway where a drunken late-night reveller will be sick over you. Then your dog will be stolen by a Romanian woman in a shawl, and then someone will make you take so much heroin that you technically become an Afghan.

And to make matters worse you'll spend your days scouring the city streets for out-of-date sandwiches, while stinking, and all the while you'll be surrounded by Jade Moss and Judy Law, who will be popping out to the shops because there's no more room in their houses for any more of their money.

Genuinely, I don't understand why people who've lost their homes think that all will be well if they stow away on a train to London. And nor do I understand why people who were in London to start with don't move out the moment they realise that it's 10.30 p.m. and that they don't have anywhere to stay.

London, when you have money, and a job and friends, is truly one of the greatest places on earth. But the capital, when you have nothing, must be more depressing than listening to Leonard Cohen from the wrong side of a cocaine high.

In the countryside things are a lot more cheery. For a kick-off the chances of being turned into a rent boy are smaller. There is also less heroin, and if you sleep in a field the chances of a late-night reveller being sick all over you are very small indeed.

What's more, food simply isn't an issue. I spent most of last week working in a rural part of Warwickshire and couldn't believe how much there was to eat in the hedgerows. Blackberries, elderberries and what I thought was a tomato. It wasn't.

In fact, if you do move to the countryside, avoid any small red plant that grows in hedgerows and looks like a tomato because it's disgusting; instead, try truffling in the fields.

In one I found several thousand potatoes, and in another, right outside someone's kitchen window, I found carrots and marrows. There were even some nearby cows that could easily be killed and eaten.

Then there's the question of clothing. In a big city like London it matters what you wear because people are looking. You have to steal the right kind of Nike trainer, for instance. Whereas in the countryside there isn't anyone around for miles, so you can keep warm in fertiliser bags, which can be held together with baler twine.

The news is good too when the sun sinks because you don't have to hole up under a railway bridge. There are countless stables full of straw and, I'm told, it's still – just – possible to find a barn that hasn't yet been converted into an agreeable home by someone called Nigel.

Not only would living rough in the countryside be infinitely better than living rough in London but I'd go so far as to suggest it might even be fun.

Not as much fun as, say, being the Queen, but certainly not bad. You could make traps and watch birds and make dens and it'd be like being nine.

In fact, come to think of it, I'm rather surprised that the countryside isn't awash with tramps, but in the 12 years I've lived out here, I haven't seen one. There's a bloke who sells *The Big Issue* in a nearby town. But I think I saw him the other day in a BMW, and sleeping in that doesn't count.

Sunday 17 September 2006

There's a literary future in the iLav

I like magazines. I like looking at the houses in *Country Life*, and I like looking at the pictures of people who've been eaten by sharks in *Nuts* and *Zoo*. I even like looking at what horrible trinketry is on the mantelpieces of the rich and orange in *Hello!*.

For you, a trip to the dentist is a hideous brush with the concept of torture, pain and despair. But me? I'm there two hours early so I can spend some time lost in a world of *The Lady* and *Dogs Today*. I even like to bury my nose in the spine of a magazine and take in some of the glue.

I love that smell, and it certainly helps at the dentist's because by the time I actually get to the chair I'm so off my face there's no need for those savage Novocaine injections. He could actually cut my whole head off with a bread knife and I wouldn't feel a thing.

But it seems I'm alone on this one because magazine sales are beginning to stall.

What Car?, for instance, has sold 150,000 copies a month since the Druids used their newfangled 'wheel' to build Stonehenge. But in the past year or so sales have tumbled to just 120,000. And they're still going down.

Of course, it's easy to see why. If you want to find out about your next car, why spend £4.25 at the newsagent's when you can simply go online and get all the information you want, from the people at *What Car?* themselves, for nothing?

And why buy *Zoo* to see what someone looks like when they've been bitten by a shark when the web is full to overflowing of people being run over and catching fire and eating their own arms?

This, of course, is great for you and me but it does raise some interesting questions. Like, for instance, how can these websites support themselves? I mean, you don't pay to see them, and the operators can't rely on advertising revenue because nobody has yet figured out what the rates might be, or even if advertising on the net actually works.

This means a teenager in his bedroom, putting up happy-slapping video clips for a laugh, now has the power to completely unpick the fabric of the world's publishing empires.

'Pah,' said a colleague of mine, in a meeting to discuss this very issue last week. 'Men will always need to take a dump, and that means the magazine is here to stay.'

It's an interesting point. The notion of going to the lavatory without taking something to read is simply incomprehensible. The joy of being in there, on your own, lost in a world of idyllic country houses and *Private Eye* and shark attacks, away from the phone, and away from the demands of the kids, is even more wondrous than being invited to spend the whole afternoon with a jar of honey and Kristin Scott Thomas.

But then, the day after we discussed the reading habits of men, came news from Sony of a new electronic book which, it's said, will do for reading what the iPod did for listening to music.

It's the size of a wallet and can store a library of up to 70 books in its memory chip. What's more, the screen has no flicker and no backlight so you can read for hours without hurting your eyes. And judging from the pictures it appears to be easy to use, with just one button for 'turning the page'.

Critics say it'll never catch on because, as a general rule, people only ever have one book on the go at a time. And they go on to ask why, when you've read it, you might want to store it electronically rather than on your shelves, by the fireplace.

Fair enough, but they're missing something. When we go on holiday, my wife needs one suitcase for her books about women in beekeeper hats doing bugger all for 650 pages, and I need another for all my speedboat and Nazi gold thrillers. An electronic reader would solve all that.

But it's the applications beyond novels that really fire my imagination. Those of you who watch the epic TV show 24 know that Jack Bauer is forever arriving outside a building full of terrorists and then having the schematics of the building in question sent to his PDA. Now I don't know what schematics are, and nor, if I'm honest, am I fully wised up on what a PDA might be, but it seems he gets the plans of the building with all the staircases and the points of egress. Sometimes there are little red blobs showing him where the baddies are too.

Now if it's possible to do this, surely it is also possible to download a copy of *Shark Attack Weekly* or *Country Life* directly from the editorial offices via my wireless internet connection into my khazi.

That doesn't solve the problem of how publishers might

generate ad revenue but if you work out how much could be saved by not having to buy the paper, and do the printing and put the magazine on lorries to the Isle of Skye, then who knows, maybe they won't actually need advertising at all.

That's not good, of course, for those who have printing-press companies or those with thin glasses who work in advertising. But even here, I have a suggestion.

Start a company making a selection of exciting new haemorrhoid creams.

Because if the nation's men can relieve themselves with, ooh, five or six hundred magazines at the time, the only thing that'll ever get them out again is their piles.

Sunday 1 October 2006

Life's ultimate short straw

My local petrol station has employed an elderly chap to run the pumps, no doubt to satisfy the recent European diktat that bars age discrimination.

Good. I'm pleased as punch that the old boy can now fill his days. However, I do wish the owners of the garage had explained to him how the computerised petrol pumps work, that the cash till is electronic, and how best to operate the chip and pin system while wearing bifocals.

By the time you walk out of there with a receipt, and your Smarties, all the fuel you bought has evaporated.

In a world that worked, petrol stations would all be run by spotty young men from Poland or Pakistan. But that simple dream can now be undone by four separate pieces of legislation. Age, sex, race and disability.

This means that if British Nuclear Fuels wants a person to monitor the reactors at Sellafield, it is duty-bound to at least consider someone whose CV reveals them to be a hormonal Afghan school leaver with a keen interest in Middle East politics, a degree in chemistry and epilepsy.

Of course, at this point you'd expect me to work myself into a state of righteous indignation and say: 'Idealism? Pah. It's a lovely thing to have, but God, it's a dangerous thing to use.'

My wife has said on many occasions that she'd like to have Jamie Lee Curtis's body. And I agree. I'd very much like to have Jamie Lee Curtis's body. But it cannot happen because life is not fair. Some people win the lottery. And some don't.

If you are born to a wealthy, intelligent family, then you will go to Eton, get a brilliant education and end up, having expended almost no effort at all, in a hedge fund, wealthy and contented.

If you are born ugly and with ginger hair, to a stupid family, things are likely to be a little more difficult.

However, here's the thing. I absolutely support legislation that forces employers to consider people from all walks of life, no matter how much they dribble, or how many times a day they need to pray.

Sure, for every idiotic Stan who wants to become Loretta and have babies, there's a Douglas Bader who overcame the loss of his legs to get back in a Spitfire, or a Michael Bolton who overcame that astonishing haircut to become a pop star. Ian Dury. Franklin D. Roosevelt. David Blunkett. Admiral Nelson. History is littered with disabled people who have not just got by, but got on.

Andrew Lloyd Webber made it even though at some point in his teenage years his face melted. And every year 200,000 people have to overcome the massive problem of being born American.

So, if I were an employer and wanted a footballer, I'd get someone who was good at football and wouldn't care where they were from, what shape they were or even if they were a horse. If I wanted a secretary, I'd get someone who could type, and wouldn't care how long her legs were or if she had sumptuous breasts. Much.

In fact, there's only one type of person I wouldn't employ under any circumstances. A small man.

Smallness trumps everything. It transcends national characteristics and traits written by the stars. I've said before that to be born Italian and male is to win the first prize in the lottery of life, but that isn't so if you're the height of a normal person's navel.

It doesn't matter if fate deals the short-arse a hand stuffed with aces, or what new laws the government imposes to smooth his way into normal human life, he simply won't be able to achieve a state of happiness if he has to go through life banging his head on coffee tables.

If you're small, it doesn't matter whether you're rich, poor, Aries, Leo or ginger, you will be consumed with a sense that people aren't just physically looking down on you, but mentally as well. This will make you permanently angry, and equipped with a chip so deep you need to wear a tie to stop yourself falling in half.

I've never once met a small man who is balanced. They misinterpret every kind word and treat every gesture as the opening salvo in a full-on war.

It's true, of course, that each generation is taller than the one that went before. I recently had a look round the restored SS *Great Britain* and the beds on this ocean liner were not even big enough for a twenty-first-century child of six.

It is, therefore, true to say that taller people are at the cutting edge of civilisation. Those of, let's say, 6 foot 5 are bound to be the brightest and cleverest and most advanced humans the world has ever seen, and those under 5 foot 5 are somewhere between the amoeba and the ape, and there's plenty of evidence to bear this out. An American man who is 6 foot 2 tall is 3 per cent more likely to be an executive and 2 per cent more likely to be a professional than is a man who stands 5 foot 10.

It's often been said that Randy Newman's song 'Short People Got No Reason to Live' is actually a metaphor for the stupidity of racism. I'm not so sure.

And nor, it seems, is the EU. Because while it's now illegal to discriminate on the grounds of age, race, sex or disability, it is perfectly legal to push small people over in supermarkets and steal their milk in the playground.

Sunday 8 October 2006

My new career as a rock god

I've spent the past 20 years or so driving round corners while shouting, but then one day Richard Hammond turned upside down and the treadmill just stopped.

There I was with a big six-month hole in my diary. There'd be no show. No driving round corners. No shouting. For the first time in my adult life I had nothing to do.

So rather than waste the time eating cold sausages and looking out of the window I decided I'd learn to play the drums.

At this point I should explain that I've taken up many hobbies in the past and am something of an expert on the matter. And what I know most of all is that when you decide to do something you must rush out in a blizzard of ignorance and hope and spend a fortune on all the toys.

This is why our house is littered with toolkits, half-made model helicopters, easels, fishing rods, pianos and now a limited-edition replica of the double-bass Pictures of Lily drum kit as used by Keith Moon in 1967. It is massive.

This, however, would never end up gathering dust because I had a mission. Richard Hammond plays the bass, James May is a classically trained pianist, and our producer fancies himself as a singer. So if I could learn the drums we could form the *Top Gear* band and have a

Christmas number one with a cover of 'Radar Love'. It was something that cheered Richard up. Something he could look forward to.

But, immediately, there was a problem. Because it turns out that when you buy a drum kit you only get the drums. The stool, the sticks, the cymbals, the pedals that cause the two bass drums to make a noise and the hi-hat (whatever that is) are all extras.

This is a bit like buying a model aeroplane and finding that the box does not contain the wings, the wheels, the cockpit canopy or the engines. And so it was a whole week before I was ready to sit down and start drumming. Right. Here we go. Er . . .

I've seen loads of gigs over the years and I sort of assumed that you just writhe around and hit stuff, but after just a few moments I realised it wasn't like that at all. So I rang a drum teacher who came round, introduced me to a drum score and gave me a lesson.

It turns out I'm very uncoordinated. I can keep reasonable time with the bass drum but as soon as I move either of my arms my leg forgets what it's doing and either speeds up or stops altogether.

I sort of knew this might happen because once I tried to fly a helicopter and each time the instructor handed me the controls we started to crash. I kept thinking, 'Look. Sarah bloody Ferguson can do this. So why can't I?'

But I couldn't. It's that whole rub your head and pat your tummy thing. Some people can do it easily. I usually end up punching myself in the face. But I'd paid the teacher for an hour's lesson so we stuck at it and eventually I was doing something similar to four-four time.

How in the name of all that's holy, I thought, can drummers do this when they've just ingested half a gallon of heroin?

By the end of the day, however, I was putting twiddly bits into the mix and two days after that I could do a passable imitation of Frank Beard's drumming on ZZ Top's 'Gimme All Your Lovin''.

Three days in and I wanted to know what it'd be like to drum while someone was playing an instrument. Luckily, I live quite close to Alex James who, before he became a columnist on something called the *Independent*, was the bassist with Blur.

And so there I was, jamming. And it was just tremendous. I have never felt so effervescent about anything.

'So where are you going to look?' said Alex after we'd finished 'Smoke on the Water'.

It turns out that drummers have to stare at something while drumming or they end up looking gormless. And I have an even bigger problem. When I drum I have to count out loud to keep time and that's like watching someone move their lips while reading.

Even worse, however, is the noise. I have installed my drum kit in a room with a powerful stereo system, but when I'm up there twirling the timber all 500 watts are drowned out completely. In some ways that's excellent. It means I can go to Tottenham Court Road and buy a new and even more powerful hi-fi system.

But it's not so good for the children, who are trying to do their homework, or my wife, who is trying to have a nap. I know of one family in London whose son plays the drums. How can they face their neighbours of a morning?

I now face a similar problem. Because Alex out of Blur announced yesterday that he wants to form a local band. And before I could draw breath to explain that I'd already been bagged by my *Top Gear* colleagues, he said he'd call Steve Winwood, who lives nearby, to see if he's up for it.

Of course, I couldn't say yes, because this would be disloyal to Richard. The disappointment might even mean it takes him longer to get better. That would mean I'd have even more time off work . . .

So, Steve, Alex and me, then.

I'll let you know the details of our first gig.

Sunday 15 October 2006

My designer dog is a hellhound

Alarming news from the pet shop. If current trends continue, then at some point in 2007 more families in Britain will own a fish than will own a dog.

Experts suggest this is because of changing lifestyles: children prefer virtual dogs on the computer, and working parents don't want to leave a real dog at home all day, in case it eats the blender and ruins the Fired Earth natural organic carpet, which cost £47.50 a yard.

Rubbish. We read last week about a Scottish hill farmer who suffered a stroke while out in the glens, and was saved from certain death by his faithful collie dogs who snuggled up with the stricken chap to keep him warm, and then ran around barking when they saw the search and rescue helicopter circling near by.

This would not have happened if he'd been up there with Shep and Rover, his trusty sheep-fish.

And when you hear a noise in your house at 3 a.m. you are entitled to feel frightened if all you have downstairs is a brace of carp. Whereas, if you have a huge dog with big spiky teeth, you can roll over and go back to sleep. Dogs bring peace of mind, then, whether you are being burgled or if you've had a stroke.

Nevertheless, between 1985 and 2004, dog ownership in Britain fell by 26 per cent and now fewer than one in five households has one.

I have three. There's a mother, a quiet and wise old thing, and a daughter, who's stupid and yellow and who spends half of her time at the local rugby club, eating whatever she can find in their dustbins. And the other half bringing it all back over my organic natural flooring.

She swallowed some slug pellets when she was younger and after a £740 stay at the vet's emerged as a cabbage patch dog. I feel sure that if I were to have a stroke while on the moors, she would eat me. And then regurgitate my wallet through a burglar's letter box.

Despite this, and the dog-logs they leave in the yard, and the incessant barking, and the smell, I find it comforting to have dogs around the place, so when my daughter said she'd like a new one for her birthday, obviously I said yes.

Things, however, have changed. Not long ago, you bought a dog for 40p, taught it to sit and fed it a tin of diced horse once a day.

Not any more. Because now, in addition to the usual array of normal dogs, there are all sorts of hybrids, usually with a poodle in the mix somewhere. I don't know why. Poodles are horrid, vicious things. But anyway, you can have a cockerpoo or a pekeapoo or the one chosen by Tiger Woods, Graham Norton and my daughter, a labradoodle.

Do you have any idea how much such a thing costs? Go on, take a guess. Nope: you're miles off because the price of what is basically a mongrel is £950. And I'm sorry, but how can something discovered accidentally in Australia possibly be worth more than a 1991 BMW?

Of course, it arrived as cute as cute could be but,

alarmingly, within 15 minutes had become the size of a small mule. Now, eight weeks down the line, it has to duck when it comes through the door, and it doesn't chew my wellies, as you'd expect from a puppy; it swallows them whole. Some people think we may have accidentally bought a poodlephant.

But no. Stroke it and you quickly realise that what we've actually got is a massive bath mat draped over a skeleton. This is the world's first meat-free dog.

When he's wet, he completely disappears. It's spooky.

He is also, I'm afraid, the subject of some bitter controversy in dogdom.

Both the poodle owners' club and the labrador society – normally sworn enemies, I presume – have put out statements saying that the labradoodle is a wicked piece of interracial designer dog experimentation built only to quench the thirst of ungodly media luvvies. They wonder what disease and madness may result.

Labradoodle owners, therefore, have been driven onto the web, arranging secret dogging locations where they can dog quietly, away from armed vigilante groups of labradors and poodles.

It's terrible. We're now on a Kennel Club blacklist, we've had to tune the house to accommodate our labracow, my wellies have been eaten and we're £950 worse off.

And this is just the start. Because if you've spent that much on a dog, then it's wise to get it insured, and they will insist that in addition to the collar it has a microchip inserted in its skin, so it can be tracked by satellite. And this, it turns out, annoyingly, cannot be inserted by an electrician. You've got to get a vet, which costs another million pounds.

I haven't finished yet. You've also got to factor in the fact that designer children's designer dogs like designer food, which is made from panda bear ears and the lightly fried scrotum of a fin whale, and they need vitamin supplements and holistic liver oil from a cod. And a fully machine-washable bed, made from myrrh.

That's why the fish is about to overtake the dog as Britain's number one pet, because these days running a dog is more complicated and more expensive than running a nuclear power station. And, of course, when a dog dies, you can't really flush it down the lavatory.

Sunday 22 October 2006

The ideal pet? Here, nice ratty

Last week I wrote about my daughter's new designer dog which, in eight weeks, has grown to the size of a garden shed and is now costing £2 million a minute in food and satellite-tracking devices. Small wonder, I concluded, that the people of Britain are now replacing their dogs with pet fish.

The thing is, though, that ever since I wrote that, it's been bugging me. Sure, I can understand that a dog is jolly expensive, but replacing it with a fish is like replacing your house with a potato.

I have two and they are utterly, utterly useless. They don't come when they're called, they don't bark at strangers, they won't fetch sticks, they're not cute and, being fairground goldfish, I'm fairly sure they wouldn't be delicious either. Honestly, it'd be more rewarding to own a pet rock.

And don't think things improve if you move up the evolutionary scale and go for a koi carp. My dad did that, and spent many happy hours watching them gliding around his garden pond, gorging on the psoriasis flakes that fish call food.

Then one Christmas I bought him half a dozen 'ghost koi' which looked very splendid in the tank at the pet shop. Unfortunately, in my dad's pond we learnt why they are called 'ghost' fish. It's because they are completely invisible. And what's the point of a pet you can't see?

Sadly, I also discovered that in the fish world they are the SAS among carp, approaching their prey silently and killing without pity or remorse. So within a day, all my dad's beloved orange fish were upside down on the surface, leaving him with a pond full of apparently nothing at all.

My advice, then, is simple. If you want a fish, get it from the chip shop.

If you want a pet, look elsewhere.

Happily, I'm able to give you a few pointers because, over the years, I've owned, loved and inadvertently killed nearly every animal on the planet.

One little thing I can tell you straight away is that you should never name a brace of animals after a famous pairing.

I did this as a child and after Gilbert and Squeak died, I ended up with Bubble and Sullivan.

I became so fed up with all my pets being killed, in fact, that I eventually bought a couple of tortoises, which came with a hardened outer shell and a life expectancy of 2,000 years.

Sadly, however, and for reasons I don't fully understand, given that they had a top speed of one mile a year, they managed to escape into a field of wheat that was then harvested. Even to this day, I open each packet of Rice Krispies with fear and trepidation.

Of course, this endless cycle of life and death taught me a great deal about the ways of nature and I was keen that my children should be similarly educated. So I recently bought them each a cute little guinea pig.

Just a week later, however, I came home to find them gone and a fox-sized hole in their cage. I should have told the kids the truth, that they'd been torn apart, for fun. But I didn't have the heart. So I invented a pathetic story about how they'd escaped and gone to live near a stream in the sunshine, with some water voles.

Great. But the next day I found half of one of them in a hedge and fearing the children might find the rest of him, or his mangulated mates, I had to call in a team of helpers to go through every bush and thicket within a radius of two miles looking for legs and arms.

We failed and I'm still frightened that one day, when they're playing hide and seek, there will be a shriek as one of the children discovers a severed head, and, in doing so, exposes my sunshine and water vole story as a lie.

I wouldn't mind but I loathe guinea pigs unless they're on a spit. And rabbits.

Rodents of this type are just fish with fur. They're utterly, utterly useless too.

The best pets I have are my donkeys. Unlike my wife's horses, which break down all the time, and lose their shoes, and are frightened by puddles, and plastic bags, my donkeys are totally reliable in all weathers, they come when you call them, and they hee-haw when they see a burglar.

But that said, there are some drawbacks, compared to dogs. If, for instance, you invite them inside to sit by the fire on cold winter evenings, they do take up a lot of space and, of course, they can't be house trained.

So what, then, with my wealth of experience of the animal kingdom would I recommend if you don't want a dog any more? Well, not a cat, obviously – despicable animals, the four-legged equivalent of a footballer's wife: pretty, well groomed and clean but, fundamentally, only after your money.

You want something that loves you, something scary for thieves, something that doesn't make too much of a mess and something, above all, which costs almost nothing to buy and run. Well, how about a rat?

Rats get a lot of bad press. Sure, they did kill half the world's population once but it wasn't their fault. It was the fleas that lived on their backs and it was a long time ago.

Today's rat can be taught to respond to its name, if you go for a male, it will clean up after itself and it will be very loving. And what's more, you can use a rat's back to grow yourself another ear.

Sunday 29 October 2006

The conspiracy not to cure the cold

I am extremely ill. I have a runny nose, a sore throat, a nasty hacking cough and every few minutes my eyes fill with water: all the ingredients you need to make a convincing Lemsip commercial for the television. So of course all you women out there will now expect me to claim that I have flu. But I don't. I have a cold.

Flu, I've always thought, is a working-class invention designed specifically as an excuse for not going down the mine that day. 'I'm not coming to work today because I have a cold' sounds a bit wet and homosexual. Saying, 'I can't come to work because I have flu' sounds more manly and butch.

But you may as well say you aren't coming to work because you've caught cancer. If you have flu, the American navy will come round to your house, inject you with plasma and take samples of your liver to their biochemical-warfare centre in Atlanta.

And when they've gone away, men in nuclear-spillage boiler suits from our own Ministry of Defence will want to know if you've had any contact with Chinese chickens or Vietnamese swans or German soldiers. And then, when they've gone away, you will die. Flu is nasty and claiming you have it when all you have is a cold makes you look ridiculous.

Mine, of course, is the worst recorded cold in the

whole of human history and I am defying medical science by being here, at my computer, writing this column.

Technically, I am dead.

Legally, you would be allowed to remove my organs and give them to a poorly child.

And as I sit here, shivering and tense with a headache and a tickly cough, I can't help wondering why there is still no cure. And whether or not we might be on the brink of creating one . . .

For hundreds of years people thought the cold was caused by being cold. 'You'll catch your death out there,' people in eighteenth-century blizzards would say.

It was in the 1920s that we understood the cold to be a viral infection, a nasty little blighter that invades your body, multiplies and then causes you to sneeze so that millions of its brothers can shoot up the noses and through the eyes of everyone within five feet.

Since then, we've been to the moon, invented the personal stereo, devised the speed camera and created the pot noodle. But still no one knows how to keep the cold virus at bay.

Aids came along and within about 10 minutes Elton John had set up his charity and was rattling the ivories from Pretoria to Pontefract so that now, while there's no cure, there is a raft of drugs to keep the symptoms and effects at arm's length. But the cold? Not a sausage.

In 1946 the British government began something called the common cold unit, based close to Porton Down in Wiltshire. It conducted endless experiments until in 1989 it was shut down. And sitting here with two bits of kitchen towel rammed up my nostrils, I rather wish they'd kept it going.

The American Centers for Disease Control and Prevention is an immensely well-funded organisation. It's here that they work on ebola and proper flu and all the really nasty viruses that could wipe out the world if they ever got on an aeroplane. And do you know what advice they have for those who don't want to catch a cold? Wash your hands with alcohol.

I'm beginning to wonder if the sort of scientists who might have been engaged in defeating the cold are now being swallowed up by the exciting and glamorous green movement; that the very man who might have developed a cure for the cold is, as we speak, sitting on an ice floe off the coast of Canada watching bloody polar bears.

Or perhaps he was thinking about taking up medical research but thought that rather than spend his life in a chilly lab in Cardiff with nothing but a pot of viruses for company he'd be better paid and happier if he went to Soho instead to be an ad man for Lemsip.

I worry about this in the same way that I worry about the loss of Concorde. It has not been in man's nature to just give up on a project, but we really do seem to have given up when it comes to the cold.

Scientifically, it's not that hard to beat. Back in 1999 British researchers worked out a way to stop the viruses infiltrating human cells in a test tube. But when it came to replicating the tests in the human nose, they all seem to have given up and gone off with Greenpeace to drive rubber boats at high speed round Icelandic whaling ships.

There is, however, some hope because apart from the Groucho Club, where people have colds in the summer, most people only catch a cold in the winter. So what we need to do is get rid of it and that, thanks to global warming, does seem to be happening.

In the last weekend of October I was sitting outside in the sunshine wearing nothing but a T-shirt. Only now that the wind is coming from the north have the viruses invaded my nostrils.

If, therefore, we can push the winter so far back that by the time it comes along we're already into the spring, all should be well. To cure the common cold we simply need to get rid of its breeding season. This means producing as much carbon dioxide as possible. Yup. The cure for the common cold may well turn out to be the Range Rover.

Sunday 5 November 2006

Real men don't go home at 7 p.m.

Speaking to an audience of wimmin in Glasgow last week, Mrs Blair revealed that back at the start of her husband's career he was told by Labour party officials that he wouldn't get very far if he kept going home at 7 p.m. to see his wife and children.

Cherie's message was clear. Men should spend quality time with their family no matter how many wars they've inadvertently started and no matter how many constables are knocking on the door wanting to know about cash for ermine.

I'm sorry, but I don't understand. If you were an Iron Age man and you came home from a hunting expedition empty-handed because you wanted to play with your children, you'd starve. If you were a penguin and you came back from a fishing trip with nothing but snow in your flippers, your baby would die and the following year Mrs Penguin would find a new mate.

This is the problem. I am designed to kill foxes, bend every woman I meet over the nearest piece of furniture and give her a damn good seeing-to.

But in an evolutionary nanosecond, it's all changed. After several million years of programming we've been told that what women really want is a husband who leaves his colleagues in the lurch at 7 p.m. and comes home to make a delicious quiche.

That's like telling your faithful family toaster after a lifetime spent making toast that you want it to become a washing machine. And it's not just a bunch of baggy-breasted feminists making the point either. It's every single girl from the age of puberty to the menopause.

Last weekend my colleague James May hurt his wrist while performing a stunt at the MPH show in London. Being male, mostly, he shrugged it off and kept going, which caused all the backstage women to treat him like a leper.

If he'd wanted to impress them he should have abandoned the show, gone home, sold his heartwarming story to *OK!* magazine, and spent the next six weeks watching *Love Actually* with his cat.

I pride myself on the fact I don't cry over films – apart from *Educating Rita*, obviously. But apparently this is all wrong. I should sob hopelessly every time I watch the news.

No, really. Look at the film stars who melt the hearts of womankind these days: Johnny Depp, Judy Law, Orlando Bloom. Are they hunter-gatherers? Maybe they'd pass muster on a Saturday morning in Carluccio's but in a jungle they'd be eaten within 10 minutes.

Back in the 1960s Paul Newman and Robert Redford were much loved as they trotted around Wyoming on their horses shooting people. But when they were reunited last week, women forgot all that and in a desperate bid to justify the stirring they felt 40 years ago, talked about how Paul has been married to the same woman for a million years and how he makes a lovely sauce.

I wonder sometimes if Steve McQueen would get a break if he appeared on the scene today. Back in the sixties he really did seem to have all the bases covered: silent but strong smouldering sexuality, the sort of man who could punch a horse to the ground while driving a Mustang sideways through the streets of San Francisco. He even managed to get Faye Dunaway's knickers off just by playing chess.

Who's his modern-day equivalent? There's nobody. Stallone has disappeared. Schwarzenegger is in politics. Gibson is setting fire to synagogues. And now we're expected to believe that a dwarf like Tom Cruise could knock someone out with a single blow from his hair product.

It's the same story in music. Robert Plant used to send women wild with that lion's mane hairdo and half a mile of hosepipe down the front of his loons. But now everyone in music is a doe-eyed pretty boy with a Ken and Barbie androgeno-crotch and nothing up his nose except moisturiser.

I work with Richard Hammond, who is about as manly as Graham Norton's knicker drawer. But girls say he has bunny-rabbit eyes and that he looks like he needs to be mothered. Pah. He looks like a Smurf.

In sport, women seem to love overpaid nancy-boy footballers who fall over all the time and cry, whereas proper men who play rugby and keep going even when their head has fallen off are largely ignored.

I'll tell you this, though, Mrs Blair. If you were a penguin looking for a mate, you'd go for Steve Thompson in front of Colin Firth any day.

All of which gets me back to the case in point; that after a million years of not coming home until you actually have an impala to eat, men are now being told by the prime minister's wife that, no matter what, we should up sticks at seven and go home with a box of tissues and something gooey from Belgium.

Right. So when the director says that he needs a few more shots and I say, 'Tough,' and drive off, that's okay, is it? It's okay that the BBC spends thousands of pounds of your money getting everyone back the next day because Jeremy wanted to get home and read his children a Winnie-the-Pooh story?

Cherie says my attitude is macho and she's right.

It is.

It might not be very attractive in this day and age. But that's because I'm a man.

I know this because I much prefer Uma Thurman, who's all woman, to Kate Moss, who, from behind, could well be a boy.

Sunday 12 November 2006

Schools are trying to break children

All of us wrap up our children when it's cold. We put them on booster seats in the car and make them wear helmets when they're on a bicycle. We strive constantly to keep them out of harm's way, and then we send them off to school so they can be tortured and killed.

I suppose we all think, rather naively, that school today is exactly the same as school back in the sixties, apart from the fact that children are now allowed calculators. And get hit by the teachers rather less often.

'Fraid not. School today is completely different. There's very little bullying, and no smoking behind the bike sheds because there's no time; not when you need to be fluent in 17 languages by four and you've got those pesky quadratic cosines to finish off by break.

I'm not kidding. I do not understand any of my son's maths homework.

And what's more, I bet he knows more about advanced mathematics now, at the age of 10, than most of the NASA scientists did when they put Armstrong on the moon.

People say Gordon Ramsay works very hard, what with his restaurants, his autobiography and his swearing empire to manage on television.

But he's a work-shy benefits dodger compared with the average 12-year-old these days.

My daughter, who already speaks Latin better than Julius Caesar, comes home from school at 6 p.m. every night, bleary eyed and drunk from the pressure. But before she can collapse into bed she has to do four half-hour homeworks. Supper? MSN? A bit of light texting? Forget it.

And on the basis that a parent can only be as happy as their least happy child, this makes me pretty damn miserable.

She's not alone, either. I read the other day that a four-year-old child had been diagnosed with 'stress' and I'm not surprised. Chances are she'd been made to miss her playtime and lunch so she could finish her paper on how the gross domestic product of Iceland was affected by EU fish quotas.

When I was at school I remember being told that if I spelt my name properly on my common entrance paper I'd be halfway there.

Exams were a hiccup in the day; not the be-all and end-all of absolutely everything.

What's changed is simple. We now have bloody league tables, a handy cut out 'n' keep guide to how well the school performs. Well, forgive the expletive, but that's bollocks.

Printing a list of 'best schools' purely on the grounds of academic achievement is as idiotic as printing a list of 'best foods' purely on the grounds of calorie content. It tells you nothing.

A couple of years ago a sixth-form student I know wanted to study for a science A level so she could pursue a noble career in engineering. The school campaigned vigorously for her to do something useless instead, like media studies or knitting. But she and her parents were adamant.

So she sat the science A level and got a D. And because of that single failure the school fell 50 places in the league tables. One child. One exam result. And a 50-place fall. Still think league tables make sense?

There's more. Another child I know was sent home recently from her school with a note saying that by the age of 10 she really should have a rudimentary grasp of quantum physics and that because she didn't she must have some extra tuition.

Unfortunately, on the back of this hurriedly written note the teacher had been doing some sums. There was a list of every child who was having extra lessons, how much each parent was paying and at the end, under the total – which was £16,000 by the way – he'd written 'Yippee'.

Now I'm sorry, but people pay an eye-watering fortune to have their children educated privately, and to be honest we do not want to end up with an emaciated wreck simply so the school can maintain its place in some point-less national academic championship.

Recently, I made a decision on which secondary school my children will attend. I won't tell you what it is but I will tell you that I have no idea where it came in last year's league tables. I have not looked. I absolutely couldn't care less. I chose it because I know several people who've been there, and they loved it. I chose it because I liked the cut of the housemaster's jib. I chose it because the children I saw mooching from lesson to lesson were mostly smiling. I chose it because it 'felt' right.

Of course, I want my children to leave there with a basic academic foundation; enough to get them to £32,000 on *Who Wants to be a Millionaire?*, say. But more than that I want them to learn social skills so they can interact properly with other human beings. I want them to learn to play the guitar, and how to smoke without being caught.

I want them to enjoy it, to have fun. I can't bear the thought of paying a small fortune every year so they can be put on a treadmill and emotionally flogged until they're bulimic, suicidal and riddled with tics and angst. School is supposed to prepare a person for life, not wear them out.

This is what we all seem to have forgotten. Yes, we must do everything we can to keep our children safe. But we should also do everything we can to make them happy as well.

Sunday 19 November 2006

That Henry II, he was dead right

I joke often about how, if I were in power, I'd employ police marksmen to sit on motorway bridges picking off people who drive too slowly. But actually I've never thought that the death penalty is a good idea.

When a state calmly and coolly, and in sound mind, decides that it's going to kill someone, that's actually premeditated murder. And when they administer the lethal injection in front of an invited audience of priests and officials on a sort of stage, well, that's just bizarre.

There are two ways a truly civilised and advanced nation can be defined. One, it has a fleet of nuclear submarines, and two, it does not have the death penalty. That leaves you with France and Britain. And that's about right.

Think about it. When you empower the judiciary to kill someone, you are not even hoping that the person will be rehabilitated. It is pure punishment. But who's the punishment aimed at? Sure, it can't be very pleasant sitting in your cell dreaming up some ludicrous last-meal request that will stump the jailhouse chef, but actually, after the poison has done its dirty work, you're dead and that's sort of that.

The people who actually suffer most are your parents and your children.

And they weren't the ones who did the crime.

I'm not saying we should be soft on vagabonds and

thieves. I'd like very much to lock them up in a cell and tell them they can eat only what they can cultivate in their body hair. And I wouldn't heat the jail either, or provide plumbing. But I absolutely couldn't support a state that declares murder is wrong and then hammers the point home by publicly and openly murdering people.

That said, a state that waits for people who are a bloody nuisance to order dim sum, then silently pokes them in the buttocks with a nuclear-tipped umbrella seems somehow less revolting.

I can think of many people who could and should be removed from the scene in such a way that no one can really explain what happened. George Monbiot. Ken Livingstone. Various hard-line Muslim fanatics. Most human-rights lawyers. Anyone with a rally jacket. People in Babyshambles. People with beards. Anyone with a sign on their desk that says 'You don't have to be mad to work here', anyone in a jungle in Australia, anyone who claps along to the oompah music at the Horse of the Year Show, and everyone at the Ideal Home Show.

This Henry II attitude to good governance – 'who will rid me of this turbulent priest' – is not premeditated murder. It's more like a crime of passion, and that's understandable. You feel sorry for the leader as he sits there thinking: 'I'm trying to run a country here and how can I do that if I've got this infernal priest nicking all my churches and making everything worse? So can someone go out there and stick a sword in his gizzard.

'And then on the way home can someone please pop into the *Daily Mail* Ideal Home Show and mess with the Earls Court boilers . . .'

That's pretty much the same as a husband trying to run a family and finding that every time he comes home from a hard day at the office his wife is in bed with the paper boy. Eventually, he's going to snap and shoot them both. And not even the Americans would electrocute him for that.

Of course, once the state gets a taste for the quiet assassination of troublemakers, there's always a danger that you end up with Uday Hussein feeding hookers to his pet tigers and making old men dance after they've had the soles of their feet beaten to a pulp.

That's bad, obviously. But what you do to solve this is have him quietly killed as well.

There's a scene in an eighties film called *Defence of the Realm* where a journalist is blindfolded and dragged to a grand-looking room in Whitehall where three old-school-tie types grill him a bit. And then after he refuses to play ball they attach a small bomb to the record player in his flat and blow him to pieces.

He was going to print a story that would have resulted in the American forces leaving Britain in the middle of the cold war. So what do they do? He couldn't be arrested and tried because he hadn't committed a crime. And he couldn't be allowed to run the story. So he had to explode.

I sort of like the idea that this Ludlum stuff is going on, behind our backs. But I fear it doesn't any more.

Thatcher, yes. There's no doubt in my mind that she might not have lost too much sleep if her security services had taken out the odd person threatening national security in a Geneva railway station. But Blair? Hmmm. I doubt he'd have the balls, because he'd be worried about what he could say if Cherie found out.

Then there's David Cameron. Did you see those pictures of him in Darfur last week? He was wearing cords and a short-sleeved shirt, and I'm sorry, but Boden Man is never, in a million years, going to order the quiet assassination of a turbulent cleric.

If he had a full packet in his underpants he might surely be tempted to lose it with his minions and shout at them to put a dollop of killer lead in Polly Toynbee's tofu. Instead of which he's now going to let her shape his party's stance on social justice.

It won't work. My Henry II plan will.

Sunday 26 November 2006

Making a meal of Sunday lunch

Most nights, like most people, I shovel food into my mouth with one hand while using the other to stab away at the remote control, desperately trying to find something on television that isn't about penguins and polar bears.

But on Sundays the television is turned off, a big fire is lit in the dining room and the whole family gathers round to gorge on a feast of roast meat, gravy and what country pubs call 'all the trimmings'.

This is the traditional Sunday lunch, but actually it's traditional in the same way as going to work in a bowler hat. It's a perceived cornerstone of the British way of life but in fact few people actually do it.

Recent figures show that only 29 per cent of families eat together more than once a week and that of this minority, 77 per cent do so while watching penguins falling over. A quarter of households in Britain don't even have a table.

This, I think, should be a new measure of poverty. We in Britain like to think we're rich because we have aspirin and, for some of the year at least, access to clean drinking water.

We like to think we're advanced because you can't join the army at nine, and civilised because people don't die in the streets of diphtheria.

But, I'm sorry, even the poorest African families have a table. And here, 25 per cent of us don't.

There's no real excuse either. On eBay there currently are 3,764 dining tables being sold, with prices starting at just £16 – less than three packets of fags. So buy one, turn the bloody polar bears off and let's get this family Sunday lunch thing under way.

It all begins at the butcher, and what you need to know is that you will describe whoever you choose as the best butcher in the world. Out here in the Cotswolds it's the next topic of conversation after schools.

'We use the "little man" at the bottom of the town. He's much better than the one at the top.' 'What? You don't use our chap in Chuntsworthy? Everyone does. He's the best butcher in the world.'

The marvellous thing is that nobody knows what they're talking about. Beef is not like wine. Yes, those with a sensitive palate could tell the difference between the scarlet plonk-meat sold in supermarkets and the Châteauneuf-du-Pape meat sold by a proper butcher.

But could you really tell the difference between the butcher at the bottom of the town and the chap at the top? Not a hope in hell.

So you buy a joint of meat from whichever butcher has the fewest flies in the window and you put it in the oven and then you try to get your children to set your eBay table.

This will make them very angry because they're busy watching that man on YouTube who tries to light his fart. And they won't be jollied along by the thought of the whole family sitting down together because the only people in the world they hate more than their siblings are their parents.

Frankly, they'd much rather be sitting down in a bus shelter with their friends.

Cajoling them to break out the cutlery and put it on the table in something like the right order, without stabbing one another, takes so long that you forget about the broccoli, which is now in need of some culinary Viagra if it's to become firm again.

No matter. An hour after the first ingredient is ready, the last will be vaguely edible as well, so it's time to carve.

This, for reasons I don't fully understand, is a man's job. Perhaps it's because he hasn't done the cooking or argued with the kids and is therefore in a better frame of mind to deal with the carving knife which, somehow, after a week in a drawer, has become as sharp as Vanessa Feltz's backside. Last weekend I would have been better off chopping up the pork with a rolling pin.

So after a while and a lot of swearing, I went to look for that electric sharpener thing that every couple are given when they get married.

Unfortunately, while foraging about in the bottom of the bottom drawer, among the juicers and the traditional scales and the £100 brushed screw-pull corkscrews, and all the other stuff we received on that happy day 13 years ago, I came across some old photographs.

And by the time I'd finished being distracted by these, the broccoli was stone cold and the gravy had become so congealed that it could have been used as a football.

My wife was very angry about this, and how the children had laid the table without mats, serving spoons, glasses or indeed anything you might need to actually eat a lunch. And I'd laid the fire with coal that smells of cancer rather than wood, which I think is naff.

Eventually, though, we were under way. The family all together. Eating good, wholesome, traditional nourishing food.

And talking about all sorts of things, such as the need to sit up straight, the need to eat with your mouth closed, the need to ask for seconds rather than just leaning across the table, and how it's important to eat without your elbows taking on the shape of a Vulcan bomber's wings.

That afternoon, feeling heavy and lethargic, I curled up in front of a drowned polar bear and thought about those 3,764 dining tables for sale on eBay.

I'm surprised there aren't more.

Sunday 3 December 2006

Nice jet, shame about abroad

Air travel has done more for world peace than any other single entity in the history of mankind. The more countries you visit, the more you understand that people from other cultures and races and places are just like you – except America, obviously – so you're less likely to want to shoot them.

The reason why there's been peace in western Europe for more than 60 years has nothing to do with the European Union or NATO and everything to do with Ryanair.

I'd give the chairman the Nobel peace prize, frankly.

But somehow Gordon Brown has got it into his head that aeroplanes are hurting the sky through which they fly and that he must therefore double airport tax. This means the cost of your annual Christmas holiday in Barbados will rise from £9,482 to a staggering £9,487.

Anyway, to mark Mr Brown's decision to save the world, I decided to go to Budapest. For lunch.

I've often said that if I came to power, the first thing I'd do is declare war on Hungary. This is because it's the only country in western Europe I've never visited. And what you don't know is scary. Hell. Malignant tumours. Strange noises in the house in the middle of the night. Hungary. They've always been the same in my book.

So when a friend rang and asked if I'd like to go

Budapest, for the day, I said, 'Er.' Then he said we'd be going on a private jet so I said, 'Yes.'

It belonged to a company called Gama Aviation, which charters its fleet out to the likes of Michael and Winner, and it was jolly lovely. But not half as lovely as the airport in Farnborough, Hampshire, where it's based.

Check-in time is one minute before the scheduled departure. Or one hour afterwards, if you can't be bothered to get up. It doesn't really matter because all you have to do is show your passport to a man who, for reasons I couldn't fathom, was wearing a high-visibility jacket. Perhaps he thought he might be knocked down by a vacuum cleaner.

Whatever, soon we were on board in a big swivelly seat, wondering whether to have our champagne neat or with a swan in it.

After we landed, a woman called Victor introduced us to our driver. He was called Victor too and he only had one word of English, which was 'moment'. That, in the big scheme of things, was not terribly useful.

For instance, when he parked outside a big hotel in the middle of a rather boring square, and we asked why, he said: 'Moment.' Plainly, he was KGB and we were all going to be killed.

But no. After 20 minutes, another Victor arrived and told us to go shopping.

Budapest, it turns out, is the worst shopping city in the whole of the world. Walking down the pedestrianised main street is exactly like walking through the centre of Croydon 40 years ago, except that all the men are sweeping leaves and all the girls are wearing knee-length shorts with turn-ups. This is not a good look at the best of times, but it's even worse when you have an arse like a championship pumpkin.

We took a trip down memory lane by going into C&A. Other than this, the only shops were Vision Express and Hungarian trinketry emporiums that sold a wide variety of 3-foot-tall motorised gnomes.

Eventually, we came across a market where two burly-looking Victors were hitting lumps of red-hot metal with hammers, and you could buy hats.

They were not like any hats I'd ever seen. Fashioned from what was undoubtedly carpet underlay, they were shaped like tubas and were 3 foot tall.

Obviously, I had to have one, which meant trying to work out how much they cost. I don't know what currency they use in Hungary – pigs, I think – and nor could I work out how many sucklings you get to the euro. This is because Victor, the hat seller, only had one word of English, which was 'moment'.

After the shopping trip we had a look round. And here's what you need to know.

There is a bridge that links Buda with Pest. There are some green statues of people you've never heard of, there's a long thin building and everything is grey. The shops are grey. The river is grey. The cars are grey.

And the sky is as grey as the shorts with turn-ups.

So we went for lunch where a man called Victor brought us pâté, and goulash and duck and it only cost four pigs. 'Do you want Hungarian wine?' he asked. Not really.

After our feast, we couldn't think of anything to do so

we rekindled the lost art of having a food fight and then went back to the airport, got on our Falcon, and came home.

Conclusions? Well, as I sat in my apartment block in London that night, trying to get half a ton of paprika out of my hair, I decided that I'm sold on private jets and that I no longer want to declare war on Hungary. It would be like waging war on a mental institution.

But there's something else I thought of too. My noodle delivery man was French, the girl in the coffee shop downstairs is Polish, the lift is always full of Americans speaking two-stroke and the girl on the till in my local supermarket is proof positive that Mars is definitely capable of spawning life.

So, actually, we don't need air, or even space, travel any more. Because these days, the best way of meeting other people is to stay at home.

Sunday 10 December 2006

It's English as a foreign language

As you know, it is impossible to speak French because everything over there has a sex. Tables. Ships. Birthday cakes. Throat lozenges, even. Everything is either a boy or a girl and they snigger when you get it wrong.

I'm told, however, that English is even harder to learn because although we recognised many years ago that tables are essentially asexual and invented the word 'it', there are several million alternatives for every object, subject or emotion.

This makes life very difficult for those to whom English is a second language.

George Bush, for instance.

When those 'trrists' flew their planes into the World Trade Center he went on television and referred to them as 'folks'. That's not right. 'Folks' are people who line-dance. 'Folks' are dim-witted but essentially quite likeable souls, whereas people who use Stanley knives to hijack planes and then fly them into tall buildings are 'bastards'.

I understand his dilemma. Because 'men' can also be called lads, blokes, chaps, geezers, guys and so on. And you try explaining to a foreigner which word to use and when.

I've just spent the week in Moscow with a Russian publisher whose English was so perfect he'd started to delve into the furthest reaches of *Roget's Thesaurus*. This was a mistake. It meant he kept referring to Russian secret-service agents as 'lads'.

I wanted to pull him up on it, but you try explaining to a Russian why someone who puts polonium in a chap's lunch is not a 'lad' or even a 'bloke'. And while he may be a 'chap' to his senior officer, to the rest of us, and to his girlfriend, he's a 'guy'.

Worse, one of the girls I met over there had a book called *Cockney Rhyming Slang*.

You cannot even begin to imagine how wonky this made her sound.

Even if English is your first language, it's easy to get in a bit of a muddle.

I, for instance, think that the word 'whatever' as in 'I heard what you just said and I can't be bothered to even think of a response' is one of the greatest additions to the English language since 'it'.

But I've been asked by my 12-year-old daughter to stop using it. Not because she finds it irritating but because she says it sounds wrong coming from a balding, fat, middle-aged man. 'Whatever' is a word solely for the pre-teens, and I'm jealous of them because all I had at that age was the almost completely useless 'groovy'.

It's not just a question of age, either. It's also region. Pete Townshend, for example, can say 'geezer' and just about get away with it because he's a sixty-something Londoner. In the same way that a plump postmistress from Derby can call you 'duck' and I cannot.

The worst example of getting it wrong, however, comes from Americans who, having lived in Britain for a while, think they can start talking English. Every time

Christian Slater calls me 'mate' I'm filled with a sudden desire to shave his face off with a cheese knife. Americans cannot say 'mate' any more than Germans can say 'squirrel'.

And it's even worse when they stop using the word 'pounds' and, in a Californian drawl, say 'quid'. I'm told – and you should be aware of this – that we sound similarly idiotic when, in America, we use 'bucks' instead of 'dollars'.

It must be particularly difficult for foreigners if they are ever exposed to British advertising, because here we find all sorts of words that work well in a commercial break but nowhere else. 'Tasty', for example. Or 'nourishing'. Or my least favourite: 'refreshing'.

My point this morning is that English is indeed a very hard language to master.

It's full of nuances and subtleties that take a lifetime to understand. But, and this is important, it does mean that for people who were born and raised here there is never an excuse for getting it wrong. Our wonderful mother tongue is always able to produce the 'bon mot'.

So why, then, is official Britain so monochromatic? Why do the police close roads because of an 'incident'? Why is every fight, from a pub brawl to a fully fledged riot, a 'disturbance'? And why is the shipping forecast so bland? Why instead of 'stormy' don't they say the sea's 'a frothing maelstrom of terror and hopelessness'?

And most important of all, why can't doctors be a bit more elaborate with their choice of words when describing the condition of a patient?

Last week, for instance, we heard about a young chap

who had been using his mobile phone on the third storey of an office block when the lift doors opened. Without looking, he stepped through the gap only to find the lift wasn't actually there.

In the resultant fall he broke his back in two places, punctured a lung and snapped several ribs. But even so, doctors later described his condition as 'comfortable'.

Now look. Someone lying on a squidgy daybed under the whispery shade of a Caribbean palm tree is 'comfortable'. Someone lying in an NHS hospital with a broken back and a shattered rib poking through one of his lungs just isn't.

'Crumpled' would have been better. As would 'miserable', 'broken', or 'cross'. They could even have said: 'Well, he won't be playing on his Wii console for a while.' Even my Russian friend could have come up with something better than 'comfortable'.

He'd have said 'the lad's a bit bent'. And it would have taken about two years to explain why that's wrong as well.

Sunday 17 December 2006

I didn't drop the dead donkey

I'm finding it rather difficult to get into the spirit of Christmas this year, because Geoffrey, one of my much-loved donkeys, has just died.

Other than the fact he had a bit of a long face last Saturday afternoon – which is fairly normal – he seemed to be fine. But then on Sunday morning he was on his side in the bottom paddock, as dead as I don't know what.

I always assumed that the expression 'donkey's years' meant an unspecified, but very long time. However, it evidently means 'eight years'. Because that's all Geoff was when he smothered our Christmas preparations with a big sad blanket and went off to that great nativity scene in the sky.

There was, as you can imagine, a great deal of wailing from the children and, if I'm honest, a lump in my throat too. I liked Geoff. He was, as I said in this column only very recently, a straightforward antidote to the silly media world in which I live. Put simply, he had absolutely nothing in common with Janet Street-Porter. Apart from the teeth, obviously.

Anyway, after an hour or two we'd all dried our eyes and were trying to bring some normality to our shattered Sunday. Except, of course, it wasn't normal, because right in the middle of the bottom paddock was a dead donkey. And what are you supposed to do about that?

Recently, I told you about the problems I had with a dead seal that washed up on the beach outside our holiday cottage. Getting rid of that took several gallons of petrol, a tractor, a strong stomach and, eventually, quite a lot of explosive. But we weren't dealing with a seal here. We were dealing with Geoff, and I'm sorry, blowing his body to pieces simply wasn't an option.

Bury him? 'Fraid not. You aren't allowed to bury a donkey because someone has decided that his rotting carcass will poison the water table.

So, the knackers' yard, then? Well, yes, but this would cost £250 and anyway, when we explained that Geoff would come out on the other side as two tubs of Evo-Stick and a few tins of Kennomeat, the children started crying again.

Happily, I was told by friends that it's possible these days to have your horse or donkey cremated and, at face value, this seemed to be the best and most dignified course of action.

But despite the solemn promises made by these companies that your pet will be incinerated with respect, and that they'll light a candle in their chapel of remembrance, and that you'll get its ashes back in a mahogany sculpture of the animal itself, I'm afraid I was sceptical.

If I ran one of these places I'd tell the bereaved family that their animal had gone through the curtains to the accompaniment of Robbie Williams singing 'Angels'.

And then after I'd got their cheque I'd give them a box full of whatever I could find in the vacuum-cleaner bag.

I spoke to one girl who'd got half her dead horse back in a box not much smaller than a garden shed. Apparently, the burners hadn't been able to cremate him properly so they'd thrown half the skeleton away and finished the job with hammers.

I decided that Geoffrey would not be going this way and, anyway, my chief concern as the afternoon wore on was that he'd been murdered. No, really. What if yobs had shot him with an air rifle? I became so obsessed with the notion that by the evening I was making up 'reward' posters and cleaning my shotgun.

My wife, more worried that he'd caught some terrible equine disease that he might have passed on to her horses, decided that before I started running round the town shooting anyone in a baseball cap, it'd be best to call the vet and ask for a post-mortem.

Unfortunately, when we explained what that was to the children their crying became what is known among psychiatrists as hysteria. 'They're going to chop Geoffrey up in our field,' they wailed.

Plainly, he had to be towed to a quiet spot, but I know from my experience with the seal that dead animals tend to come apart when they're being dragged. So we had to borrow a forklift and, afterwards, the vet discovered that he'd had a heart attack.

That was a relief but we still had a dead donkey in the garden. Actually, don't tell my children, but we had two halves of a dead donkey in the garden.

In the end we told the children that Geoff was going to a taxidermist so he could be stuffed and used in school nativity plays – neat, eh? – and then we called a local underground movement known simply as 'The Hunt'.

Today, still wanted by the government, they survive as

soldiers of fortune. If you have a problem, if no one else can help, and if you can find them, maybe you can hire the Heythrop.

They arrived in a souped-up black van, we put both of Geoffrey in the back and I gave them a hundred quid to take him away. Today, I suspect, he's in their hounds, which when no one's looking will use Geoff's energy to kill foxes, so that they can't attack and maim our children.

On that happy note I'd like to wish all of you a very happy Christmas, especially my editor who rang last week to ask if I'd write a column about Christmas shopping. He actually used the line, 'Can you drop the dead donkey?' Priceless.

Sunday 24 December 2006

Let's all stay with Lord Manilow

When choosing a holiday destination, I listen to friends, examine data from the Met Office and think hard about where the nearest paparazzi photographer might be. What I don't do is thumb through my record collection, pick out my favourite, and rent the lead singer's villa. You probably know where I'm going with this: the extraordinary holiday locations chosen by Mr and Mrs Blair.

Recently, it has been Sir Cliff's sumptuous villa in glittering Barbados and now, thanks to a wonky landing at Miami airport, we know he's staying at a waterfront mansion owned by Field Marshal Robin Gibb of the Bee Gees.

Of course, I doubt either of these choices came from His Tonyness.

Having been to a public school in the 1970s, I should imagine his preferred choice of holiday location might be the Dutch canalside house of Thijs van Leer of Focus, or maybe the organic bean farm now run by Supertramp's Roger Hodgson.

Unfortunately, most of the rock stars to whom Tony undoubtedly listened in the 1970s are now tweedy land-owners in Wiltshire who like to shoot anything that moves and drive very fast from grouse to grouse in Range Rovers. I can see them in their delightful Tuscan villas discussing the Boden catalogue with Dave and Sam, but

I can't imagine that they have much in common with Tony and Cherie.

So, we can deduce that they're actually working their way through Cherie's record collection. Next year, I imagine, it'll be Lord Manilow's penthouse in Vegas and then, perhaps, General James Last's schloss in the Bavarian Alps.

I'm actually rather surprised by this. I've always had Tony clocked as Snowball, and Cherie as Napoleon, a steady hard-a-port hand on the tiller. So I've rather imagined that her musical tastes started at Billy Bragg, moved through Kirsty McColl and then sort of ended up with the Pogues.

Plainly, though, I'm wrong. She obviously goes down the middle of the road so firmly that I'm surprised she doesn't have a bruised arse from running over all the Catseyes.

Anyway, a bit later than planned, I shall now get to the point of this new year missive: that you can learn an awful lot about someone from their choice of holiday destination.

In the past couple of years I've been to Corsica, Iceland and Botswana. Next year it'll be Canada. So you know from this list that we're not an entirely conventional family and that, as a result, we'd make good dinner-party guests.

Likewise, if you meet someone who's been to Ibiza you will know straight away that they are drug addicts and nymphomaniacs, and that if they've just come back from the Greek islands they are either homosexual or their husband has recently run off with his pneumatically breasted secretary.

Anyone who goes to France votes Conservative. Anyone who goes to Italy votes Labour, and anyone who goes to Spain has, at some point in the recent past, held up a post office. The only person who ever went to Germany for a vacation was Arthur Scargill.

Those who go on long-haul holidays can be split into two neat groups. If they go west they are likely to be shallow, materialistic and fitted with hair that isn't entirely normal. Those who go east will be interesting, dynamic and have unruly pubes.

Dubai is right out. It's all very well having an indoor ski slope in the desert and guaranteed sunshine and lots of things to do in the empty quarter, but you cannot drink outside your hotel. And I'm sorry, but anyone who puts quad-biking and wadi-bashing above the need for a glass of something chilled is plainly out of their tiny minds.

So what about taking a holiday at home? Tricky this, because obviously Rock is tremendous if you're 19 and you're being propelled through life by a cocktail of testosterone and cannabis. And Norfolk is also wonderful if you have developed a television programme and you want to meet commissioning editors in the local oyster bar.

But the worry I have about people who go on holiday in Britain is that they might be caravannists or, worse, environmentalists. They might think, in other words, that by not going on an aeroplane they have in some way saved the life of a Tasmanian butterfly.

Happily, however, Napoleon and Snowball have rather blown this argument into the middle of next week by going to stay *chez* Lord Sir Field Marshal Gibb.

We know from the plane crash that they did not go to

Florida on an organic sailing boat, and we know from the press coverage that they are being transported to and from the Big Pink restaurant in a big black Cadillac SUV.

His Tonyness has told us again and again that man's effect on the environment, and in particular on climate change, is large and growing. He's asked us to reduce our carbon footprints. And so, while we're all at home eating our low-energy light bulbs, it's a bit annoying to find that to satisfy his wife's lust for the Bee Gees he's straddling the Atlantic with a big carbon stomp.

In the olden days Labour leaders were more careful. Harold Wilson holidayed in the Isles of Scilly, Michael Foot liked Venice and John Smith would go walking in Scotland. Not because he wanted to meet Sheena Easton but because he liked the mountains.

Of course, back then, all the animals were equal. But now, thanks to Napoleon and Snowball, some really are more equal than others.

Sunday 31 December 2006

Brought down by bouncing bangers

Last week Britain severed its last tie with the 1950s. The monarchy has modernised itself. Homosexuality is now desirable. And Dave doesn't wear a tie.

But, until now, we've never been able to free ourselves completely from our grimy, black-and-white, music-hall past, thanks to the umbilical cord that is Little Chef.

Little Chef seemed to exist in a world of post-war catering, where the banana was considered exotic and nylon tights were decadent and risqué. The coffee was brown, simply because the main ingredient was mud. But now you can rejoice because last week it went into administration. And now it's been sold.

According to press reports, 20 million people a year visited Little Chef's chain of restaurants. I bet they did. They'd walk in, think they'd gone through some kind of time portal and that Tommy Trinder might leap out of the next booth, and then they'd not so much walk straight out again as flee.

I know a very great deal about Little Chef and its picture-book menus because its restaurants were always a handy main-road rendezvous point when I had to meet film crews in the back end of beyond. The only thing I ever found to eat in there was the sugar.

Even film crews, who are known throughout the civilised world for their capacity to eat absolutely anything, up to and including wheelie bins and manure, would draw the line at the Little Chef all-day breakfast.

There was a letter in the *Sun* last week from a woman who plainly shares their views. She ordered an omelette and was told they hadn't come in that morning. Apparently, they were delivered frozen and then simply heated up.

It's lucky she didn't go for a Little Chef sausage or she'd still be in there, wondering what on earth they'd made it from. Mashed-up tennis balls probably, because, and I've tried this, the Little Chef sausage is the only sausage in the world which, when thrown to the floor, will bounce.

Then there's Little Chef's 'traditional' fish'n'chips. No no no no no. You look at it on your plate and you think: 'Jesus H. Christ, did a cod really give up its life to end up here?' And then you put it in your mouth and you think: 'No, it didn't. I don't know what this is but it sure as hell isn't a fish.'

To me, it tasted like a dishcloth.

Sometimes, my wife would have the salad which, this being 1953, was a bit of lettuce and some tomato. Celery, in the world of Little Chef, was a bit too la-di-da. And eggs in their time zone were, of course, powdered.

Nonetheless, it's hard to imagine that you could go too far wrong with lettuce and tomatoes.

Oh yes you can. Especially if you select only the oldest lettuces that have been left in the sun for too long, and tomatoes which have that squishy 'Best before the Boer war' texture.

What were the management thinking? They must have known that all over Britain people would get up in a morning, have some espresso from their zinc kitchen appliances, then drive out of their towns, past the internet cafés and the Bang & Olufsen centres, while listening to some RnB on their MP3 interfaces.

So what made the bosses think that these cool, funky, twenty-first-century people would get 30 miles down the road and think: 'Ooh, what I fancy for elevenses is a taste of the 1950s'?

It's only 15 months since Little Chef last changed hands. It was bought by what was called 'the People's Restaurant Group'.

One of the backers was a chap who'd been on the Gumball Rally, sold surfer gear to dudes, and helped fund Café Rouge. A modern sort of guy, you might imagine.

But what did they do with Little Chef? The worst thing. They slashed the prices so that customers could enjoy a traditional fishcloth'n'chips, plus a mug of tea, for £4.99.

Do the maths. How much for staff costs, for heating, for rent and rates? How much for the tea, the water, the milk, the sugar, the potatoes, the peas and the batter? Now deduct the profit margins and you're left with the inescapable conclusion that somehow he was buying each fish for a unit of currency so small that it doesn't exist. It was ration-book catering for the Jamie Oliver generation.

John Major probably gave them hope. Famously, the former prime minister admitted once that he liked Little Chef. But of course he would, because John wanted to go back to basics.

In his 1993 speech, he urged us all to gather round the Light Programme every night, and have side partings. This was a man who thought that putting Currie in his mouth was dangerous and exciting.

But, as we now know, he was out of step, and the administrators had to be summoned. So what should the new owners do to jazz the place up?

Well, all of us fancy the idea of a proper fry-up, so why not simply take the Little Chef formula and do it like the war is over. Get your eggs from the back of a hen, use bread that doesn't contain any Crimplene, and serve sausages that are made from dead pigs.

You will also need someone to cook it, rather than heat it up. Get a Bulgarian and don't worry about the cost. People have come in a car. They can afford it.

In essence, don't make a trip to Nottingham a trip back in time.

Sunday 7 January 2007

TV heaven is an upside-down skier

With the demise of Dibley's vicar, home-grown comedy continues its downward spiral, and now, to compound the problem, they've neutered the funniest programme ever shown on British television: *Ski Sunday*.

I like skiing very much. And the thing I've always liked most of all about it is flopping into an armchair and watching other people do it for me.

Ski Sunday was always the highlight of my viewing week. In the olden days you had David Vine in the commentary booth, talking us through the brilliance of some tanned and muscular young man from Norway.

You'd marvel at how he made it look so easy, his skintight suit revealing every sinewy twitch and, according to my wife, whether he was a cavalier or a roundhead.

But let's be honest, all of us, really, were waiting for the falls.

Oh sweet Jesus. The falls. They were the best accidents a man can have without actually exploding, and they always went on for hours, a tangle of flesh and ego bouncing down the mountain until it crashed into the crowd in a technicolour explosion of joy, Gore-Tex and snow.

And better still, you knew that after the paramedics had collected all of the limbs and hosed most of the blood off the piste, you were going to get it all over again in super-voyeur slow motion. And it would all be set to

David Vine's completely humourless commentary, which somehow made it funnier still.

We watch the Horse of the Year Show for the same reason. Not because we want to see Sanyo Music Centre score a clean round but because we hope it will brake suddenly, sending Harvey Smith through the fence in an ear-splitting jangle of splintered wood and bone.

Bernie Ecclestone probably thinks we watch Formula One because we want to see Michael Schumacher's supreme car control. Wrong. If he wants the big viewing figures back he must arrange that in every race some floppy-haired Brazilian playboy disintegrates.

Skiing, however, has always been the best because the contestants are going so fast, and they are protected from the forces of nature by nothing more substantial than a big Durex. We could actually see their arms coming off.

So, a single half-hour of *Ski Sunday* provided more naked laughs than a million crying babies falling in paddling pools on *You've Been Framed*.

Nowadays, however, the show is presented by two greasy-haired dudes who I suspect may be snowboardists.

Now snowboarding, so far as I'm able to determine, is a sport where you dress up in clothes from the Dawn French Baggy Collection and then ingest as much cannabis as possible. The last man still making sense is the winner. This is not great TV.

Mind you, in last weekend's episode of *Ski Sunday*, we were treated to the edifying spectacle of one young chap from America who spent an age plugging an iPod into his ears and selecting the right track before setting off. Much to my intense pleasure, he fell over almost immediately.

Amazingly, the commentary team didn't seem to realise that any sport where the participants wear iPods doesn't really cut the mustard. So instead of pointing out that the competitor was an imbecile, we cut straight to a link where one of the presenters was addressing us while skiing backwards through a forest.

I can't tell you what he was on about because, like absolutely every one of the show's viewers, I was on my knees, praying to God that he'd slither backwards into a tree. More than a long life full of health and happiness, I wanted to see him try to finish the piece to camera with half a fir tree poking out of his bottom.

This is the whole point of skiing. We don't flog to the Alps every winter simply because we like the mountain views, or because we want to perfect the stem christie. Mainly, we go because we know that snow's slippery, and that there's a good chance we'll see someone fall over.

Why do you think YouTube is so popular? Because of the irony, or the subtle use of hyperbole in a situation that's both morally uplifting and tragic? No. It's banana-skin humour: a million billion clips of people falling off bicycles, and as often as not catching fire.

The Office and *Alan Partridge* were both brilliantly written. My respect for Gervais and Coogan is boundless. But did you ever laugh while watching Dave Brent? I doubt it. Not like you laugh when someone comes a cropper on *Deal or No Deal*, or trips over a paving stone in the town centre and falls flat on his face.

This is what the *Ski Sunday* team seem to have forgotten. They showed us how much flare should be in evidence in our skiing pants, and how the glove should be worn in relation to the cuff. And all the time, I kept thinking: 'Oh for God's sake. Show me a Norwegian falling over.'

Instead, we got a whole segment on snowboarding, and that won't do. There's nothing unusual in a stoned Finn getting all wobbly, because that's what people do when they've had a spliff. And my wife doesn't like the big clothes because, she says, she can't see their tackle.

The whole point of *Ski Sunday* is to take the ludicrous art of skiing and present it in a sensible fashion. It's the juxtaposition of the sane and the insane that works. Someone falling over is brilliant. Someone falling over and then pretending they meant it to happen: that's comedy gold.

Sunday 14 January 2007

No pain no gain (and no point)

On the surface, the human being appears to be a flawed design. Obviously, our brains are magnificent and our thumbs enable us to use spanners. Something an elephant, for instance, cannot do.

However, there seems to be something wrong with our stomachs. It doesn't matter how many pints of refreshing beer we cram into them, they always want just one more roast potato. And then, instead of ejecting all the excess fat, they feed it to our hearts and veins, and we end up all dead.

Of course, we can use willpower to counter these demands, but this makes us dull and pointless. You need only look at the number of people in lonely-hearts columns who neither drink nor smoke to know I'm right. If they did, they'd have a husband. It's that simple.

What I tend to do when it comes to the business of being fit is not bother. I eat lots, and then I sit in a chair. The upside to this is that I have a happy family and many friends. The downside is that I wobble and wheeze extensively while going to the fridge for another chicken drumstick.

Unfortunately, all this now has to stop because in April I'm going on an expedition. I can't tell you where because it's a secret but I can tell you that it's full of many perils, such as being eaten. And that if it all goes wrong, I may have to walk many miles over the most difficult terrain you can imagine.

Last week, then, I was sent to a training camp, where the instructor, a former Royal Marine, simply could not fathom what unholy cocktail of lard and uselessness lay beneath my skin. The upshot was simple.

Unless I did something dramatic about my general level of fitness, I would not be going. So I bought a rowing machine.

It cost a very great deal of money and is bigger than a small van. Modelled, I presume, on something from the KGB's cellars, you tie your feet to a couple of pedals and then move backwards and forwards until your shoulders are screaming so loudly that they are actually audible.

According to the digital readout – powered by my exertions, I might add – I had covered 35 yards. This was well short of the four kilometres I'd planned, so I had to grit my teeth and plough on.

Eventually, after several hours, I'd made enough electricity to power Glasgow and I'd reached my goal, so I tried to dismount. But it was no good. My magnificent brain was so stunned by what had just happened that it had lost control of my legs. I also felt dizzy and sick. Fondly, I also imagined that I had a tingling in my left arm and chest pains.

Part of the problem is that to go on my expedition, I must be six pounds overweight. This means losing a stone so I have been living on a diet of carrots and Coke Zero, which simply doesn't provide enough calories to rock back and forth in my conservatory for half a day.

Actually, conservatory is the wrong word. I had pro-

duced so much sweat while moving about that, technically, it was a swimming pool.

Now one of the things I should explain at this point is
that I am always hugely enthusiastic about new projects,
but only for a very short time. If I was to get fit and thin,
it needed to be done fast, before I lost interest, so once
some feeling had returned to my legs, I went for a walk.
And since then time has passed in a muddy blur of cycling,
trudging, rowing and discovering that it's uphill to my
local town, and uphill on the way back as well.

This has made me dull, thick and, because there's no
beer or wine in my system at night, an even bigger insom-
niac. And all the while I have this sneaking suspicion that
what I'm doing is biologically unhealthy.

Pain is designed to tell the body something is wrong
and that you'd better do something fast to make it go
away. So why would you get on a rowing machine and
attempt to beat what God himself has put there as a
warning? That's like refusing to slow down when an
overhead gantry on the motorway says 'Fog'.

Today, then, my magnificent brain is questioning the
whole philosophy of a fitness regime. If God had meant
us to have a six-pack, why did he give us the six pack?

In the olden days, people had to run about to catch
deer so they all had boy-band torsos and good teeth.

But now, we Darwin to work in a car. Trying to look
like a twelfth-century African is as silly as a seal trying to
regrow its legs.

No, really. The thing about evolution is that each step
along the way has a point. Cows developed udders so they
could be plugged into milking machines. And humans

developed the remote-control television so they could spend more time sitting down.

Fitness fanatics should take a lead from nature. Nobody looks at water and suggests it would be more healthy if it spent 20 minutes a day trying to flow uphill and nobody suggests a lion could catch more wildebeest if it spent less of its day lounging around.

Plainly, then, our stomachs are designed to demand food and feed fat to our arteries for a reason. I don't know what the reason might be but I suspect it may have something to do with global warming. Everything else does.

Sunday 21 January 2007

The end is nigh, see it on YouTube

I have the most horrible feeling that the only possible conclusion to the problem of Muslim extremism – and I'm looking 30 or more years down the line here – is mass deportation and an all-new cold war between Mecca and Rome.

I am also fearful that unless we stop thinking of ways to prevent global warming, and start to address the problems it will cause when it gets here, our children are going to finish their days in an overcrowded, superheated vision of hell.

Where they can't even get a cold drink, because all the corner shopkeepers have been made to go and live in Pakistan.

Unless, of course, America goes bust in the meantime . . . which it will. It is a mathematical certainty, unless George W. Bush announces, today, a tax hike for both individuals and companies of 69 per cent or he cuts federal spending to zero. Not just for a month or two. But for ever.

Since George Bush is unlikely to do either, the world's biggest economy will collapse, which means we can't rely on Uncle Sam when your neighbourhood mullah beats your daughter with a stick for not going to school in a tablecloth. Because it's 47°C out there and getting hotter, and Jonathon Porritt won't let you have air-conditioning.

Strangely, however, my biggest fear for the future of the planet and the well-being of our children is YouTube.

At present it is full, mostly, of young men falling off their bicycles and catching fire. But in addition to this you can log on if you wish to see next week's episode of *24*.

This means the producers of *24* have gone to all the trouble of making a show, and paying the actors, and getting all those phones to go 'beep beep eeoooh' and then finding that no television company in the world is all that bothered about screening it, because everyone's seen it already on the web.

Naturally, the company that makes *24* – and I suppose I should point out that it's Fox, which is part of News Corporation, the parent company of this newspaper – has started proceedings against YouTube.

Fine, you might think. YouTube will be forced to treat the copyright laws with a bit more respect and that will be that. Except it won't. Because the internet's like mercury, so as soon as it becomes impossible to post copyrighted material on YouTube, some other computer nerd in Bangladesh will, for an outlay of 35p, start a new video-sharing site. And you'll be able to post it there.

This morning there are 921 Jeremy Clarkson clips on YouTube, for which, obviously, I receive not a penny. Of course I could sue them – and now they're owned by Google I think I might – but then the 921 clips would simply appear on the new sharing site based in Bangladesh. And what's the point of suing someone whose only assets are a laptop and a loincloth?

The upshot is that films, television shows, magazines,

newspapers, songs, anything published or recorded, can be put on the internet. And the person who published it or recorded it doesn't get any money. So what's the point of publishing or recording anything?

Obviously, if Jonathon Porritt were to write a book, it would be jolly funny to buy the first copy and put it all online, so he ended up with a royalty cheque for 50p. But it's not so funny if you are Jonathon Porritt.

At present, everyone is obsessed with the internet. Every large media company in the world is investing millions in their websites and not one, so far as I can tell, has even the remotest idea of how it can possibly generate any money.

A prime example is iTunes. It doesn't. Apparently, Apple doesn't make a penny from the music you download to your computer. But if you want to put that onto a portable device you have to buy an iPod, and they make lots of dosh from that.

It's a brilliant wheeze, but now the Norwegian ombudsman has decided that Apple must make its loss-making music library available to anyone, no matter what sort of hardware they have. France and Germany are thinking of following suit. And if the rest of the world falls into line, that's pretty much that for Apple.

It's all a nonsense anyway, because there are countless sites out there in cyberspace where you can download music for nothing and then put it onto whatever sort of MP3 player takes your fancy.

Small wonder that last week Music Zone, a chain of Manchester-based record shops, went belly up. Who would buy a CD these days when with two or three clicks they can have it for nothing? That's as idiotic as saving up for a BMW motorcycle when you live in Branscombe.

And it's not just the media that are under threat. Why go to a doctor when there's NHS Direct? Why have sex when there's always some bird in Latvia who's happy to get her knickers off? Why buy an encyclopaedia when there's Wikipedia (apart from the fact that everything on Wikipedia is wrong)? Why go to Tesco when you can shop online? Estate agents. Property developers. Motorcycle dispatch riders. They've all had it.

The only people I can think of who won't lose their jobs to the internet are those who empty cesspits. And nobody seems to have spotted this.

One day, of course, they will. The world will wake up and realise it's unemployed; that we've all been terminated by machines. And please don't try to argue that men will always triumph over machinery because we can always turn it off. Because that's the thing with the internet. You can't.

Sunday 28 January 2007

Robbie and I know about pills

I wish to state from the outset that, mostly, I have no problem with people taking drugs. If you want to shovel a ton of coke up your nose before going to the Brits, that's fine by me. Just so long as I don't have to sit next to you.

In fact, I read last week that Robbie Williams has checked into rehab because he's getting through a handful of happy pills, 36 espressos, 60 cigarettes and 20 Red Bulls every day, and I thought 'Pussy'. If you substitute the happy pills for Nurofen, that's my daily diet as well, and I'm fine. 'Fine, d'you hear.' Apart from the fainting.

However, I must say at this point that I intensely dislike all drugs that affect my ability to think properly. You see people in the garden at parties, hiding behind trees, claiming loudly that Jesus is out there too, and wants to eat them. And you think, 'Where's the fun in that?' And why are you now in the fridge, sprinkling frozen peas onto a sherry trifle?

I once saw a group of people who'd taken some magic mushrooms, lying on the floor laughing hysterically at a tube of toothpaste. And toothpaste, so far as I can tell, has exactly the same comedic properties as Russell Brand.

Magic mushrooms, then, do not make you clever, or horny, or buzzy, all of which would be fine. They make you mental, and that's not fine at all.

I don't even like to take alcohol in such large quantities that no matter how carefully I marshal my thoughts into a coherent sentence they come out as a stream of incoherent gibberish.

Once, in Houston, Texas, I arrived back at my very large hotel and couldn't remember either what room I was in or my name. So I had to spend the whole night trying my key in each of the doors, a job made doubly hard because they each appeared to have 16 or 17 locks. Fun? No, not really, unless the alternative is being eaten by a shark.

The worst drug, though, by a mile, is the common or garden sleeping pill. I tried one once, on a flight from Beijing to Paris, and was so removed from anything you might call reality that to this day I have no recollection of the emergency landing we made in Sharjah. Being so out of it that you can sleep through a plane crash: that's bloody frightening.

So last weekend, when I was offered a couple of pills for the flight back to London from South Africa, I smiled and said no. But the paramedic was very pretty and very persuasive and said they were only antihistamines rather than proper sleeping pills, so I relented and as the plane took off popped them into my mouth.

The first indication that something was wrong came 20 minutes into the Martin Scorsese film I was watching. It didn't make any sense. Mark Wahlberg had become Leonardo DiCaprio who, in turn, looked just like Matt Damon. I didn't know what was going on. I didn't care. And then I fell into such a deep sleep that, legally, doctors would have been able to remove my spleen for transplant.

The next thing I knew we had landed at Heathrow

and Richard Hammond – or it could have been Matt
Damon – was shaking my shoulder, pointing out that I
had to get off. 'This isn't the Circle line,' he said. 'You
can't just sleep till your stop comes around again.'

I vaguely remember collecting a bag from the carousel
– I think it was mine – and driving into central London
to the accompaniment of many blown horns and harsh
words. And I dimly recall climbing into bed thinking, 'I'll
just have an hour's kip before I go to work.'

And then it was five hours later, and I still wasn't
entirely sure how the world worked. I stared at my coffee
machine for what must have been 20 minutes until the
sheer complexity of the thing made me feel all weepy. So
I went to work, made a mess of everything, and then
went home for more sleep.

I'd love to report that the next day I felt refreshed, but
in fact everything was worse. I wanted to be well, but I
couldn't shake off the immense soggy blanket that had
been laid on my head. Or the dead horse that had been
nailed to my back.

And do you know what? I'd only taken a couple of
antihistamine tablets. Whereas in Britain 16 million full-
strength sleeping-pill prescriptions are issued every year.

Only some of which go to Robbie Williams.

Research estimates that anything up to 1.75 million
people are going through life in a state that puts them
somewhere in the middle of the River Styx.

Which certainly explains why I meet so many bores in
the course of a normal day.

Technically, anyone on temazepam is not really what
scientists would call 'alive'.

Certainly, I would like to see a law imposed whereby anyone who takes a prescription for sleeping pills is forced to hand over their driving licence. And their children, for that matter.

You may write to me saying that you have trouble nodding off at night but I have no sympathy because I too lie in bed every night, in a fug of smoking primrose oil, with a tummy full of lettuce, counting sheep, and I can't sleep either.

But I know that getting through the next day on half an hour's shut-eye is better than trying to get through it with the reaction times, humour and conversation of a boulder.

Sunday 18 February 2007

Drip-drip-drip of a revolution

The news last week that olive oil, Marmite and porridge cannot now be advertised during television programmes aimed at children confirms something I've suspected for a few months. There's a revolution going on in Britain and no one seems to have noticed.

When the French and Russian proletariat rose up against the middle and upper classes, they made a lot of noise and used pitchforks. Whereas here the revolutionaries are using stealth and a drip-drip-drip policy of never-ending legislation.

It started when they let ramblers trample all over your flowerbeds and then, of course, there was hunting. We know that the antis couldn't really have cared less about the well-being of foxy woxy, but they hated, with a passion, the well-heeled country folk who charged about on their horses shouting tally-ho.

Then came the attack on four-wheel-drive cars. 'It's the environment,' they smiled, but it's no such thing. Otherwise they'd be up north taxing people with clapped-out Ford Orions and telling fat people in council houses to get out of the chip shop and lag their bloody lofts.

No, they go after Chelsea Tractors because these are symbols of middle-class success. You have to remember that trade unionists and anti-nuclear campaigners didn't go away. They just morphed into eco-mentalists because they realised that global warming was a better weapon than striking, or doing lesbionics for mother Russia in Berkshire.

Think about it. They tell you not to go to Tuscany this summer, and they throw withering looks at the Ryanair flights to Gascony. But when Kentucky Fried Chicken starts advertising a bucket of supper with disposable plates and non-biodegradable plastic cutlery so you don't have to get your fat arse out of your DFS sofa and wash up, do we hear a murmur? You can cup your ears as much as you like but the answer is no.

Instead we get Ofcom listing what it considers to be junk food and therefore unsuitable for children. Chicken nuggets? Plain white bread? Oven chips? Diet drinks? Nope, along with a lot of oven-ready 'meals', these are all fine apparently.

But Marmite, porridge, raisins, cheese and manuka honey? 'Fraid not. This is what middle-class kids eat so it's all wrong, and now it can't be advertised on television in the afternoon.

Meanwhile, you have John Prescott insisting that each new housing development can only get a planning green light if it 'spoils some Tory bastard's view'.

It gets worse. Ken Livingstone has not extended the congestion charge into Tower Hamlets or Newham. Nope. He's gone for Kensington and Chelsea. And we learnt last week of plans to turn Sloane Square, the epicentre of middle-class shopping and conviviality, into a tree-free crossroads.

I've checked and strangely there are no plans to build a new road through the statue of Harold Wilson in the north's equivalent of Sloane Square – George Square in Huddersfield.

There are, however, plans afoot to give Janet Street-Porter and others of a Gore-Tex disposition access to a 10-yard-wide corridor around all of Britain's 2,500-mile coastline. So you worked hard all your life and saved up enough to buy a bit of seclusion by the sea? Well, sorry, but Natural England, a sinister-sounding bunch, has advised DEFRA, which sounds like something the Nazis might have dreamt up, that your garden should be confiscated and that there should be a 'presumption against' giving you any compensation.

You see what I mean? On its own, that's no big deal. But lob everything else into the mix and it becomes clear that traditional Britain is under attack. It's porridge and Jonathan Ross's back garden today, but tomorrow Mrs Queen will be transported to Scotland and summarily shot. You mark my words.

I bet the chief executive of Barclays agrees. He announced last week that the bank had made record profits, and was probably feeling pretty chuffed, right up to the moment he was summoned to a television studio and presented as the unacceptable face of capitalism who goes round the countryside at weekends stamping on puppies.

I felt it too, on Thursday, because for reasons I can't be bothered to explain I was in London with a Rolls-Royce and no one ever let me out of a side turning.

Why? As I've said before, Simon Cowell, who is a rich man, gives the exchequer more each year than is generated by all the speed cameras put together. If you combined the tax contributions of all those who have Rollers, I bet you'd have enough to pay for Britain's air traffic control system.

And that's before you start on how much Britain's rich do for charity. Last year a bunch of hedge-fund managers raised £18 million in a single night to help Romanian orphans. At one party Lady Bamford's mates stumped up £3 million for the NSPCC. And I had lunch on Thursday with a chap who, so far as I could tell, single-handedly looks after every disadvantaged child in the land.

And yet, when he climbs into his Bentley to go home at night, a bunch of communists and hippies, egged on by faceless former Greenham lesbos in government think tanks, makes sure he can never pull into the traffic flow.

Not that he's going anywhere anyway, because Ken Livingstone has taken £8 a day from middle-class Londoners and given it to a crackpot South American lunatic in exchange for cheap oil, which means the capital is choked with buses full of Bulgarian pickpockets fleeing from the police.

I notice this morning that the blossom is out on my trees. And yet, somehow, it doesn't feel like summer's coming.

Sunday 25 February 2007

Fear and loathing in Las Manchester

We keep reading about plans for the supercasino in Manchester, and everyone seems very bothered about whether it'll be like Las Vegas or not.

Well, in one important respect it won't be. Las Vegas is situated in the middle of the Nevada Desert, not far from Death Valley, the hottest place on earth. Manchester is known for its year-round drizzle and its summertime peaks of 57°F.

As you approach Vegas from Los Angeles, especially at night, it is a genuinely impressive spectacle. All that power. All that energy. And so many air-conditioning units that as often as not the city generates its own overhead cloud cover to cool the gamblers down.

As you approach Manchester you usually think, 'I'll turn my wipers on now.' And then you keep right on going to somewhere better.

We can't forget the police, either. In Vegas they wear shorts, ride bicycles and – I'm not kidding – have flashing lights on top of their helmets. And no one laughs at them.

Then we have the hotels. At the MGM Grand in Vegas there are 5,044 rooms and the turnaround time is phenomenal. You check out, and even if it's three in the morning someone else will be in your room just 20 minutes later.

The last time I stayed in Manchester, my hotel room

had nylon sheets that made my hair look like it had been styled by a Van de Graaff generator, and the biggest diversion was the Corby Trouser Press.

However, in one important respect Manchester's supercasino will be very similar to Las Vegas. The customers will be poor and fat when they get there.

And a little bit poorer and fatter when they leave.

When I first started gambling, back in the early eighties, it was a rather elegant way of passing the time. I'd go to the Connoisseur on the Fulham Road, or Le Casino in a Lower Sloane Street basement. This was a wonderful spot, with just four tables, a fire and a maître d' called Roget who'd always offer to find me a taxi at 4 a.m., knowing full well I was always penniless and would have to walk.

Then there was the Moortown Casino in Leeds, where I first encountered the cooking of Marco Pierre White. The only problem here is that it was always full of old Jewish ladies, and getting on the blackjack tables was a nightmare.

So we used to ring from the phone box outside and ask to speak to Mrs Cohen. An announcement would be made over the club's PA and then we'd simply push past the crowd of old ladies coming to the reception desk and, hey presto, we could play where we wanted.

Vegas too, in those days, was a laugh. The Strip was a great place for cruising. You could stay at the Aladdin for $8 a night, see the Doobies, play a little blackjack, develop a rapport with the dealer and it was all jolly lovely. Even though you knew your losses were being used by men called Don to buy guns in Chicago and cocaine in New York.

Last week you probably read about someone called the Fat Man who has dropped £23 million in the last few years at Aspinalls, a place described as lovely and luxurious and full of 'the right crowd'. The way they talk, Lord Lucan is still in there chatting to Pamela Harriman, and so you probably think gambling is still a fun thing to do.

It isn't. Le Casino and the Connoisseur were taken over, amalgamated and then resurfaced in a glittering, noisy barn under the Gloucester Hotel in South Kensington. I've been there a couple of times and it's always full of Chinamen losing their tempers.

And Vegas. Oh. My. God. I went last summer and it's now crammed.

You can't move on the Strip, 24 hours a day, and as you sit at the bar being insulted by the uninterested staff you get the impression that it's just a giant cathedral to the worst sort of capitalism. You know that it's all owned by the corporations, who are using it to rape the terminally stupid.

They sit there, some of them on five or six bar stools, with a bucket of money on one phlebitis-ridden thigh and a bucket of lard on the other. And you just don't want to join in.

I love playing cards for money. I really, really adore it. But that night I felt a bit sick watching the Sheriff of Nottingham simply empty the serfs' pockets.

There's no style any more. No panache. When you check in at the MGM there's an army of valet parkers who direct you to one of the 16 lanes so that you are in the casino and at the tables that little bit faster.

In the past the receptionist would tell you about all the

shows in town. Now you give them a credit card and you're in your room, where the bed is still warm from the last sucker who breezed into town. It is horribly depressing.

And that's what it's going to be like in Manchester. Oh sure, you'll get a handful of the nation's orange people from Cheshire over there, dropping vast wads on black to make themselves more sexually attractive. But mostly it'll be poor, fat people gambling away money they barely had in the first place.

And meanwhile, 160 miles to the south, Tessa Jowell will be sitting in an agreeable flat wondering what on earth became of her socialist principles.

I haven't got any at all. Never had. But if I were her I'd feel a bit of a chump.

Sunday 4 March 2007

Bullseye! The pub is dying

Good news. It seems that the centuries-old tradition of being forced to pop down to the local for a pint and a game of arrows with your mates is coming to an end.

A survey of regular pub-goers last week found that only 10 per cent had played darts in the past year, compared with 41 per cent five years ago. Better still, four out of ten men in their twenties had never played in their lives and a similar number had no idea what a bullseye is worth.

I loathe darts. You settle down with your mates for a bit of a chat and a few drinks and then one of them suggests a game. Why? Why do I want to spend my time in the pub, standing up, doing maths?

Darts is a game for people who can't make conversation, or who are so bored by seeing the same faces night after interminable night that they have to do something apart from talk.

We're told that Henry VIII was a keen darts player and I can understand that. Because he didn't have a PlayStation and he needed something to take his mind off an alarming collection of sores that were multiplying in his underpants, I can believe that throwing some shortened spears at the bottom of a beer barrel might in some way be deemed entertaining.

When syphilis became less popular, I can still see how darts might have flourished. You'd come out of t'factory with t'lads and there was no point going home because the bog was at the bottom of t'garden and half your children had rickets. So you may as well go to t'pub.

But now, anyone who can't think of what to say to their friends while in a pub can spend their time texting other friends who aren't there. Even that is better than bloody darts.

Of course, it doesn't help that I'm not very good at it. My ability to hit the treble 20 is governed not by hand–eye co-ordination but by the laws of averages and probability. Mostly, I fail to hit the board at all, or the dart bounces back and pierces my shoe.

And then I'm expected to stand there, with my foot nailed to the floor, trying through a fog of pain to deduct 17 from 263.

Some people call this a sport. Rubbish. A sport is something that requires specialist clothing, whereas all you need to play professional darts is a loud shirt that you don't tuck into your trousers, a stomach the size of Staffordshire and an idiotic nickname.

They're all called 'the Viking' or 'the Viper' or 'the Assassin' when in fact they should all be called 'the fat bastard who hates his wife and kids so much he'd rather spend his evenings throwing arrows into a bit of bristle with his fat and disgusting friends'.

Show me somebody who likes playing darts and I'll show you a social misfit with so much worrying imagery on his hard drive that if it were ever discovered, the courts would lock him away for a thousand years.

That's why I'm glad to see it's dying out and that pubs are replacing their oches with abstract art and bits of furniture from Conran. But you know what? I won't really be happy until the pub itself has gone.

People, normally those who have their own arrows and can get breaks of 50 or more in snooker, lament the passing of what they call 'the rural drinking pub'. They paint a picture of traditional England with low ceilings, horse brasses, a fire and people from the village gathered around to swap stories over a pint of handmade beer.

'Mmmm' you might think. But the reality is that you have to stand up, the beer's got twigs in it, the landlord is a psychopath, you can't hear what anybody is saying, the fire's too hot, you can't stand at the corner of the bar because 'that's where Jack stands and he'll be in in a minute' and if you inadvertently spill someone's drink you'll be invited into the car park to do pugilism. Oh, and the only cigarettes in the dispensing machine will be Lambert & Butlers.

Often, these rural drinking pubs serve a selection of sandwiches and pies, but for nutritional value you'd be better off eating the little blue tablets in the urinals.

Then you have city-centre pubs where men go to meet girls, not realising that all girls in city-centre pubs have thighs like tug boats and morals that would surprise a zoo animal. Show me a man who married a girl he met in a city-centre drinking pub and I'll show you someone who's made to wait in the loft, playing darts, while she entertains lorry drivers in the front room.

Of course, these people would sneer at what they call gastropubs but I don't see why. In a gastropub, nobody has their own tankard, nobody will throw a dart into the side of your head, there are no biker chicks who want to rape you, especially if you have a lorry, and there will be a chef who, sometimes at least, has a clue what to do with food.

Your darts player would poke his nose into such a place and then leave in disgust because it had arugula on the 'menu' and it was playing a chill-out CD.

What's wrong with that? Moby is a better listening experience than the descant of a beeping fruit machine set to the bassline of some old bore in red corduroy trousers who's regaling the landlord with a story from the golf course and keeps referring to Mrs Bore as 'the wife'.

We shook off the culture of strikes, chilly winters and Michael Foot and now we must shake off the spectre of the pub and all that it stands for: darts, bar billiards, bores and beer with the consistency of engine oil. Mine's a Bacardi Breezer.

Sunday 11 March 2007

You can't kill me, I'm the drummer

When the BBC asked if I'd become involved in the Comic Relief extravaganza, obviously my initial reaction was 'no'. I saw no reason to give up my time so a couple of African dictators could buy bigger Mercs.

But then I was told the Comic Relief money doesn't actually buy cars or bigger power tools with which Mr Mugabe can drill into his opponents' heads. It buys useful stuff such as ambulances and help for the mentally ill of Britain.

And anyway, saying no to the Comic Relief team is a bit like saying no to the man at the Tube station with the stack of *Big Issues*. In fact, it's even harder because you can't smile and say: 'It's all right, I've already got one.'

So what did they want me to do? Wear a leotard and flail about on an ice rink? Sing? Stand in a school playground while children rubbed lumps of elephant dung into my hair?

It turned out the offer was even worse. Would the three *Top Gear* presenters like to appear on a humorous celebrity version of *A Question of Sport*?

As I'd rather have spent the afternoon sitting on a ham slicer, I came up with another idea. What about *Top Gear of the Pops*? It'd be like *Top Gear*, only instead of cars we'd have music. And then, I said jovially, we could finish with a tune from the *Top Gear* band.

The Comic Relief people loved this, and commissioned it immediately. And that was great, except for one teeny-weeny detail. There was no such thing as the band.

Yes, Richard Hammond used to play bass with a band 20 years ago but gave up when, in a fit of temper, he broke his guitar over the singer's head. And sure, James May is an accomplished harpsichord player with a degree in the science of music. But while he'd be good at Brahms and Chopin, he's not so good when it comes to what he calls 'pop'.

And that leaves me. I took up the drums about six months ago and have had seven lessons. I practise infrequently and have become to the world of sticksmanship what Germany is to the world of cricket.

In my heart, I fondly imagined that one day, many years from now, when I'd become more proficient, I might team up with some like-minded souls and perhaps play a small gig to a few close friends in a pub. But here I was, volunteering to make my debut, in a week's time, in a studio full of 700 people, to a television audience of maybe 5 million.

There's no medical term for what I was going through. Doctors call it simply 'shitting yourself'.

And it became worse when we turned up, a day before the studio recording, to practise for the very first time.

I'd selected Billy Ocean's 'Red Light Spells Danger', partly because it's a good happy pop song ideal for ending a feel-good Comic Relief show. But mostly because there are only a couple of twiddly bits for the drummer. The rest, though fast, is all fairly straightforward.

Except it isn't. Not when you put other instruments into the mix. I'd always thought the drums are a sort of noise that go on in the background of a song, but it turns out the drummer is the engine room. The man who keeps time.

The single most vital piece of the entire ensemble.

Unaware of this, I did my first twiddly bit and sort of picked up with the beat where I'd left off. Much to my surprise, the rest of the band stopped playing, lowered their shoulders and turned to stare at me.

Actually, Hammond sort of glared. There was a very real sense that if I did that again he'd kill me. And since I didn't know what I'd done wrong this was worrying.

When you're behind a drum kit, bashing away as though you're in a cage, trying to get out, you can't hear any of the other instruments. You kind of assume they're playing the tune and all is well.

But no, rock music is not the anarchy I'd always assumed. It's actually pure maths. I had to hit the snare at the precise moment Hammond was hitting some aspect of his guitar, and no, he couldn't just 'miss a bit out to catch up'. When I suggested this, he became even more angry.

To make matters worse I was supposed to be achieving 180 beats per minute. And I was . . . some of the time. Everyone shouted at me a lot for this.

And when I said: 'Oh well. It's for Comic Relief. Perhaps people will find my inability to keep time funny,' they shouted even more.

Eventually, our singer, Justin Hawkins, formerly of the Darkness, turned up. He was a bit amazed to find the drummer and the bassist squaring up to one another, but after a couple of run-throughs said: 'That's as good as it's going to get', took over my drum kit and spent the rest of the day jamming with Hammond and May while I ate crisps.

And so the next day, after seven lessons and two run-throughs, we took to the stage and did our song.

And afterwards everyone was very kind to me, in the same way you're very kind to a four-year-old who's painted a picture of some flowers.

Even though they look like dogs.

The finished product was transmitted on Friday night at 10 o'clock. I hope you were all in bed and missed it.

Sunday 18 March 2007

What the hell are we saying here?

A few weeks ago I became a businessman, which means I've started going to meetings. Or, as they should be known, 'places where nothing happens and nothing gets done'.

Here's how they go. Each of the people round the table expresses their opinion on a particular subject, and each of these opinions is completely different. Then, after you've drunk a cup of what might be coffee, but could be oxtail soup, a biggish woman – and it's always a woman – says: 'Well, we're outside the box here with a new kind of hybrid venture and we can't know what the result will be until we've run the flag up the flagpole and seen which way the wind's blowing.'

Plainly, you want to argue with this, but as you draw breath to speak you realise that what she just said didn't make any sense. And anyway, she hasn't finished.

'It's mission critical that we use blue-sky thinking and that we're proactive, not reactive, if we're to come up with a ballpark figure that we can bring to the table.'

Again, you raise an index finger to make a point. But you don't know what that point might be, so you pour yourself another cup of winter-warming coffee broth, help yourself to another triangular tuna and cucumber sandwich and wait for the pastry-faced woman in culottes to finish.

'We must maintain a client focus so that we can incentivise the team and monetise the deliverables, and only then can we take it to the next level.'

You look round the table at all the old hands, the sort of people who whip out their laptops every time they're at an airport and know what a Wi-Fi looks like, and they're all nodding sagely, so you stop yourself from actually saying: 'I'm sorry but what the hell are you on about?'

Later on in the day, you ring the person who called the meeting and in less than a minute decide on a course of action. And then, when you get home, you wonder why it was necessary to have the meeting at all. So you can listen to a farmyard animal in a power suit turning nouns into verbs and talking rubbish for half an hour to mask the fact she hasn't got a single cohesive thought in her head.

To get round this problem, a friend and I developed a new scheme to make meetings more interesting. We would give each other a band as we walked through the door and then we'd compete to see how many of their song titles we could lob into the conversation without anyone noticing.

That's why, last week, I actually said: 'Every breath you take is like an invisible sun. We are spirits in the material world, or, as they say in France, Outlandos d'Amour.' And do you know what? Nobody batted an eyelid.

And nor did anyone cotton on when my friend replied by saying: 'We're on the top of the world looking down on creation, and we are calling occupants of interplanetary craft.'

Eventually, though, even this became wearisome so I went on holiday, but even in the Caribbean there was no escape. A fax arrived from my new business colleagues advising me that there was to be a conference call at 2 p.m. Barbados time between people in Los Angeles, Aspen, London and Cairo.

I've never felt so important in my whole life. Me? On a conference call? Spanning the globe? Wow. I was so excited that I completely forgot about it until 1.55 p.m., by which time I was very drunk, and on a sailing boat.

No matter, I dialled the number, entered the security pin I'd been given and was asked to state my name so I could be introduced. 'Beep' went the phone, and then on came an electronic voice to say: 'Captain Jack Sparrow has joined the conversation.'

Conference calls are great. They're exactly like a normal meeting in that nothing happens and nothing gets done and everyone talks rubbish, but you don't have to sit there remembering not to fall asleep or what Culture Club did after 'Karma Chameleon'.

You can just pour yourself another rum punch and look out of the porthole. At one point, when the boat went about, or whatever it is sailing boats do when they turn round, I fell off my chair, dropped the phone and couldn't find it for five minutes, and when I finally rejoined the conversation nobody had even noticed I'd been away.

Unfortunately, one of the decisions made in a follow-up phone call to the man who'd hosted the conference chat was that we'd have to go to Los Angeles.

Hollywood. America. And have meetings, there, face to face with the people we hadn't been talking about because they were in the box and we were outside it, at the top of a flagpole seeing which way the wind was blowing.

Gulp. American business meetings. That'd be scary. A whole new raft of power women and even more white-collar nonsense. I'd better get sober.

Strangely, however, the Americans have got meetings down to a fine art, which is probably why they have NASA and Microsoft and we have Betty's tea shoppe. You walk in and the receptionist asks if you'd like some 'wadder or something'. You are then ushered into a conference room where you say your piece, and when you've finished, their top man stands up, thanks you for coming and leaves.

They've realised that the meeting is useless for getting anything done, so they listen'n'go. And move straight to the follow-up phone call where the decisions are made.

I therefore have a new rule. If I go to a meeting, only I am allowed to speak. And then something happens.

Sunday 15 April 2007

Hell is a tent zip in the snow

I have spent the past three weeks in a tent. And I have decided that anyone who does this kind of thing for fun must be either nine years old or absolutely insane.

What disturbs me most of all is that all tenting equipment is obviously designed specifically to not work. Let us take the zip as a perfect case in point. For 47 years I have raised and lowered the flies in my trousers without getting it caught in the fabric once.

And yet, in the world of tenting, every single zip gets stuck all the time. So there you are, outside in the freezing cold, jiggling the damn thing backwards and forwards, knowing that with each tug, and each muttered expletive, more and more of the tent is being swallowed by the fastener.

Eventually, and often with the help of a knife, you get through what tentists laughably call the door − it's a cat flap − and you are presented with your sleeping bag, into which you must climb as quickly as possible because tents are essentially heat exchangers.

They are always seven degrees colder than the ambient temperature outside. And that was a particular problem for me because on my tenting holiday it rarely rose above minus 17.

So, you dive into your bag, yank the zip and instantly the entire bag disappears into it. And you can't fish it out

because your fingers are bright blue and have become
what a horse would call 'hooves'.

To warm them up, you must light the stove. Simple,
you might think. In the civilised world there are many
burners that light at the touch of a button, or with the
merest hint of a match. But this is tenting, so the stove
you've been given is designed to not light at all for two
hours, and then blow up in your face.

First of all, you must fill the fuel tank and then pump
it to create some pressure.

That's a) pointless, and b) extremely dangerous in cold
climates because skin sticks to metal and can be removed
only with the aid of a chain saw.

Finally, though, after you've used 600 matches and
emptied your Zippo, you get a flame. Which grows bigger
and bigger until it engulfs the pressurised fuel tank.

This does at least mean some feeling returns to your
hooves, which means you can feel the agony as you
plunge your hand into the inferno and carry the bomb
back through the slashed cat flap and into the snow outside. So now you have no heating, and your sleeping bag
is still stuck in its own zip.

I do not believe that these design flaws can be acciden-
tal. I believe that people who manufacture tenting equipment deliberately make their products useless and
dangerous because anyone who wants to live under canvas
plainly wants their life to be as harsh and as uncomfortable
as possible.

That's why the tent and sleeping bag come in condoms
that are slightly too small, so you can never get them back
inside again.

It's why your backpack and trousers have straps and fasteners that serve no purpose except to get tangled up in one another. It's why the fabric for the modern tent is designed to burn with the savagery of petrol and flap noisily whenever there's even the hint of a breeze.

And it's why the sleeping bag is so slim that it is impossible – impossible, d'you hear – to do up the fastener once you're inside.

You get it so far and then realise that if you keep going, your left hoof will end up deep inside your right nostril. So you attempt to zip it up from the outside, which means your entire arm is left sticking from the bag like the aerial on a satellite phone.

I didn't find a single piece of tenting equipment, in three weeks, that worked properly. I had to eat from a plastic dog bowl that shattered when you sat on it.

And when you're trying to get out of a sleeping bag, with a frozen joint of lamb sticking out of your shoulder, in a tent that's just a few inches tall, and lined with ice, and you've had no sleep because of the flapping, it is impossible not to sit on absolutely everything.

Then you have the mattress, which rolls up into an impressively small sausage. But it will not remain flat when it's unfurled.

You have to put a weight on the far end, which means crawling into your tent with snowy boots. The snow then falls off, melts when your heater explodes and then freezes in the night so you awake to find you've been set in aspic.

Food? Well, obviously you could take beans and sausages. But no, tentists choose instead to feast on dried-up copies of the *Guardian*. You simply add water, which you get by melting snow, and hey presto, you dine on Polly Toynbee's column garnished with a hint of George Monbiot.

You can't even go for a pee properly because tenting trousers have no zip. God knows what they'd eat if they did. This means you must pull down each of the eight pairs you are wearing to keep out the cold.

And I can guarantee that when you pull them back up again one or two will remain below your arse, which makes walking difficult.

Needless to say, the only way you can do your number twos while tenting is to squat, like an animal.

And because tenting is so weak when it comes to personal hygiene and washing facilities, I came home after three weeks with a peculiar growth on my face.

Doctors tell me I may have grown a beard.

Sunday 13 May 2007

If you're ugly you've got to be funny

As I career towards old age, there are many things which frighten me. All the hair on my head will start to grow out of my nose. My ear lobes will swell up. My bladder will cease to function. I will become even more baffled by new technology.

And then there will be the inevitable onset of cancer.

But the greatest fear I face is not that I might lose my sense of sight, touch or smell. No, it's that people, once they reach the age of 50, seem to lose their sense of humour.

John Cleese is a prime example of this. One minute he's strutting about in a Torquay hotel and the audience is reduced to Smash robot hysterics. The next he's in a supermarket advert, barking at customers, and everyone is behind their sofas quietly dying of embarrassment.

Then you've got his old colleagues. Michael Palin is charming and warm, but as he trundles through India on yet another old train does he make you laugh? Eric Idle is responsible for *Spamalot* and that's about as funny as a bout of chlamydia.

Terry Jones is wrapped up in 14 layers of Chaucer and we haven't heard a squeak from Graham Chapman for years. Though this might have something to do with the fact that he's dead.

Woody Allen springs to mind as well. In *Sleeper* and

Play it Again, Sam, I honestly thought that I might need the services of a doctor to sew up my sides. But in his more recent films I've wanted to sew up his mouth. I've leant on funnier trees.

The funniest man I've ever seen on stage was Jasper Carrott. His act was so hysterical that halfway through I was taken out of the auditorium by a chap from the St John Ambulance because I had lost the ability to breathe. I honestly thought I was going to die. But is Jasper funny now? I doubt it.

And the reason for this, I've decided, is very simple: sex.

I remember vividly, back when I was at school, competing with a friend to chat up a girl. He was captain of the football team and was therefore equipped with a triangular torso, firm thighs and shoulders broad enough to double up as a runway for light aircraft. Me? Well, I looked like a telegraph pole on which a stork had made its nest.

The only way round this was to try and make the girl laugh. And so, even when she'd gone off with my footballing friend and was in the bushes, moaning at the glare from his sapphire-blue eyes, I was standing near by prattling on about Englishmen, Scotsmen, Irishmen, horses with long faces and planes with only one parachute. This is the last, and indeed only, resort of the hideously deformed.

I mean it. Do you look at Stephen Fry and think 'Phwoar'? No? So what about Ben Elton or Paul Whitehouse? Did you ever think Bernard Manning was Johnny Depp in a fat suit? Paul Merton is no prettier than the town from which he takes his name and Ian Hislop looks like he ought to spend his day in a wheel, squeaking.

I could go on, so I shall. Steve Coogan looks like a plumber. Jimmy Carr looks like a moon. Rowan Atkinson appears to have been made from polyurethane. And precisely because of this, they're all funny.

They've all lost a girl to the captain of the football team. They've all stood in front of a mirror, thinking: 'Well, there's nothing for it. I shall have to be a homosexual.' Or was that just me?

I think, and I hope I don't get clobbered for this, that the evidence is even more acute for women. Jo Brand. Dawn French. Victoria Wood. Notice anything they have in common? Yes, you're right! They're all much funnier than Scarlett Johansson, Keira Knightley and Uma Thurman.

At dinner parties I look around at the yummy mummies in their short skirts and their flirty tops. And I hope and pray that I will end up sitting next to the fat bird, because that way there's at least a chance that I'll have a laugh.

So, if it's true that good-looking people aren't funny and that fat, ugly people are, then it stands to reason that humour is essentially used as a tool for whittling out a bit of sex that might not otherwise be available. And that brings me neatly to the problems when we reach 50.

No one, not even Sean Connery or Joan Collins, can stand in front of a mirror, naked, when they're starting to sag and think 'mmmm, yeah'.

I stand there and think, 'How the bloody hell can a telegraph pole with a stork's nest on top get pregnant?'

By rights, then, older people should try to compensate

for their withered looks and wobbly skin by being funny. But what's the point? Chances are you're married; and anyway these days there are many, many things you would rather do at night than have sex. Sleeping. Reading. Being dangled from a tall building by what's left of your hair, even.

So, if you're not after a mate and you're not motivated by the need for rumpy-pumpy every minute of the day, then you may as well give up trying to be funny and start writing Abba musicals.

The only hope that we all have is Viagra. Because it keeps the old chap working, even when everything else has broken down completely, it means there is still a point to making people laugh.

This probably explains why Adrian Gill can still dole out the giggles at the age of 52.

Sunday 20 May 2007

Why Brits make the best tourists

Can you imagine the horror of being able to read other people's minds: to find out what they really think about you? Well, last week we were able to do just that, as 15,000 hoteliers from all over the world explained exactly what they thought of the British.

We harbour a cheery notion that Britain and its people are a shining beacon of hope and goodness to the dirtier and less well educated. We assume that when our glorious island nation is mentioned, people all over the world imagine us going to work in bowler hats and volunteering to be out in a game of cricket, way before the umpire has actually made up his mind. When they think of us, they think of Kenneth Kendall reading the news on the BBC. In a tie.

'Fraid not. It turns out that, mostly, they think we're arrogant, badly dressed, untidy, loud, drunk and nowhere near as much fun to have around as the Japanese.

It turns out that hotel staff in Corfu don't actually like it when we do the conga through reception at two in the morning and then rush into the gardens with one another to catch chlamydia. They think this sort of thing is anti-social.

Further digging reveals that while we spend quite a lot of money while we're on holiday, it's mostly on beer, burgers and Satan's favourite snack, Cheez Whiz.

This, according to another report, from the Lonely Planet guide, is because we are all obsessed with celebrity, we worship people who have no talent, we're all binge drinkers and that back at home there's a general air of disillusionment in the wake of the London Tube bombings.

Small wonder that the people who write this book are lonely. You won't get any friends if you mooch about all day in an Eeyore blanket of drizzle. Cheer up, for God's sake.

The fact is that Britain, right now, is a jolly place to live. Tony Blair is going. Everyone's house is worth a million pounds. And the summer, thanks to a few dedicated souls like me and that chap at Ryanair, is likely to be warm. That's why we do the conga at two in the morning: because we're happy. And that's why the hoteliers don't like us: because they're jealous.

They have to live in a country where the wine's made from creosote, the women don't shave their armpits and you need to bribe the plumber with something from Fabergé to get him to mend your dishwasher.

And they can't cope when they see us lot bouncing into the hotel with our sexually liberated girlfriends and our big strong pounds.

I know this to be true because anyone who's ever been abroad knows full well that on any international league table of bad behaviour, we are a long, long way from the bottom.

Have you ever shared a hotel swimming pool with a South African? What they like to do, and you've got to remember they're all fairly big-boned, is climb to the top of the diving board and jump on your head. And as you helplessly flop about with a broken spine, the rest of their equally big-boned family hoots with derision and orders another round of Castle.

Or what about the Swedes? You think we can drink. Ooh you ain't seen nothing till you've seen a party of Thors locusting their way through the swim-up bar. The only difference is that when we get drunk, we like to catch a venereal disease. When they get drunk, they like to commit suicide.

Apparently, the hoteliers like the Germans very much. They say they're very quiet.

Well, yes, they would be. They have to stay sober and be in bed by nine because, as we know, they do like to get up early . . .

Interestingly, the Americans come second in the poll, behind the Japanese. They're billed as polite, interested in new cultures and good at tipping. I agree, but sharing a restaurant with a party of nasal sceptics with their two-stroke vowel sounds is like sharing a restaurant with a Flymo. And they do have the most annoying habit of talking to their friends as though they are 600 yards apart.

At the other end of the scale we find the French. Apparently, they are the worst holidaymakers. The pits. Except for one thing. Stop carefully and think: have you ever seen a French person on a foreign holiday? Italy is full of Germans. Spain is full of Brits. Greece is full of dust and homosexuals. The Dutch are everywhere. The Swedes are all dead, and is that someone with a strimmer? Oh no, hang on. It's a party of Americans coming up the hill.

But the French? They don't seem to do foreign holidays and with good reason. Does God leave heaven every August and take a vacation in hell? No. Well, why would anyone go abroad if they live in France?

The fact of the matter is that the French are nowhere to be seen and that means – no arguing please – the Russians are the worst tourists in the world. Of course, they spent most of their childhood eating concrete and trying not to be tortured so who can blame them for exploding onto the world's beaches in a tizzy of frills, Versace sunglasses and extraordinarily tight Speedos.

The only problem is that they all look so sinister with their pastry complexions and their special-forces tattoos. You get the impression when they look at you that they're imagining what you would look like with no head.

A lout from Liverpool may vomit on you and that's nasty. But a Russian would happily garnish your pizza with a dash of polonium. And that's so much worse.

Sunday 27 May 2007

Save the planet, eat a vegan

Good news. It seems that your car and your fondness for sunken light bulbs in every alcove are not warming up the planet after all.

In fact, according to new research, power stations and transport produce lots of carbon dioxide, but in addition they also produce lots of aerosols that, in the short term at least, help keep the planet as cool as a deodorant model's armpits.

So who has come up with this new theory? Some half-crazed nitwit with a motoring show to protect? George Bush? A bloke in the pub? No. In fact, it comes from an organisation called EarthSave, which is run and funded, so far as I can tell, by the usual array of free-range communists and fair-trade hippies.

The facts it produces, however, are intriguing. Methane, which pours from a cow's bottom on an industrial scale every few minutes, is 21 times more powerful as a greenhouse gas than carbon dioxide. And as a result, farmed animals are doing more damage to the climate than all the world's transport and power stations put together.

What's more, demand for beef means more and more of the world's forests are being chopped down, and more and more pressure is being put on our water supplies.

Plainly, then, EarthSave is encouraging us to go into the countryside at the first possible opportunity and lay waste to anything with more than one stomach. Maybe it wants me to shoot my donkeys. Happily, what it's actually saying is that you can keep your car and your walk-in fridge, but you've got to stop eating meat.

In fact, you've got to stop eating all forms of animal products. No more milk. No more cheese. And if it can be proven that bees fart, then no more honey either. You've got to become a vegan.

Now, of course, if you don't like the taste of meat, then it's perfectly reasonable to become a vegetablist. It's why people who don't like, say, John Prescott become Conservatives. But becoming a vegan? Short of being paraded on the internet while wearing a fluffy pink tutu, I can think of nothing I'd like less.

Eating a plate of food that contains no animal product of any kind marks you down as a squirrel. Eating only vegetables is like deciding to talk using only consonants. You need vowels or you make no sense.

Of course, there are certain weeds I like very much. Cauliflower and leeks particularly. But these are an accompaniment to food, useful only for filling up the plate and absorbing the gravy. The idea of eating only a cauliflower, without even so much as a cheese sauce, fills me with dread.

There are wider implications too. Let us imagine that the world decided today to abandon its appetite for sausage rolls, joints of beef and meat-infused Mars bars.

What effect would this have on the countryside?

Where now you find fields full of grazing cows and truffling pigs, there would be what exactly?

Hardcore vegetablists like to imagine that the land

would be returned to the indigenous species, that you could go for a walk without a farmer shooting your dog, and that you'd see all manner of pretty flowers and lots of jolly new creatures. Wolves, for instance.

In fact, if animal farmers were driven away, the land would be divided up in two ways. Some would be given over to the growing of potatoes – the ugliest crop in Christendom – and the rest would be bought by rock stars. Either way, Janet Street-Porter and her ridiculous gaggle of ramblers in their noisy clothes and stupid hats would still get short shrift.

What's more, there'd be no grassland because there'd be no animals to graze. And there'd be no woods either because without pheasants what's the point? I'm sure EarthSave dreams of a land as pristine as nature intended but it'd be no such thing. Within about three weeks Britain would look like Saskatchewan.

So, plainly, the best thing we can do if we want to save the world, preserve the English countryside and keep on eating meat, is to work out a way that animals can be made to produce less methane.

Scientists in Germany are working on a pill that helps, but apparently this has a number of side effects. These are not itemised, but I can only assume that if you trap the gas inside the cow one of the drawbacks is that it might explode. Nasty.

And unnecessary. We all know that the activity of our bowels is governed by our diet. We know, for instance, that if we have an afternoon meeting with a bunch of top sommeliers in a small windowless room it's best not to lunch on brussel sprouts and baked beans.

Recently, I spent eight days in a car with my co-host from *Top Gear* James May, who has a notoriously flatulent bottom. But because he was living on army rations – mashed-up Greenpeace leaflets to which you add water – the interior was always pine fresh and lemon zesty.

So if we know – and we do – that diet can be used to regulate the amount of methane coming out of the body, then surely it is not beyond the wit of man to change the diet of farmyard animals.

At the moment, largely, cows eat grass and silage, and as we've seen, this is melting the ice caps and killing us all. So they need a new foodstuff: something that is rich in iron, calcium and natural goodness.

Plainly, they can't eat meat so here's an idea to chew on. Why don't we feed them vegetarians?

Sunday 3 June 2007

Stuff the tiger – long live extinction

As the population of China becomes more wealthy, demand for illegal tiger parts is booming. Up to 600 million Chinese people believe that tiger bones, claws and even penises will cure any number of ailments, including arthritis and impotency. And as a result we've just been told, for about the hundredth time, that if nothing is done extinction looms.

Well, not complete extinction. Obviously, tigers will continue to exist in Las Vegas for many years to come. And in Asia there are so many backstreet big-cat farms that they outnumber cows. But they will cease to exist in the wild.

Right. And what are we supposed to do, exactly? Send an international force tooled up with the latest night-vision gear and helicopter gunships to hunt down and kill the poachers?

Really? And what are these mercenaries supposed to say to the locals? 'Yes, I realise that you have no fresh water, no healthcare, little food and that your ox is broken, but we are not here to do anything about that. In fact, we're going to put an end to the only industry you have.'

Yes, say the conservationists, who argue that unless this is done now our children will grow up never being able to see a tiger in the wild. And that this is very sad.

Is it? I have never seen a duck-billed platypus in the

wild or a rattlesnake. I've never seen any number of creatures that I know to exist. So why should I care if my children never see a tiger?

In fact, come to think of it, if they're on a gap year trekking through the jungles of Burma I fervently hope they don't.

There's an awful lot of sentimentality around the concept of extinction. We have a sense that when a species dies out we should all fall to our knees and spend some time wailing. But why? Apart from for a few impotent middle-class Chinamen, or if you want a nice rug, it makes not the slightest bit of difference if Johnny tiger dies out. It won't upset our power supplies or heal the rift with Russia. It is as irrelevant as the death of a faraway star.

So far this century we've waved goodbye to the Pyrenean ibex – did you notice? – and the mouthful that is Miss Waldron's red colobus monkey. Undoubtedly, both extinctions were blamed on Shell, McDonald's, the trade in illegal diamonds, Deutsche Bank or some other spurious shareholder-led attempt to turn all of the world into money and carbon dioxide.

But if we look back to a time before oil, steam and German bankers, we find that species were managing to die off all on their own. The brontosaurus, for example. And who honestly thinks it's sad that their children will never get to see a tyrannosaurus rex in the wild?

In the nineteenth century 27 species went west, including the great auk, the thicktail chub, the quagga, the Cape lion and the Polish primitive horse. Apparently, the Poles tried their hardest but it was no good. It was just too primitive.

Eco-mentalists ignore the fact that between 1900 and 1919 we lost most of the young men in Europe and prattle on about the passing of the passenger pigeon, the Carolina parakeet, and the Tasmanian wolf.

Honestly, who cares, because there are quite literally millions more fish in the sea. Only last week we heard that scientists in the South American rainforest have found 24 previously unknown species including 12 dung beetles, a whole new ant, some fish and a rather fetching frog.

It may not be as cuddly as a baby tiger or as primitive as a Polish horse, but it is groovier since its purple fluorescent hoop markings appear to have been drawn by Steve Hillage himself.

So is the world rejoicing at the sensational news that we've been joined on earth by a hippie frog? Is it hell as like. What the world is doing instead is crying into its eco-handkerchief because of what's going on in the Arctic.

We're told that because of the Range Rover, HSBC and Prince Bandar all the ice at the North Pole is melting and that as a result the polar bear has nowhere to live. Apart, that is, for the 3 million square miles of northern Canada that are completely untouched by any form of human encroachment.

Anyway, ignoring that, we are told that the polar bear is now at risk and as a result we're all supposed to kill ourselves.

Why? Contrary to what you may have been led to believe by Steiff's cute and squishy cuddly toys, the polar bear is a big savage brute, the colour of nicotine, with a mean ugly pointy face and claws that, if they were to be found in Nottingham on a Saturday night, would be confiscated as offensive weapons.

If the polar bear dies out it will make not a jot of difference to you or anyone you've ever met. The only people who'll even notice are the Inuits, and its passing will actually improve their lives because they'll be able to go out fishing and clubbing without running the risk of being eaten to death.

I do not believe that we should deliberately kill stuff because we find it ugly or offensive. Unless it's a virus or a mosquito. But I do wish the world's conservationists would learn a lesson from some of the more enlightened species in the animal kingdom: that when push comes to shove, the only creatures that really matter are those in our social group. And our children.

Sunday 10 June 2007

I went to London and it had gone

Yesterday I saw something unusual. While sitting in a jam near London's Parliament Square I noticed a huge queue for one of those old-fashioned phone boxes. The complicated red jobbies that take some poor chap six years to paint.

Why, I thought, are people queueing to use a phone box? Everyone has a mobile these days. And why is the woman who's actually using it not using it at all? She's half in and half out, with one leg in the air and a silly grin on her face.

It turned out she was a tourist posing for a photograph in the only slice of olde England she could find. And what's more, all the people behind her were also tourists queueing to have their pictures taken with it as well. This made me rather sad.

How far have they travelled, I wondered? And how much have they spent on this once-in-a-lifetime trip to the former capital of the free world?

And this – this crummy old phone box – is the only evidence that they've landed in the right place.

The policemen have replaced their *Dixon of Dock Green* helmets and cheery demeanour with body armour and sub-machine guns, the home county turds in the river are now otters, no one is allowed to feed the pigeons in Trafalgar Square and the absolute last language you will hear spoken on any street is English.

There's more too. Today the beefeaters are women, the Cutty Sark has melted, Greenwich is a dome, the Queen has become Helen Mirren and the old double-decker buses are gone, purged by the maniac Livingstone, who sees everything from yesterday as an example of the global corporations' love affair with money, slaves and carbon dioxide.

You get the impression that if some City chap actually walked across Waterloo Bridge wearing a bowler hat and carrying a rolled umbrella he'd be mobbed by a grateful Sony-toting horde.

On my trip to London last week I did a river trip, saw the Eye, tootled about near Tower Bridge for a bit and went to Piccadilly Circus. And after a while I began to think I might be in a strange place, the result of an unusual sexual liaison between Geneva in 2027 and Moscow in 1974.

Hanging from every single lamp post in the West End – and that's a lot of lamp posts – there's a big sign saying 'DIY Planet Repairs'. I have no idea what this means, any more than the workers in the People's Tractor Factory No. 47 knew what the politburo's encouraging slogans meant.

I guess it's a sort of diktat from the commissariat, urging us to take exercise, work harder and gain strength through joy. Certainly, in every bus shelter there's a poster from the mayor that says, 'London was made for cycling'.

No it wasn't. London was made for people to come and do business. There was a gap of several hundred years between the invention of Londinium and the day when some idiot invented the pedal and handlebar.

To take refuge from the constant political bombardment, I sought shelter in a well-known restaurant where a pot of tea for four and some cake cost me £78. That is not a misprint.

Then there's the river. Oooh, the banks these days are a funfair of funk and groove with lots of smoked glass and teak decking. But you can see all the Korean ladies on the cruise ships not knowing what the bloody hell to take a picture of.

There's absolutely nothing that says to the folks back home 'I've been to London'.

Rather, it looks like they've been to a retirement home for people whose silly architect specs were so thin and so fashionable they couldn't actually see what they were designing.

Of course, despite the idiotic prices and Ken's best efforts to ruin everything, London is a better place to live now than it was 20 years ago. But in the drive to make it 'modern' and 'edgy', the period features, the things that make people want to come here, have been thrown out. No, really. How many people sit down with the travel brochures every year and think, 'This year, for our summer holidays, let's go somewhere really multicultural and green'?

None. What people want when they come to London is pomp and circumstance. And this brings me on to the Union Jack. I know it's offensive to certain portions of the Muslim community and I know it got a bit hijacked by the British National party.

But do you think it might be possible to fly it somewhere? You won't even find it on Tower Bridge.

Helen Mirren does a good job. All the way from Admiralty Arch to Buckingham Palace, the DIY Planet Repairs nonsense has been replaced with a lot of big flags.

And as a result the Mall is a seething mass of relieved tourists happily filling up their memory chips with something other than the lone red phone box.

But the truth of the matter is this: London is now further away from its image than any other city in the world. The postcards still paint a picture of the day when Rules ruled, but the reality is a city where tourists are greeted at reception by a Latvian and shown to their room by someone from Poland. They eat arugula from titanium plates and are reminded every time they go outside that the mayor thinks he's Stalin. They want steak and kidney, and we give them Tate Modern with a hint of the Baltic.

Coming to London now is a bit like tuning in to an episode of *The Ascent of Man* to find it's being hosted by Pamela Anderson. In a lime-green thong.

It's not wrong. It's just not what anyone was expecting.

Sunday 17 June 2007

Playing the fool at Glastonbury

On Friday morning my wife got dressed up like Worzel Gummidge, put some bog roll in a bag and roared off in her Aston Martin to watch a bunch of useless teenagers singing in the rain at Glastonbury.

I think she may have gone mad.

And she's not alone. Helicopter companies all over the south-west have reported a booming demand for charters. Everyone in the de luxe tenting business is now on a beach in Barbados and all last week Brixton was doubtless awash with hedge-fund managers and BBC programme controllers trying to buy drugs.

And getting the wrong sort. 'Yeah, man. You gotta try some of this horse tranquilliser. It'll even you out.' Honestly, I bet that this morning Glastonbury is full to overflowing with your accountant calling all the policemen pigs and trying to reverse onto a selection of other men, having ingested six gallons of crystal meth.

I understand the mentality, of course. You're middle-aged. You have children. Your life is so boring you actually look forward to the arrival of the milkman. And you fancy, for just one weekend, the idea of transporting yourself from the humdrum and into the fetid sleeping bag of your youth.

I have no problem with that. I'm not going to spend the next foot of newsprint berating you for not acting your age and laughing at you as you try to remember how to roll a joint. But I do have a problem with Glastonbury.

Rock music is ours. By which I mean it belongs to anyone born between 1950 and 1971. We invented it, and we made the rules. You sit in a darkened room, in headphones, listening to *Dark Side of the Moon*, trying to work out whether it's about hope, death or despair.

And not just a lot of nonsense from five blokes who were out of their heads.

For us, concerts were all about spectacle and volume. Jimmy Page strapped a laser to his violin bow and split the sky with a noise so huge that today it would not be allowed through the amps without a hi-vis jacket and half a dozen warning notices.

The Who rocked up at Wembley one year with a laser and hologram show of such immensity that officials were genuinely scared that it might bring down airliners on their final approach into Heathrow. You watched that while Daltrey belted his way through a rendition of 'Listening to you, I get the music' and it made the hairs on your lungs swell up.

These are the sensations my wife is hoping to relive this weekend. She wants to be drunk, wet, deafened and assaulted by a blizzard of showmanship and spectacle. For one glorious weekend she wants to pretend she's eight.

But what she'll get is a bunch of reedy-voiced, stick-thin teenagers who've nicked what is rightfully ours and mangled it out of all recognition. A bunch of useless, talentless ne'er-do-wells who'd love to play you their next song but only after they've delivered a sermon on the evils of corporate America, global warming and how we should all club together to help some poor African kid with flies in his eyes. Oh for God's sake. Either turn on the lasers or eff off.

Of course, there was a lot of peace and love and get the troops out of Vietnam at Woodstock, but that didn't matter because the people on the stage were in tune with the people in the audience. At Glastonbury this weekend it's all out of kilter.

It's billed as a hippie festival and is, of course, sponsored by the newspaper of choice for those who like tie-dye – the *Guardian*. So, naturally, visitors are urged to leave their tents behind so they can be shipped to the Third World. They are asked to try horse dung as an alternative to Disprin. And some will be encouraged to hunt down ley lines using a forked stick. 'They're how pigeons navigate, you know, man.'

But of the 177,000 people due to attend – at £145 a pop – only six will be druids called Merlin. The rest will have Volvos and Bell JetRangers. And we don't need ley lines to navigate because we're clever and rich and we have sat nav.

Does anyone really imagine for a moment that my wife gives two stuffs about global warming? She certainly didn't appear to be all that bothered on Thursday evening when, during the great carbon-saving switch-off, I ran round the house furiously turning on every light, hairdryer, dishwasher and toaster.

She can't like the music very much either. Certainly, I'd rather spend the day listening to the score from *Confessions of a Window Cleaner*. And then Shirley Bassey will come on.

Sweet divine Jesus. What's that all about? I would walk naked over a field of molten steel to avoid the shouty Welshster, but there she is, providing a respite for a bunch of delusional parents on a ley line in bloody Somerset. And I bet you a million pounds she gets the same rapturous reception afforded to Rolf Harris when he cropped up at Glastonbury a couple of years ago with his cardboard Aboriginal version of 'Stairway to Heaven'. It's all just too ridiculous.

I'm not proposing for a moment we ban festivals. There are some good ones, where old bands, who know what they're doing, play old favourites to old people on rugs.

But I do think the time has come for new bands to be banned from playing or performing rock music. It's ours. They should go and invent their own plaything.

Sunday 24 June 2007

Kick the fans out of Wimbledon

As the All England Lawn Tennis Championship edges towards its thrilling conclusion in front of half-empty grandstands, there will be the inevitable calls for corporate fat cats to go away so the real fans can come along in their anoraks and their *Daily Telegraph* small-ad sandals.

It started on the first day with a million Henmaniacs clogging up the internet's message boards, all saying it was disgusting that instead of watching His Timness, most of the audience was to be found slumped on a bar, yelling about City takeovers and drunkenly attempting to swab mysterious stains from the front of their chinos with their old school ties.

Blah blah class war blah toffs blah blah all right for some.

Hmmm. It's certainly true that businessmen and their guests do tend to get stuck into the fine wines at lunchtime and some decide they'd rather spend the afternoon ogling the waitresses than utilise their precious Centre Court tickets.

And it's also true that even those who do wobble back to the match often have no clue what's going on, calling the racket a bat and generally leaving their mobile phones switched on. Some, and you know who you are, even spend the whole match speculating on what the crusty old ladies are doing to themselves under their tartan rugs in the royal box.

Last year I sat next to Johnny Vaughan who, probably excited by having such a large audience for once, decided he would regale pretty much everyone with a series of increasingly funny stories. I'm afraid I was party to the gales of laughter that provoked much shushing from the real fans and, inevitably, the intervention of a man in a blazer. Whom I called Stewart, before I realised his badge actually said steward.

Frankly, I can't see what's wrong with any of this. Quite apart from the fact that corporate guests spend pots of money on tents and exotic cheese, which allows the club to send its roof away for a polish, I'd rather watch an empty seat than some of the extraordinary specimens you see cheering and applauding when the real fans are allowed in.

I think the rot began with the creation of Henman Hill. It swarms each year with the sort of people who clap along in time to the music at the Horse of the Year Show and have all of Cliff's records. Naturally, they all adored Princess Diana, principally because she stuck one to those swan-eating toffs in Buckingham Palace.

You'd imagine, as you watch this sea of flab cheering and hollering in their nasty clothes, that they're having a brilliant time. But all they're doing, in fact, is determinedly showing the fat-cat wallahs that they – the people – are having more fun. Which they're not.

I don't care how much you yell and wave your arms about, you will never convince me that sitting on a patch of mud eating a wizened Israeli strawberry is anything like as much fun as getting sloshed with Johnny Vaughan over a plate of poached salmon and some Jersey Royal new potatoes.

It just isn't.

You may well say, 'It's all right for some', and I'd agree. It is certainly all right for George Clooney, who was born with an attractive face. Or whatsername who's going out with Shrek-ears Rooney. Some people are lucky. So sit down, shut up and get used to it.

Small wonder Terry Wogan, normally the most genial man in the world, announced on his radio show last year that he'd like to go down to Henman Hill and 'machine-gun the lot of them'.

Let them inside the courts themselves and, oh dear, things really start to go wrong. Replete with their sunburn marks and their Millets wet-weather gear, they applaud absolutely everything. Double faults from anyone who is taking on their beloved Tim Henman. The arrival of Sir Cliff Richard. Even a decision by the referee to keep on playing even though it's technically the middle of the night.

But the thing they applaud most of all is when the umpire asks one of the corporate fat cats to switch off his mobile phone. They love that. Some toff full of swan being publicly humiliated. It gives them such a warm glow that the wiring in their Playtex bras actually starts to melt.

Unfortunately, what you have to remember is that Wimbledon attracts enormous television audiences from all over the world and I often wonder what these sophisticated people from abroad are going to think of Britain when they see some hysterical fat woman with raspberry-ripple arms and American Tan tights, fanatically applauding a pigeon that has just landed on Court One.

They're going to think we're all ugly and mad.

They'd know for sure if they could get into her head and find out that her idea of heaven, what she dreams about in the wee small hours, is a threesome with Tim and Cliff.

I would therefore urge Wimbledon to take a lead on the matter and start to get the real fans out of sport.

The place would look better, and remember: the fat cat's host at Wimbledon has paid £23,000 for a five-year debenture. What's more, corporate hospitality shovelled £1.4 million into the Natural History Museum's coffers last year and keeps events like Ascot and Henley afloat.

Eventually, this idea could be rolled out into football as well. I went to the Cup Final this year – my first ever game – and I loved it. I might even be tempted to go back, so long as I can sit in a box, with a nice claret, and not squashed up against a fat man with a spider's web tattooed on his face.

Sunday 1 July 2007

Hands off 007 or I'll shoot you

I am not a jealous man. I do not sit around all day coveting my neighbour's helicopter or your new hair system. Some people are fortunate and others are not, and anyone who fights that truism is on a path that leads to madness and communism.

That said, however, I fell to my knees and wept with envy and rage last week when I opened my morning newspaper to discover that Ian Fleming's estate had asked Sebastian bloody Faulks to write the next James Bond book.

'Nooooo,' I wailed, in the manner of someone whose daughter has just fallen from a cliff, as I learnt that the manuscript has already been blessed by Bond movie producer Barbara Broccoli.

Getting Faulks to write a Bond book is like asking Polly Toynbee to write the next Die Hard film. It's like casting Vinnie Jones as Mr Darcy. In the whole history of getting things wrong, this is right at the top of the list.

I met Sebastian once and he seemed like a nice chap. I have also read many of his books and they are marvellous. The scene at the end of *On Green Dolphin Street* where the woman howls was so powerful I thought I might have a feminine side after all.

Not a big side, you understand. Not big enough to make me even think of placing scented mini-cushions in my underwear drawer, but certainly big enough to have me reaching for the box of tissues.

And let's be honest. Any author who can get 16 stone of beefheart blokeishness all teary-eyed and snivelling over some silly woman's doomed and entirely fictional love affair is plainly very good at his job. But we're talking about Bond here.

And I'm sorry, but when it comes to shooting people in the face with a harpoon, that job, by rights, is mine.

I suppose I should admit at this point that I've never read any of Fleming's originals. But I don't see why this should hold me back. If his estate and Broccoli were to tell me that Bond was a dark and brooding loner who managed to be both gallant and a seducer all at the same time, I think I could manage.

I'd simply begin by saying: 'Bond woke up in bed with a girl who he liked very much. Darkly and broodily he hauled himself from under the sheets, kissed her on the ear and said, "My darling. You are marvellous. But I am a loner and I must go now because I have to blow up an oil rig".'

Then I could get into the meat of what matters in the big wide world of Bond: gadgets, explosions, wisecracks and improbably large men who've had their hands replaced with spiky lumps of ebony.

Oh and the car chases. I bet I'd be a bloody sight better at those than Sebastian nancy boy Faulks with his *Birdsong* and his bloody *Dolphin Street*. Bastard.

Apparently, his new book, which is probably called *Bond Joins the RSPB*, is set in 1967 when 007 is damaged (yawn), ageing and is called in as a gunfighter for one last heroic mission.

Wrong wrong wrong. Bond cannot be damaged. Even if he were to fall out of a hot-air balloon and into the spinning blades of a Hughes 500 – and I bet Faulks thinks that's some kind of lawnmower – he should emerge with nothing more than a slightly disarranged tie knot.

And he cannot age. He simply morphs from a Scottish milkman with a tattoo on his arm into a safari suit and keeps right on going.

Normally, when you compare a book with a film, the book is always better. But with Bond, a collection of old stories about a dark and brooding loner, written a million years ago by a man who spent most of his day snorkelling, cannot possibly hope to compete with a film franchise that has spanned the world for 40 years. Bond is now a product of the multiplex, not the library.

And if we have to have Bond books at all, they should reflect that. Instead of worrying how 007 might have been seen by a long-dead author, the powers that be should think more how he has been seen by 2 billion cinema-goers.

I have no doubt at all that Faulks will give 007 layers of character so intense and so well rooted that it'll be page 148 before he shoots anyone.

And then I bet he spends the following 148 pages agonising over what he's done. Who cares? Who goes to a Bond film to see a man in a bar agonising? And who goes to see Charles Gray's bath-o-sub being dropped into a shark-infested lagoon?

That's why you need me to be the next Bond author. Because I get this.

I'd have Bond shoot someone on page two and then,

instead of analysing how this felt, I'd explain in quite a lot of detail about how the baddie's head erupted in a thin grey and red mist as Bond leapt onto his jet pack and hurtled through a wall of noise into the night.

In fact, I'm so angry that I wasn't asked by Mrs Cauliflower or whoever to write the next book I might write a spy thriller anyway. It'll be about an agent who's more shallow than a summer puddle. After shagging a netball team for fun, he'll walk into a bar where Bond is agonising over something. And shoot him in the back of the head with a short-nosed Heckler & Koch machine pistol.

Get out of that one, Faulks. I'm going to shoot your superhero in the head. Then you'll have to go back to your birdsong and your howling women and I'll get what was rightfully mine in the first place.

Sunday 15 July 2007

Get back in your stockings, girls

We know from Big Brother that today's young ladies have replaced their appealing thongs with pants the size of spinnakers, and now comes news that the sales of stockings are in free fall. Down from £10 million sales in 2002 to £5 million in 2006.

According to the *Sun*'s woman editor – as opposed to the real editor, who's a woman – this is because girls have better things to do these days than get dressed up like a Parisian hooker every time they go to the shops.

I absolutely understand that. Getting dressed in the morning is something that should never take more than 20 seconds and putting on a pair of stockings and suspenders can take anything up to three hours.

Actually, this is only a guess, based on how long it takes me to undo a suspender belt. Even when I'm armed with a head torch and a pair of scissors.

Anyway, I fully appreciate that in a post-Mrs Robinson world, where women work and raise children, stockings are to the wardrobe what the quill is to online banking.

But here's the thing, girls. Tell us that you won't wear stockings because they are impractical and you may well find that we'll give up as well.

At the moment we tend not to pick our noses when in your company because it is a bit slovenly. But if you're going to slob around in a pair of footless tights and a sack, then you won't mind if we bury an index finger in each of our nostrils and dig away.

I was at London's City airport this morning surrounded by a group of middle-aged chaps who, I presume, were going to Scotland to watch some golfists.

At home, each of these men would, I'm sure, eat all their yoghurt and pretend to be interested in Victoria Beckham's opinion on interior design.

But at the airport, with no wives and girlfriends to keep them in check, they quickly reverted to type.

By 7.45 a.m. they were on their third pint and as I boarded my plane, I believe they were beginning a farting competition.

This is not a criticism. I recently spent a couple of weeks camping in Africa with 20 or so other men and you wouldn't believe how neanderthal we became. Or how quickly.

Every morning would begin with a conversation about who'd been for their number twos, what the number twos had looked like, what they'd smelt of, how much more there was to come, and whether any records for sheer tonnage had been set.

Then we'd move on to who'd crept into whose tent the night before, what it had felt like, and how long, if we were the last 20 people on earth, it might take for one of us to sleep with James May.

You might argue that your husband is not like this, but I assure you that beneath the veneer you see at home, he is.

He may do the washing-up and take the children to the park, but when you're not around, he's like the light in a fridge. He's a completely different animal, obsessed with bottoms, buggery and belching.

So, girls, do you want that sort of thing at home? Really? No? Well, get down to the petrol station, then, and buy some bloody stockings.

You may say that tights are practical and warm but have you seen what they do to a bank robber's face?

And hold-ups won't do either. Thanks to all that elasticated rubber, they ruin the shape of your thighs and, in all probability, cut off the blood supply to your feet, causing gangrene. And no man fancies a girl, no matter how sparkling her eyes and wit might be, if she is gangrenous.

Pop socks, meanwhile, would be completely banned if I were in power. And anyone found wearing them would be made to parade in nothing else through their local town, and then shot.

It must be stockings, with a suspender belt, because what this combination does is mask everything that doesn't matter and lay bare everything that does. A picture is nice, but before you hang it on the wall it needs a frame.

And apart from anything else, if you flash your stocking tops at a man you can, and I mean this literally, get him to do anything you want. Unless you have the figure of a bison, obviously, in which case he won't do anything at all. Because he will be too busy being sick.

Assuming, however, you have legs which clearly belong on a human, you only need let a man know you're wearing stockings and you will be empowered to a point you may have thought impossible.

I honestly believe that if David Milibandilegs really wanted to solve this Russian crisis, he could simply ask Rene Russo to re-enact that scene from the remake of *The Thomas Crown Affair* and Putin would have the Litvinenko murder suspect on the next flight to London.

And please, let's not have any of this 'ooh, stockings make us sex objects' nonsense because that simply isn't true.

We all saw Sharon Stone cross her legs in *Basic Instinct* and we all tittered in a schoolboy way. But when Rene popped a stockinged leg from that split skirt, I damn nearly fainted with admiration at the size of her brain.

Plainly, she'd worked out that what she really needed to gain control over the entire New York police department was not a degree from Harvard. But a pair of £4.99 stockings from Pretty Polly. That makes her smart. As well.

Sunday 22 July 2007

Save rural Britain – sell it to the rich

For the past 19 years the European Union has argued that it's expensive and wasteful to run a grain mountain. So, to get round the problem, it's been paying farmers large lumps of our money to grow nothing at all.

It's called the set-aside policy and I've always hated its communist overtones.

So I should have been delighted yesterday when I heard that this autumn it's expected to be abolished. But I'm not. I'm filled with an awful sadness, a sense that something truly terrible is about to happen.

The problem is that unlike the rest of the world, where all the most beautiful views were created by nature, here in England almost all the countryside was made by man.

If you gaze up Swaledale it's the labyrinth of drystone walls that mark it out as special. If you scan the Vale of Burford it's the patchwork of fields that make it all so splendid. And, of course, the last time *Country Life* had a competition to find the best view in England it was won by a scene that had Salisbury Cathedral parked slap bang in the middle.

Great. But now 1.2 million acres of Britain, which for the past 19 years have been sitting around doing nothing, have suddenly got to become economically viable again.

This is a huge chunk of land. The National Trust only owns about 620,000 acres.

Mrs Queen's farming land only runs to 110,000 acres. Add them together and you are still short of what's currently set aside for yellowhammers and lapwings. And what must soon start to generate cash.

You can forget the notion of it all being covered in barley or lavender. There just isn't the demand. And you can forget grassland for cows and sheep because these days there are too many stupid vegetarians to make that work.

So now put yourselves in the stout working boots of Johnny Farmer. You've got 70 acres down by the bottom pond and you've got to think of something that'll make it pay.

Some will be lucky. They will be given the equivalent of a lottery cheque in the shape of planning permission to build 400 new executive homes for people in IT and call centres. But some won't. And what if you're in this camp? How long's it going to take before you realise the answer is to be found in the country's current obsession with global bloody warming?

ScottishPower announced recently that some of its power stations will soon be running on willow and cereal. The crops will take up a staggering 12 per cent of Scotland's agricultural land – but will replace only 5 per cent of the coal currently used. Pretty soon, then, the Lowlands will start to look like Winnipeg.

Meanwhile, in Wales every single south or westerly facing escarpment is being smothered in wind farms.

Giant tubular bird mincers that whir and moan 24 hours a day and eventually, after a year or so, produce just enough energy to light up Mrs Llewellyn's bedside lamp.

Then there's England, which will be smothered with

so many polytunnels it'll start to look like the freezer cabinet of an American supermarket. Oh, and the bits that aren't under polythene will be smothered in a yellow sea of asthma, bronchitis and eczema as our friend in the stout boots realises that the only crops anyone wants these days are the ones that you can put into the petrol tank of your infernal Toyota Prius.

In other words, to save the sky we will completely wreck the land.

There's no point turning to Gordon Brown for help because he represents some godforsaken pebble-dashed constituency in Scotland, lives in Westminster and believes that everything in between is full of Tory bastards who need burying in executive homes, polythene and asthma. And that all their horses should be fed through an eco-windmill.

Nor can we rely on the Campaign to Protect Rural England. It's terribly noble, especially now it has Bill Bryson as its president, but the simple fact is that it took it 20 years to get the government to save the nation's hedgerows. On that basis, saving 1.2 million acres would take it about 4,000 years.

So, as usual, it falls to me to come up with a plan. And I have.

You may have read recently that Sir Tom Hunter, who is a businessman, decided to give £1 billion to charity because he feels the gap between rich and poor is now too wide. This is all very worthy and they will probably give him another knighthood.

However, Sir Sir Tom is wrong. What he should do is spend £1 billion buying up as much of the countryside as possible. And then he should encourage the rich to become richer so they can do the same.

I even suggest that we tax the poor, who cannot buy land, and give the money to the wealthy so they can buy even more.

No, really. If the land is taken out of the hands of the farmers, who earn on average £10,000 a year, and bought by private individuals, the need to make money will be shoved aside by the need for better aesthetics.

And not only would the countryside look better, there would be no overproduction of crops, no intensive farming, no need for set-aside payments, no more polythene or windmills. There would be a much greater diversity of animals and birds because they won't all be choked to death by the oilseed rape, and the few remaining miners could continue to produce coal for the power stations.

And the quality of cheese in our supermarkets would improve.

Everyone wins – except for Janet Street-Porter, and she doesn't count.

Sunday 29 July 2007

Dunked by dippy floating voters

I'm confused. When I left for a short working trip to Spain 10 days ago Gordon Brown was languishing in the polls and everyone knew that, at the next general election, Tory golden boy and all round floppy-haired good guy David Cameron would win.

This made perfect sense because Gordon's jaw doesn't work properly, he has no discernible sense of humour and the charisma of a boulder. And what's more, in the past 10 years, he has been number two in a government that has almost completely ruined Britain.

Today you can't land unless the tray table is up, you can't smack your children, you can't smoke in a pub, you can't take shampoo on a plane, you can't climb a ladder if you're a policeman, you can't eat more than six grams of salt a day, you can't urge your dogs to kill a rat, you can't sell food unless you explain on the packet precisely what's in it and where it came from, you can't reverse without a banksman, you can't go to work unless you have a yellow high-visibility jacket, you can't have an operation if you smoke, you can't tell Irish jokes to your friends, you can't say 'ginger beer' on television, you can't talk on your mobile phone in a traffic jam, you can't sit on a coach unless you're wearing a seatbelt and you can't drive a boat if you've had a beer.

Of course, you can't blow up an airport terminal

building either, and that makes sense. But then you cannot blow up someone's armbands at a municipal swimming pool. And that doesn't.

David Cameron, meanwhile, has never done anything to annoy you. In fact, so far as I can tell, he has never done anything at all.

So why, then, when I got back from Spain, had he somehow become public enemy number one?

What the hell had happened?

It must have been something dramatic because the opinion polls were suggesting a massive swing in Gordon's favour. When I left, the only people who said they'd vote for him were his wife and two former steelworkers in Sheffield. But when I got back he had nearly 40 per cent of the vote in the bag and the bounce showed no sign of abating.

Had Gordon suddenly decided to abolish taxes and give away a free George Clooney to any woman who buys two books of stamps? Or had David Cameron announced that he wants to eat anyone who doesn't earn at least £150,000 a year?

I checked back through a stack of newspapers and could find no evidence of either thing. A shark had appeared off Cornwall, someone with pretty knickers had left the *Big Brother* house, it had stopped raining – and that was about it.

I therefore checked to see what the leaders had been up to and, again, it's nothing much. Gordon had been to America where, it seems, people were very impressed by his suit. And David had been to Afghanistan where he'd been photographed smiling at some children. Nothing there that could cause the nation to change its voting intentions.

But then I did some more digging and an awful truth began to dawn. Gordon Brown had enjoyed a huge leap in the polls because during the recent flooding he put on his nice suit and a serious face and went to Gloucestershire to thank the emergency services for actually doing what he pays them to do, instead of selling spurious stories to the *Daily Mail*.

Meanwhile, David Cameron had been transformed from golden boy to a splodge on the Tory party's windscreen because instead of standing in a puddle up to his welly tops in Charlbury he'd been in Rwanda lecturing the government there on global warming.

What possible difference could it have made if he'd stayed at home? No, really. If your sofa has just floated out of an upstairs window why does anyone think your life would be improved by a politician posing for pictures in the lake that used to be your front lawn?

And how in the name of all that's holy can this possibly be a basis for choosing a system of government? Are you really saying that we must endure another five years of Labour's bossiness and bullying simply because its leader went to see some fat old crow in Tewkesbury whose ghastly button-backed DFS furniture had got a bit soggy?

I knew politics had become shallow but I didn't realise you could now succeed in it without it even coming up to your knees.

What staggers me most of all, though, is that almost all the people I know have either voted Conservative all their lives or Labour all their lives. And I've always been led to believe that swings in general elections come down to a tiny number of people on a tiny number of streets in a tiny number of marginal constituencies.

But, plainly, this isn't so. There must be millions and millions of people out there who will change their mind about which party to vote for on an hour-by-hour basis, using only the smallest amount of information on which to base their volte-face.

It's not *Big Brother*, for crying out loud. It matters. And you can't change your mind just because one of the candidates has picked out a nice suit.

Or because he was in Africa talking about global warming when you think he should have been in Oxfordshire talking about global soaking.

Choosing who to vote for on this basis could be an unmitigated disaster. Because if Ming Campbell put on a particularly appealing tie one day we may well end up being governed by the Monster Raving Lunatics. Or, as you know them, the Liberal Democrats.

Sunday 5 August 2007

The hell of being a British expat

Alarming news. It seems that all the world's clever people have gone missing. We know where the stupid people are. They're in the White House, or they're on *Big Brother*, or they're singing for Simon Cowell's supper. But while we are absorbed with this lot, the rocket scientists and astrophysicists have disappeared.

Seriously. America claims that the huge influx of Mexicans is in no way compensation for George Clooney, who has moved to Italy, and Madonna, who now lives in Wiltshire. And that it has a net brain drain.

It's the same story in Egypt, Iran, India, Russia, New Zealand and France. Germany claims to be in the middle of the biggest brain drain since the 1940s. Everywhere you look, governments are saying that while they're up to here with housekeepers and swimming-pool attendants, their graduates are all moving out.

So where are they going? Could it be, I wondered, that all the Tefalheads have come to Britain? Certainly, we seem to have so many scientists that there aren't enough serious projects to go round. On Thursday, for instance, two Manchester doctors announced that they'd been studying dinosaurs and found that the T-rex had a slower top speed than Frank Lampard. Wow.

Further evidence came to light on Thursday with the GCSE results. Every 16-year-old in the land, except those who have recently been shot, had scored at least 415 per cent in advanced Latin and applied maths.

Yes! I thought. Britain is pinching all the Russian billionaires, the American singers, the French chefs, the Egyptian doctors and the German businessmen. We may not be the happiest nation on Earth or the richest. But we are the brainiest.

And then came the latest migration figures, which showed that while Britain received 5.4 billion west African pickpockets last year, we lost what the *Daily Mail* calls 196,000 British citizens. White, middle-class families who have moved abroad.

These figures would lead us to suggest that, like everywhere else, Britain is suffering from a brain drain. That all our well-educated, well-spoken young professionals are being replaced by Borat.

Unfortunately, this argument fails to hold any water when you look at where these middle-class people are moving to. Australia is the number one choice, apparently, with 1.3 million British emigrants living there.

Fine, but in the whole of human history, nobody has ever woken up and thought, 'I know. I have a wonderful family, lots of money, a great job and an active social life. I shall therefore move to Australia.'

Australia is where you go when you've made a mess of everything. That's why the 1.3 million Brits who live there are known as whingeing Poms. Because they're all failures.

Another popular destination is Spain, which is home these days to 761,000 Brits.

Are they all brain surgeons? Inventors? Did Sir Christopher Cockerell invent the hovercraft and then move to Puerto Banus? No. Spain is where you go when you've sold your taxi.

What about America, then? We imagine that the Brits living there are successful and bright, like David Beckham and, er, Kelly Brook. But mostly, I suspect, the people who move from Britain to the States do so because they are interested in guns and murdering.

Twice I've bumped into expats while in America and both times they were wandering around in woods carrying preposterously large guns and wearing combat fatigues.

One was chewing tobacco which, when combined with his broad Birmingham accent, made him appear to be the stupidest person in the world. He probably was.

The fact is, I'm afraid, that anyone who emigrates from Britain, no matter where they end up, is a bit of a dimwit.

I mean, why leave? Because you have no friends? Well, what makes you think it'll be easier to make friends somewhere else? Because of the weather? Oh come on.

Sunny days work when you're on holiday but when you're stuck in an office, you need it to be 57°F and drizzling.

Maybe you're fed up with the crime in Britain. What, and you think California has fewer murders than Bourton-on-the-Water? You think there are no syringes on Bondi Beach?

Public services? Puh–lease. Even if you can convey to the chap on the other end of the phone that you are up to your knees in raw sewage, he will still take two weeks to dispatch some walnut-faced thief who'll make everything worse and charge you £800.

Maybe you fancy a tax haven? Great, you save a few quid but you end up with a bunch of other ingrates in a cesspit like Monaco. Seriously, would you rob a bank knowing you could keep the money but that you'd have to do some time? No. Well, don't be a tax exile, then, because it's the same thing.

Honestly, every single expat I've ever met is the same: hunched at a bar in a stupid shirt, at 10 in the morning, desperately trying to convince themselves that they are not alcoholics, that the barman really is their friend and that it's only 11 hours till bedtime.

And then, when they clock your accent, they launch into a slurred tirade about Gordon Brown and the British weather and how their prawns are the size of Volkswagens. And then they ask if by any chance you've got a copy of *The Week*.

Anyone who fails to realise that this is how they'll end up is monumentally idiotic and we're better off without them. So go, and we'll see you back here when you need some brain surgery.

Sunday 26 August 2007

Binge drinking is good for you

Who are they? The people who decide how we should run our lives. The busybodies who say that we can't smoke foxes or smack our children. The nitwits who say that we should have a new bank holiday to celebrate traffic wardens and social workers.

Where do they meet? Who pays their wages? And how do they get their hare-brained schemes onto the statute books?

Honestly? I haven't a clue. But I do know this. It's very obvious that their new target is people who drink alcohol – i.e., everyone over the age of eight.

Over the years we've been told that we can't drive a car if we've had a wine and that we should avoid alcohol if we're pregnant. But now they seem to be saying that all people must steer clear of all drinks always.

Having told young people that they must stop drinking while on a night out, in case they are stabbed or end up having sex with a pretty girl, they now say that older people, who think it's acceptable to enjoy a bottle of wine with their supper, are clogging up hospital wards that could otherwise be used to treat injured foxes.

We are told that alcohol rots your liver, makes you impotent, gives you stomach ulcers and turns your skin into something that looks like a used condom's handbag.

Only last week we were shown photographs of a

stick-thin man with a massive stomach who had died at the age of 36 because he'd had too many sherry trifles.

The BBC says that if you drink too much your brain stem will break and you will die. The British government tells us that if a man drinks more than two small glasses of white wine a day he will catch chlamydia from the bar-maid in the pub garden after closing time. Rubbish. If a man drinks two small glasses of white wine every day it's the barman he needs to worry about.

Me? Well, what I love most of all is binge drinking. Really getting stuck in.

Hosing back the cocktails until the room begins to swim and my legs seem to be on backwards.

It's not just the recklessness and freedom that result when massive quantities of alcohol unlock the shackles. It's the promise that in the morning you can share your pain with a bunch of other similarly afflicted friends.

Normal pain, such as an eye disease or toothache, is a lonely and solitary pursuit, but a group hangover is a problem shared and that seems to bring out the best in us. Like the Blitz. Like when you've just stepped off a terrify-ing roller-coaster ride. Everyone's in it together. And a problem shared is a problem pared.

Of course, the trouble these days is that the binge drinking that is necessary to produce collective hardship is a complete no-no.

They say that if you go out and get blasted you'll die in a puddle of blood and vomit down a back alley long before you get the chance to catch chlamydia from the barman, and that no one will come to your funeral.

Happily, this is rubbish. I've just done a calculation and

on holiday this year I drank 55 units of alcohol a day. I would start at 11 o'clock with a beer which, because it was hot, was like trying to irrigate East Anglia with a syringe. So I would have three more.

Then I would guzzle wine and mojitos throughout the afternoon, the evening and the night until I fell over somewhere and slept. Am I now dead? No. In fact, because I drank so much I was more relaxed, which means that I'm back at home now feeling fresher and more rested.

So there you have it. Serious binge drinking is not only a nice thing to do and jolly good fun, but also — and here's something that you won't get from the mongers of doom — it's good for you too.

The point of binge drinking is that you drink and then you stop drinking. And this is the key. The real problem is when you drink — and you keep on drinking. This is known as alcoholism and that, so far as I can tell, is the worst thing in the world.

There is nothing quite so pitiable and wretched as an alcoholic. I know plenty of people who take drugs, drive too fast and kill foxes. And they're all good company. But honestly, I would rather do time in a Turkish prison than spend time with a drinker.

They ramble, they fall over, they think they are 10 times more interesting than is actually the case — and if they get the slightest inkling that you disapprove or are bored a great many become aggressive.

These are the people whom the busybodies should be concentrating on. Not with stern words and dire warnings, neither of which will make the slightest bit of difference, but with help and understanding and patience.

Seriously, telling me that I'm an alcoholic because I binge drink on holiday and share a bottle of wine with my wife over supper every night is the same as persecuting everyone who breaks the speed limit.

We need to make a distinction between someone doing 32 mph and someone doing 175 mph.

And it's the same story with child abuse. By telling me that I'm breaking the law every time I smack my children's bottoms, you are taking the pressure off those who lock their kids in a broom cupboard and only let them out to go thieving.

My handy hint this morning, then, is simple. Leave the normal people who do normal things alone. Forget about the people who drink for fun and worry only about those who drink to live.

Sunday 2 September 2007

Public school is the hell we need

Over the years I have filled this column with many things. I've suggested Yasser Arafat and Ariel Sharon should have a fight in the Albert Hall. I've revealed that Mars once crashed into my chimney pots and I've explained that if you painted a picture using a sheep's dingleberries instead of oils you could sell it to Walsall borough council for £150,000.

In other words, when it comes to subject matter I have plumbed the bottom of the barrel and then kept right on going. But I have never written about one of the most discussed topics in Britain today. Education.

There's a very good reason for this. I don't understand any of the debates.

I've talked to David Cameron about grammar schools, about how he doesn't want any more but he doesn't mind if councils build lots, and I'm afraid my eyes glazed over – partly because it all sounded like politico-gobbledegook and partly because, if I'm honest, I don't actually know what a grammar school is.

I think they are places for pupils who can tie up their own shoelaces, as opposed to comprehensive schools, which are big ugly buildings on the outskirts of town for pupils who wish to be stabbed.

Then you have assisted schools. Again, I'm afraid I'm not your man for guidance.

All I can say for sure is that you should avoid them like the plague because, having read Alastair Campbell's book – *Why I Am Brilliant* – it seems they are entirely filled with the children of new Labour ministers.

What does interest me are public schools. I went to one. My mother went to one. And I've always sort of known that my children would go to one as well.

Of course, you may well sneer at that. You may say it is entirely unfair that some children are given a better start in life than others. And I would absolutely have to agree with you. In the same way that it's entirely unfair that some people are born fat or ugly or dyslexic or disabled or ginger or small or Welsh. Life, I'm afraid, is tragic.

And besides, I use exactly the same argument with private schools that I use with private medicine. People who can afford it should be required to indulge because it stops rich bastards clogging up the system for everyone else.

Why should my kids take a place at our local comp – which is excellent, I hear – when it could go to someone whose parents can't afford the alternative? Answer me that, Mr Lenin.

And no. Please don't say that you've read somewhere that state schools now provide a better education than those in the private sector. I've read the stories too and never, in all my years, have I seen so many mangled statistics. In essence, they find one state school that has (just) outperformed one private school and whoopee-do. It's a red-letter day in the *Guardian*.

Well, I'm sorry, but that's like watching Doncaster

Rovers beat Derby County in an FA Cup match and then arguing that all League One clubs are better than all clubs in the Barclays Premiership.

Here's something to chew on. In order to be the school lad at Repton, all I had to do was rub a gallon of creosote into the housemaster's cormorant. Had I wished to be the school lad at my local comp, I would have had to burn it down.

That's why I laugh at all those stories about misbehaving public-school kids wreaking havoc in Cornwall every summer. Oh do me a favour. What sort of havoc are we talking about here?

Smoking joints on the beach? Vomiting Pimm's into your hydrangeas? Did one of them debag the vicar? And is that so bad? Or would you rather your village was taken over each year by a gang of yobs from Croxteth with their sub-machine guns?

Again, you might say you can't bear spoilt rich kids with their trusts and their floppy Boden hair. Fine. But if you are going to use extremes then I hope you don't mind if I respond in kind. I can't bear gormless louts who hang around in shopping centres, shoplifting and catching venereal diseases.

But let's stop the insults. I've always felt that sending a child away to boarding school helps them learn, very quickly, that if they upset others, there's no running home afterwards. They have to deal with it. This means they are more likely, in later life, to be 'good in a room'.

Then there is the range of opportunities. The state system, we keep being told, struggles to find an inflated football, let alone somewhere it can be kicked, while most public schools have their own underwater hang-glider display team.

And, of course, gone are the days when you packed your boy off at 13 saying: 'See you when you're 18. And try not to get buggered too much.' Nowadays, almost everyone employed by the main public schools isn't a predatory homosexual.

As you can see, I am entirely blinkered and useless when it comes to schools. I've always been the biggest fan of private education, the boarding-school system, and I have to be physically restrained when it's criticised.

Right up to the point last week when I dropped my eldest off at her new boarding school. After the death of my father, it was, without doubt, the most painful experience of my life. Leaving my daughter in a strange place, in the hands of a group of people I barely know. And then just driving away.

It's a barbaric and hateful thing to do. And what makes it worse is that she's going to absolutely love it.

Sunday 9 September 2007

Dial M for a mobile I can actually work

There are a great many mobile telephones on the market these days. All are made by companies with preposterous mission statements, all have idiotic names and all are full of ridiculous features that you neither need nor want. So where do you go for some no-nonsense advice?

Films are reviewed in all the major newspapers so that you can avoid the expense and embarrassment of accidentally seeing one with Vin Diesel in it. And it's the same story with books. You want to know what's worth reading and what's not, you tune into *Richard and Judy*.

Everything is reviewed. Cars. Restaurants. Holidays. You name it. But the only place you're going to find advice on mobile phones is on the internet.

On paper this is a good idea. We're not being regaled by people who we suspect have been bribed with a press junket to Bali. We're reading the words of real people who've spent real money on a product. Their experiences, then, should be worthwhile.

They're not. The page always starts with one post that says the product is excellent value for money, well designed and sold as standard with a battery that lasts for a thousand years. This, you know, has come from the marketing department of the manufacturer in question.

So you skip it and get to the meat. As a general rule each phone has about 1 million reviews, all of which fall into two distinct camps. When presented with the opportunity to be a reviewer, people think they have to either gush or damn.

Hand them a choice of giving a rating of anything from one to 10 and all you get are ones and 10s. Six, in the world of amateur reviewing, does not exist.

So the phone you're reading about is either better than Uma Thurman's bottom or the worst use of plastic since Leslie Ash asked for a lip job.

Absolutely none the wiser, you will go to a shop and seek advice from the nine-year-old boy at the counter. 'Which mobile is best for me?' you'll say in a language that marks you out as being English. A point he plainly doesn't notice because, and I guarantee this, he will reply in a tongue you simply will not understand.

He will tell you how many 'pixels' the camera has. How many 'gigs' the music player contains. He will talk about 'Waps', 'browsers', 'USB connectivity', 'Bluetooth' and, unless you are quick with your fists, 'Eee-zee finance deals' that his company happen to be offering at the moment.

What I want is a mobile phone with a battery that lasts for more than six seconds.

This means no colour screen. A colour screen uses more electricity than the Pentagon. I do not want it to take photographs. I do not want it to play music. I do not want to receive emails. I want it to be a telephone.

No such device is offered. Can you believe that? Seriously. Not one single mobile-phone company in this vast and glorious world is offering a phone that is just that. A phone. A device that enables you to speak with someone a long way away.

Why? When I go to my local off-licence to buy a bottle of wine, I am not told that the bottle also contains a packet of Werther's Originals, a typewriter, some insect repellent, the throttle cable from a 1974 Moto Guzzi and a million other things that will simply impair my enjoyment of the wine. I am very angry about this.

My previous telephone was made by Motorola (mission statement – Web. Email. Music. Blade thin. Experience it – along with a picture of a stupid-looking black man).

It was called a Razr (not so much a name as a spelling mistake) and it was great if you wanted to download pornographic images from cyberspace into your pocket.

But, unfortunately, if you tried to make a telephone call it would let you say 'Hello' and then the battery would be exhausted.

My wife suggested I buy a RaspBerry, but I dislike these phones with the passion I normally reserve for ramblers and John Prescott. This is because people who have RaspBerries do nothing all day but fiddle with them. Since my wife got hers all she has said to anyone is 'Mmm?'

Nokia was high on my list as a replacement possibility. Its mission statement – 'Connecting people' – gave me hope that it might do just that. But no. It should be 'Connecting people, photographing them and annoying them with a vast range of mindless ringtones'.

And it was the same story with LG – 'Life's good', Samsung – 'Where imagination becomes reality', and Sony Ericsson, which claims to sell simple talk and text phones, but that's like claiming the Bible is a book about a man.

It's ridiculous. They're making phones only for 12-year-old girls who want something cool, or businessmen who want something enormous so they look impressive in departure lounges. There's nothing for normal people. Nothing with a screen you can read. Nothing for people whose fingers are finger-sized. And nothing for people who don't do e-speak.

But, despite this, it's important that you buy now because soon you will be able to use your phone to bet on the horses and watch television.

It will become a device of such mind-boggling complexity that you will be lost and its battery will be flat anyway.

I ended up buying the nicest looking. It's called the V8 and, in the best traditions of phone reviewing, I'd give it one.

Sunday 16 September 2007

Biggles, you're a crashing bore

Last weekend, a friend of mine was killed when his helicopter crashed in Scotland.

And then, just hours later, another friend was lucky to
walk away when his chopper flipped onto its side while
making an emergency landing in Essex.

Strangely, however, it's not a fear of dying that puts
me off the idea of private aviation. It's the sure-fire knowledge that nothing in all the world is likely to be quite so
boring and pointless.

The idea of piloting your own helicopter or light aircraft, among the clouds and the linnets, far above the jams
and the pressure, is an appealing prospect for anyone who
doesn't know what to do with his money.

Better still, you might imagine that you could enliven
your journey by swooping underneath low bridges, dive-
bombing fields of cattle, looping the loop over friends'
houses and landing for the hell of it in beauty spots and
bird sanctuaries.

Only last month I flew down the Okavango River in
Botswana in a twin-engined light aircraft, following the
waterway's endless twists and turns just 6 feet up, at
150 mph. It was a joyous and brilliant thing to do. But,
unfortunately, if you tried that at home, skimming the Don
in Sheffield, for instance, a man with adenoids and a
clipboard would come round and take your licence away.

In fact, the whole process of learning to fly, it seems to me, is designed specifically to weed out those who might want a plane or a helicopter for fun.

When you want a driving licence, all you have to do is demonstrate to a man in beige trousers that you can reverse round a corner. But when you want a licence to fly, you must demonstrate to the entire Civil Aviation Authority that you are prepared to spend several months with your nose in various text books on meteorology and aerodynamics. Plainly, it only wants pedants up there.

Then you have to spend more months learning how to use a radio. Why? I know already. You just stab away at various buttons until someone comes over the speaker. Then you tell him what you want.

Oh no, you don't. You have to talk in a stupid code, saying 'over' when you've finished speaking for the moment and 'out' when you've finished altogether. Why? When I ring the plumber or the local Indian restaurant, I am able to convey the nature of my request perfectly well using English. So why, when I'm in a plane, do I have to talk in gibberish?

'Hello, it's Jeremy. Is it all right to land?' is a much easier way of saying, 'Weston Tower, this is Charlie Victor Tango on 8453.113 requesting a westerly approach to runway 27.'

But private pilots love all this sort of stuff. They love doing utterly pointless pre-flight checks, tapping dials and making sure that a bunch of goblins didn't come in the night and chew through all the wires.

They never think: 'I bought this plane to make my life more convenient but in the time I've spent checking it, I could have driven to Leeds.' And nor do they ever think: 'If these checks are so foolproof, how come that in the western United States, more small planes fall out of the sky than rain drops.'

No, really. In America, more than one person a day is killed in private-plane crashes. Light aircraft, over there, are known as 'dentist killers'.

And try this for size. You don't have to check your plane if you leave it alone for a few hours in the day. But you do if it's been left alone at night. Why?

Do the plane goblins only come out when it's dark? No. Will a comprehensive pre-flight check keep your plane in the air? No. The fact is that pilots love checking things. They love details.

I know this from glancing at the magazines they read. Boat magazines are full of boats skimming the waves with naked girls on the foredeck. But plane magazines are filled with lists of serial numbers and adverts for stuff that no one could conceivably ever want to buy. Quarter-scale cockpit models, for instance. And hideous pictures of Lancasters, at sunset, over Dresden.

Just last night, I spent some time in the company of two private-plane enthusiasts who never once talked about the speed of their machines, or the convenience, or the sheer, unbridled fun of skimming the treetops at 150 mph. Instead, they talked for hours about parking and refuelling. I bet they think the best bit of sex is unwrapping the condom.

Certainly, they seem to have a weird love for the medical, which they must take every 15 minutes. I can't see why this is necessary because medicals cannot predict a heart attack, which is about the only thing that will affect someone's ability to fly a plane.

And you know what. Hardly anyone with a plane ever uses it to go somewhere useful.

Instead, they take 'the old kite' from their flying-club headquarters to another flying-club headquarters where they have some cheese and Branston pickle. And then they fly home again. What's that all about?

And while they're flying around, spoiling the peace and quiet for everyone on the ground, they are having absolutely no fun whatsoever. This is because they are at 3,000 feet, where 100 mph feels like you're standing still. And they can't come down low for fear of the man with adenoids.

So, the recipe for flying, then. You drive to an airfield, check your plane for two hours, take off, sit still, speak gibberish into a radio, land, eat cheese and then sit still again till you're home again. Repeat until one day you hear a loud bang . . .

Sunday 23 September 2007

The kids are all right with lousy TV

Oh deary me. There was much wailing and gnashing of teeth last week when the most extensive report ever compiled into the state of children's television found that our kids are being brought up on a diet of American violence, schmaltz and pink fluffy nonsense.

The figures were terribly gloomy. Just nine years ago, 22 per cent of shows made by the BBC and ITV were for kids. Now it's just 4 per cent. And as a result, fewer than one in five children's programmes on British television are actually made here.

This produced a torrent of angry missives to the nation's blogs. Angry middle-aged people from all over Surrey and Sussex raged furiously, saying that children should be made to watch wholesome Enid Blyton stories. And that they must be broadcast mute and with subtitles in Latin.

Oh for heaven's sake. Yes, Enid Blyton was tremendous 40 years ago. I particularly enjoyed the Famous Five series. Especially, although I did not know why at the time, when the smugglers took the tousle-haired Georgina to a cave and tied her up. But times change.

And children change too. My grandfather was born up a chimney and was only allowed out when it was time for him to be beaten. My father looked forward to the orange and piece of string he was given every year at

Christmas. I spent most of my childhood watching television. And my kids pass the time doing anything but.

Apart from *The Simpsons* and *Doctor Who*, I cannot get them to watch it at all.

The rot set in during an episode of *Planet Earth*. David Attenborough had just shown us a charming little bird of paradise that danced about in a funny way and my youngest daughter was much taken with it. 'I'd like to see that again,' she said, happily.

But of course, this being television, she couldn't. So on to the internet she went, where, hey presto, she found the clip on a BBC website. And then she found lots of other clips as well. Just the good bits with all the talking taken out.

This, to her, was perfect entertainment. And why wouldn't it be? It's how we watch porn films. You fast-forward through the bits where the plumber comes up the drive, and the lady in a nightie makes him a cup of tea, and slow it down when the action starts.

Now my daughter only really watches YouTube. There's no plot. No Attenborough explaining stuff. No tedious instructions on how to make a space helmet out of a squeezy bottle. No adverts. Just loads of people falling off their bicycles and catching fire. And when she finds one she likes a lot, she watches it over and over again. For nothing.

How can television possibly compete with that? When I was eight, I watched *Marine Boy* because on a wet Thursday afternoon in October, there was absolutely nothing else to do.

Now kids have got YouTube, Xbox, MSN, MySpace, text, email, PSP, DVD and SkyPlus.

All the world's ones and noughts have been harnessed for their edification and you're not going to drag them back to the box with a bunch of jolly-what tally-ho Enid kids in big shorts getting into scrapes with smugglers. That was then, and it's as gone as the ruff and tuberculosis.

Every week (starting tonight, incidentally) I make a television programme called *Top Gear*. But I never watch it. What I do is watch my children watching it. And it's depressing. Because they only really perk up when someone falls in a lake.

Whenever there's talking, they start to unpick the stitching in the sofa. It isn't that they have a limited attention span. They haven't got one at all.

There is no solution to this. Forcing broadcasters to make shows for children is a complete waste of time. Because to make anything they want to see, it would have to be a non-stop orgy of fire, and people getting their heads stuck in lifts.

Fearne Cotton would have to be injured every five seconds and then at the end she'd have to explode. And they couldn't fake it because that's not allowed any more. She really would have to say: 'That's it for this week, kids, and now I'm going to blow up.'

The best thing I can suggest is not to worry. Ofcom says the vast majority of programmes for children are stupid American cartoons. And this is true. But they're all shown on faraway distant satellite channels. And no one is watching them.

If you look behind the hysterical headlines, you'll discover that the most-watched children's programme on television is *Evacuation*, a British-made BBC reality show that gives kids a taste of what it was like to be an evacuee in the Second World War.

The top 20 is almost all British-made. You've got *Blue Peter* at two, *Newsround* at three, *Jackanory* at ten and so on. The old wholesome favourites are still there.

It's just that in our day, they were watched by 5 million and today they are watched by about half a dozen. The rest? The missing hordes? Well, they're doing something else, but we mustn't worry because, honestly, the kids are all right.

My big problem is that broadcasters will react to the report by redoubling their efforts to win back an audience that simply isn't there any more. This will mean there'll be even fewer programmes for those who really do watch television. People who don't have a PlayStation or an account with My Book. People who don't go out on a Saturday night. We're called adults.

The message, then, is simple. Sod the children. And bring back *Minder*.

Sunday 7 October 2007

It's a man's game being a rugby ref

Unbelievable. What a match. Having proved to the Australians that they aren't even any good at sport, we took on the French in the semi-finals . . . and won.

Or lost. It's hard to say for sure because today's Friday and the match hasn't happened yet. But one thing's certain: when it does I'll be there, glued to the screen, with my boy and some beers, talking a load of absolute codswallop.

The problem is that I like rugby very much and I have many opinions about who should do what and when, but never having played I do not have the first clue what's going on. I have no idea why the forwards play at the back and the backs at the front. And nor do I understand what's meant by 'the blind side'.

I can't see why one side of the pitch is blind and the other is in full view. It all makes no sense.

And it makes even less sense when 140 tons of beef all lands in a big muddy lump on top of the ball and you have no idea what on earth is going on in there. Not until the referee blows his whistle, does some signing for the deaf and decides that someone at the bottom of the pile has let go too soon, or not at all, or come in from the side, or made the ball go forwards and that, as a result, another big muddy lump must be formed to get the game going again.

Despite all this, though, you have to love the collisions, the moments when someone with thighs made from oak and a chest the size of a tugboat smashes into a winger with such ferocity that you wonder how his skeleton hasn't just disintegrated into a million pieces.

That and the fights, those cherished moments when a man-mountain smashes his fist, which is the size of a Christmas ham, into someone else's face and all hell breaks loose. Brilliant.

And that brings us on to the referee who, instead of wading into the melee and showering the participants with red cards, simply asks everyone to calm down, pauses while the more badly injured have their noses and ears sewn back on, and then restarts the game.

Compare this attitude with the homosexual nonsense we see in football. Flick someone's earlobe in a game of football and some jumped-up little gnome, sweating like a rapist, will mince over and order you off the pitch.

What's more, a rugby referee is not so drunk on power that he won't go to the video ref if he's not sure. The commentators complain about this but I think it's marvellous: the chap knows how important this game is to the players and he wants to make sure he gets the decision right.

Football refs are not allowed to consult technology even though, so far as I can see, they never ever make a correct decision. No, really. They don't notice when the ball goes over the goal line, they send players off for breathing and do nothing when Ronaldo hurls himself to the ground and claws at his face as though he's been showered with acid.

And you can't argue with these power-crazed idiots because then you get sent off as well.

Do you know a football referee? Do you know anyone who knows a football referee? Have you ever even met anyone who sold a dog to someone who knows a football referee? No. And don't you think that's weird? I know an astronaut. I've even met someone who makes a living from sexing the Queen's ducks. But I've never met a football ref.

Perhaps they're bred on farms, like *The Boys from Brazil*. Either that or they all hide behind meaningless day jobs in PC World, emerging only on a Saturday like a troop of SuperNazis with their too-tight Hitler Youth shorts and their silly whistles.

It's not just football either. The unseen referees in Formula One motor racing distinguish themselves every year by getting every single decision wrong. Only the other week a Polish driver was made to come and sit on the naughty step because he had the temerity to try to overtake a rival.

Then there's Wimbledon. Half a trillion pounds' worth of electronic projections say the ball was out. But sometimes, and I often feel for the hell of it, the umpire calls it in.

And then docks the player points if he objects. But what's the player supposed to do? He's been on a court, solidly, since he was old enough to vomit. He's never been out with a girl, he's never had a beer, he's never been allowed to masturbate. He has dedicated his whole life to this match and this moment and now some jumped-up power-crazed lunatic has denied him the point.

Of course he's going to be angry. Of course he's going to throw his racket on the floor.

If I were in charge of tennis, I would allow aggrieved players to actually punch the officials in certain circumstances.

Either that, or I would get them all down to Twickenham to see how it should be done.

They will note that rugby refs josh and joke with the players. They give off a sense that they're pleased to be out there and – by constantly issuing instructions during rucks and mauls – that they are on hand to offer advice, as much as they are to enforce the rules.

I was going to say that they are the most important feature in rugby. But obviously that's not true. The most important feature in the game, of course, is watching Australia lose.

Again.

Sunday 14 October 2007

Feed the world – eat blue whales

We begin this morning, I'm afraid, with an alarming revelation. Never mind the war, the rugby or gun crime. It has come to my attention that in the whole of the British Isles there isn't a single eco-nutritionist.

The government's Food Standards Agency employs about a million and a half working groups who tour the nation in cheap suits making sure that Bernard Matthews is not filling his turkeys with asbestos and that Sainsbury's isn't using polonium to make its bananas more bent.

But not one of them is thinking: 'Wait a minute. If we build the 3 million new houses Gordon Brown has promised by 2020, where will we grow all the stuff needed to feed the people who live in them?'

And worse. Nobody is wondering where we might get the water. Not for our lawns and our lavatories but for the crops, the cows and the piggy-wigs. Like I said, this is an alarming problem.

Already the Atlantic has fewer cod in it than Elton John's bath, so we are having to import fish fingers from China. And you may think this is fine. Your underpants come from the Far East, and your mobile phone, so why should we not import our watercress and beef from those industrious little yellow fellows on the banks of the Yangtze?

I'll tell you why. Because China's population is growing too, and soon they won't be able to send us their fish fingers because they will have been scoffed before they get to the docks.

It is a fact that the world can just about feed 6.5 billion people. But it will not be able to feed 7 billion or 8 billion. And certainly not if, as the lunatic Al Gore suggests, Canada stops growing food and turns over its prairies to the production of biodiesel.

Maybe man is causing the world to warm, but we'll never know because, frankly, we will all have starved to death long before anyone gets the chance to find out.

Obviously, one solution is to burn the entire Amazon rainforest and turn this rich and fertile place into the world's pantry. But, unfortunately, this is not possible because Sting will turn up on a chat show with some pygmy who's sewn a saucer into his bottom lip, arguing that the world's 'indigenous tribes' are suffering because of the West's greed.

And never mind that the pygmy is wearing a Manchester United football shirt.

Another solution is that we all become, with immediate effect, vegetarians. It takes 1,790 litres of water to grow 1 kilo of wheat. But 9,680 litres to produce 1 kilo of cow. Sadly, however, this doesn't work for people like me who only really enjoy eating something if it once had a face.

I fear, too, that if we all became vegetablists, the world would smell of halitosis and we'd all start to vote Liberal Democrat. Furthermore, all the veg-heads I know are sickly and grey and unable to climb a flight of stairs without fainting.

It all looks bleak. But don't worry, because I have a suggestion that I worked out this morning.

At the moment, we eat only a very small number of things. Cows. Pigs. Potatoes. Lettuce. And that's about it. So what I propose is that we spice up our lives with a bit of variety.

David Attenborough is forever finding unusual creatures in the deepest parts of the ocean. He tells us how they can see down there in the murky depths and how they mate. He tells us where they live, how they raise their young and how they use their tentacles to find prey. But he never tells us the most important thing: what they taste like.

It's the same story with Monty Don. Each week, he crops up on *Gardeners' World* and explains how lupins form the perfect backdrop to any rockery. Yes. Fine. But can you put them on toast?

I'm looking at my garden now and wondering. I know I can't eat the yew hedge because it will bounce off my diaphragm and come right back out again. But what about the lawn? Would that be delicious and nutritious? And, gulp, what about Kristin Scott Donkey, who died recently?

Should I have given her poor body to the hunt, or should I have garnished it with some lupins and a sea horse and had her for supper?

Why not? Over the years I have eaten dog, snake, crocodile, guillemot, whale, puffin and a scorpion. They all tasted like chicken, so it's a fair bet donkeys would too. Or what about camels, which, as we all know, need very little water?

This brings me on to the final solution. There are many people who are greatly concerned for the plight of endangered species such as the tiger, the panda and the blue whale. They work very hard doing charity marathons in zany T-shirts to help keep these poor creatures teetering on the right side of extinction.

So how's this for a plan? We start eating them. I believe that if enough people demanded blue whale for supper, garnished with the ears of a panda and the left wing of a juicy great bustard, it wouldn't take very long for big business to move in.

When there's a quid to be made, pandas will be having babies with the regularity of hens and you won't be able to go to the shops for all the leopards you'll meet on the way.

It's either this or, I'm afraid, we are going to have to start eating each other.

If that happens, bagsy I get John Prescott.

Sunday 21 October 2007

It's lies that make TV interesting

There has been a great deal of brouhaha in the newspapers recently about what is real on television and what is not. The *Daily Mail* in particular is very keen that the BBC is above board, honest and fair. And doesn't spend its days making up hysterical stories that happened only in the imagination of the reporter . . .

Of course, some of the criticism is fair. You cannot ask people to vote in a telephone poll if you know full well the lines are closed. And you cannot show film of the Queen exploding when she has done no such thing.

Although, amazingly, it turns out you can make a global-warming film that contains nine proven factual inaccuracies. And they'll give you a Nobel peace prize.

Still, we've now reached a point of such hysteria that people are poking their noses into every little corner of the television world and finding out that when Gordon Ramsay emerged from the sea with some fish on the end of his spear gun he hadn't actually caught them himself. Oh Jesus, no.

And worse, it now transpires that Alan Yentob may not have been in the room when some dreary old Czech playwright was being interviewed. Seriously. Never mind the bush fires and the Iranian sanctions. Yentob's 'noddies' may have been filmed afterwards.

The problem is that the people who get arsey about

this kind of thing don't have a clue how television works.

Do you really think Gordon's production company has the money to stand around while he flounders about in the oggin, shooting bits of seabed near to where a fish had been swimming moments earlier? No. Exactly. So why not just pretend?

Then there's Alan. Let's say the dreary old Czech rambled on about the meaning of Ibsen for two hours. That needs to be cut down because the programme is only an hour long. And how do you cover the edit points? Simple. At some later stage, you film the interviewer pretending to be interested in what the man is saying, even though he's gone home. And then you use these shots to plaster over the joins.

There is no one in television who has not done this. Although what I like to do instead of nodding and looking earnest is yawn. It drives the director mad.

There's more. On *Top Gear* I whiz about for the camera until I have a feel for the car. Then I disappear into a hut for an hour or so to corral my thoughts into a workable script. And how do we occupy the expensive film crew while I'm doing that? Stand them down? Or put a researcher in the car and have him slither about until I'm ready to come back?

Yes, in the film you watch, some of the shots feature a car not being driven by me. But ask yourself a question: does it matter?

This is the most important question. In Japan recently, TV producers changed the subtitles to make foreign interviewees say something they were not saying. And because this was a programme about what gives Tojo cancer, plainly that does matter. But most of the scandals you've read about recently do not.

However, because of the furore over Gordon's fish and Ant's telephone and Alan's noddies, we have a serious problem. No one believes anything they ever see on television any more. No one believes we were attacked by a gang of crazies in an Alabama petrol station. No one believes we really did go across the Channel in a pick-up truck. No one believes we went to the North Pole. They spend their whole time looking for the smoke and mirrors.

And now there's an even bigger consequence. Television producers have become so paranoid about making sure that every little thing is real that it's beginning to have an effect on what we watch.

Last week there was a programme on BBC2 called *The Truth About Property*. And at one point the presenter, a keen young chap in a short-sleeved shirt, explained that he was on his way to look at the house where he grew up.

In a piece to camera, he said that he had lived there from the age of five and that he hadn't been back since he was 18. It would, he said, be a trip down memory lane.

Fine. In the olden days, a researcher would have called at the house several weeks earlier. Arrangements would have been made with the owners to let the crew in and show the presenter his old bedroom. He would then get all teary-eyed and everything would be lovely.

Not any more. He arrived at the house, rang the bell, waited a while and then said to the camera: 'No one is in.'

Is that what you want? Lots of foreplay and a withered

ending? Because if you want total transparency from every single show, that's what you're going to get.

You're going to have midgets sticking their heads out of their Dalek suits saying: 'Hey, kids. It's not a ray gun. It's a sink plunger.' You're going to have the people on *Blue Peter* saying: 'Here's one a researcher made earlier.' And David Attenborough explaining that meerkats don't really make that cute little snuffling noise. The film was shot mute and all the effects were added on in a lab in Bristol by a man in a jumper.

And imagine if this sort of thing were to spread to the *Daily Mail*. You'd have a paper full of stories saying that Princess Diana died in an accident, that you won't get breast cancer if you eat cornflakes, and that immigrants will not cause your house to be valueless.

Sunday 28 October 2007

A Met Office severe bossiness warning

We're told that a recession is coming. Apparently, it's got something to do with the Chinese, who have, in a complex way, affected America's sub-prime. Inflation here will spiral out of control, millions will find themselves on the dole and thousands of immigrants will be eaten by rats.

Good. Because this will give the government something to do. And maybe it will then stop sitting around all day finding new ways to boss us around.

Already, in the period of Great Boredom, they've stopped us smoking, killing foxes, reversing without a banksman, playing conkers, enjoying bonfire night and taking toothpaste on an aeroplane.

And now they are thinking of banning patio heaters, doing 30, and wearing hooded tops. Soon, it will be illegal to not be George Monbiot.

The latest wheeze comes from the Highways Agency, which is 'concerned' that over half of those interviewed in a recent survey would carry on with a journey, regardless of a severe-weather warning.

Well, of course we would, you non-conker-playing, health-and-safety-obsessed, hard-hatted, high-visibility clowns. Because, and I want to make this absolutely clear, your idea of severe weather is very far removed from anyone who's got an IQ in double figures.

You may have noticed these days that every single weather forecast tells us the Met Office has issued a severe-weather warning.

Two weeks ago they said the whole of East Anglia was to be engulfed by a flood so massive and so destructive that billions would die in screaming agony. Last week they were banging on about fog so dense and impenetrable that we'd all be eaten by werewolves we never saw coming.

I see what's going on here. The weather people are cross because they have to follow the news, which is full of interesting stuff like murder and war, and all they've got to talk about is drizzle and clouds in the west by mid-morning. So they try to spice things up a bit, to make their job look a bit more interesting.

We can all see it's a sham. British severe weather is like British severe poverty, a fairly limp-wristed affair when placed in a global context. Northern Norway has severe weather. Oklahoma, in the tornado season, has severe weather. And a Cuban has every right to say 'Wow, that was severe' after a category-five hurricane has just blown his house into the middle of Houston. But in Barnsley? No.

When you've seen the flooding in Bangladesh during the monsoon, you'll realise how idiotic Gordon Brown looked in Tewkesbury earlier this year, comforting those whose DFS sofas had been ruined. And when you've experienced an Icelandic white-out, you will cry with laughter when some hapless reporter in wellies comes on the rolling news channel to say Britain is locked in ice chaos. It's all complete claptrap.

I am 47 years old and I do not ever remember weather so severe that I could not go out. The so-called hurricane of 1987 was so pathetic it passed right over my house and I never even woke up. And the snowstorms of my youth were never so bad that we couldn't drive 20 miles to find a tobogganing hill.

Undeterred by the bothersome notion of facts, however, the Highways Agency has enlisted the help of the Met Office which, spurred on by the chance for a bit of bossiness, agrees that we should stay at home whenever it's windy, and possibly move to the cellar with some soup until the all-clear is sounded.

Only then they get themselves in a bit of a pickle because arguing that we're in for a cold winter doesn't sit well with their directive to big up climate change.

So they say we mustn't be lulled into a false sense of security by global warming because cold snaps are still possible.

How cold exactly? Minus 4? Minus 8? The coldest temperature ever recorded in Britain was minus 27.2°C and I'll admit this is far too nippy for, say, swimming. But when I went to the North Pole earlier this year, it went to minus 58°C, and even though I was in a tent, I didn't even slightly die.

As humans we can cope. We have central heating, and patio heaters that will keep us warm when we go outside for a cigarette. And at the other end of the scale, last year I worked in Death Valley for 10 days where it rarely dropped below 110°F (43°C). And that was fine too. I even got a suntan, which, amazingly, failed to give me cancer.

The trouble is, of course, that the Highways Agency nitwits don't really care about reality. What they care about is that motorists are ignoring weather warnings from the Met Office. And that, in bossy Britain, won't do.

So they've come up with a new system of red and amber alerts that will be broadcast over the radio and flashed up on motorway gantries warning drivers of severe weather ahead.

And, of course, we will ignore these too because we know that unless we've accidentally driven to Archangel the severe weather in question will be as frightening as an ageing Labrador.

Which means a law will be necessary that forces us to stay at home when the Met Office has decided it will be windy.

I promise you this. It is a cast-iron guarantee. Unless we get a recession to occupy the minds of those in charge, they will impose legislation. And when they do, the profitability of your business, the wealth of the nation and the education of your children will depend entirely on the whim of Michael Fish.

Sunday 18 November 2007

Make my day, sir, shoot a hoodie

Almost every day a politician comes onto the news and tells us all that Britain's town centres are being overrun by teenage gangs who drink vast quantities of cider and then run about all night stabbing passers-by. While the event is videoed on mobile phones for the edification of YouTube viewers.

It all sounds frightful, but frankly they could be talking about events on the moons of Jupiter because, happily, I live in Chipping Norton, where a lost kitten is front-page news. Of course, there are teenagers here, and some of them have hoodies, but mostly they are called Araminta and Harry, and I've never once got the feeling they want to plunge a kitchen knife into my heart.

It's the same story in Notting Hill, where I spend the working week. While dining in restaurants such as E&O, I have no real sense that outside the window gangs of 14-year-olds are lurking in the shadows, eager to punch me in the face for a moment's glory on the internet.

Last week, however, I had to go to Milton Keynes. It was my youngest daughter's birthday and she wanted to spend the afternoon at the town's snow dome. Directions were sent, and then more, with even greater detail about how this indoor Alp might be found. But none of this was really necessary, because you just head for the largest building ever created by man.

It's a brilliant place, all full of snow and vending machines offering energy drinks. But sadly, because of Mr Blair's smoking ban, you have to go outside for a cigarette, which puts you slap-bang in one of the happy-slapping town centres the politicians keep talking about.

I wasn't even remotely bothered when the swarm of children first approached. I figured they were fans of *Top Gear* and wanted to know about Richard Hammond's head. But no. What they wanted to know most of all was if I had any security.

I asked them politely to leave me alone. I walked away. I even walked away a bit more. But they kept coming. And so, figuring that attack was probably the best form of defence, I grabbed the ringleader by his hoodie, lifted him off the ground and explained, firmly, that it'd be best if he went back to his tenement.

He declined. They all did. In fact, they all reached for their mobile phones and began to take pictures of the altercation. And that put me in a tricky spot . . .

I have reached the age where I am no longer able to tell how old a child is. The boy I was holding could have been 18. Or he could have been eight. And if he did turn out to be eight, I figured the photographs could look a bit like bullying.

So, weirdly, I was standing there holding this boy by the scruff of his neck, and instead of worrying about being stabbed I was actually thinking: 'Jesus, I'm going to get done for assault if I'm not careful.'

I therefore put him down, and in a flurry of swearing and hand gestures involving various fingers he was gone. Leaving the entire nation with a very serious problem.

It's this. Plainly, this boy's parents are useless, allowing him to be out and about on the streets, harassing passers-by at will. Think about it. Every single time one of these children is found stabbed or shot, his mum and stepdad always tell the papers he was a 'good lad'. And that he 'didn't deserve to die'.

And nobody ever says: 'Well, if he was such a frigging angel, what was he doing on a derelict building site at four in the morning, you halfwits?' He didn't deserve to die, for sure, but you do, for having the parenting skills of a Welsh dresser.

There's an equally big problem at school. Children, as far as I can see, are at liberty to do just about anything to one another at school because there is absolutely nothing the teacher can do. Not without being hauled out of the classroom by some frizzy-haired human-rights lawyer, sacked and sent to prison.

The police? Oh come on. They are far too busy filling in health and safety forms and processing speeding tickets to be bothered with every single gang of teenage ruffians. Which means that every single gang of teenage ruffians is completely free to go out and do whatever it pleases.

And we – the normal people who see town centres as somewhere to go to buy takeaway food or organise a loan for a new house – can't do anything either because a) the politicians keep telling us all these kids are tooled up like special-forces hitmen, and b) if we stand up for ourselves we will spend the next 40 years in the Scrubs fighting off the unwelcome advances of Pinkski, the Albanian nonce.

Happily, I think I have a solution. Nothing can be done about the parents because they are too thick. It'd be like trying to train a hedgehog to smoke a pipe. We can't rely on the police either – not without unpicking every single thing done by new Labour in the past 10 years.

And, I'm sorry, but even if the law is changed so that adults are allowed to defend themselves, you'd think twice about poking a boy in the eye or slamming his head in a car door if you thought his friends had machetes down their trouser legs.

The only place where this issue can be tackled, then, is at school. So you fit airport-style metal detectors at the doors to ensure no pupil is packing heat, you put all the troublemakers in one class and you give the teacher in charge immunity from criminal charges. And a sub-machine gun.

Sunday 2 December 2007

Enough, I'm gonna torch my antiques

According to the *Daily Express*, falling house prices have now caused house prices to fall. But if I were you, I'd stop worrying about the value of your bricks and mortar and start addressing the value of your furniture.

I do not know why Britain developed a fondness for buying antiques. Perhaps it was the day, at some point in 1952, when people began to think of the past as a better place than the present. Or maybe it's because we think a Georgian dining table will hold its value well whereas something that came flat-packed in cellophane from Sweden will be worthless from the moment you take it out of the box.

Especially if you choose to make it yourself. Because it will be all covered in arterial splashback.

Giving your children an elegant Victorian hatstand means something. Giving them a red leather button-backed sofa that you bought from DFS in the sales 30 years earlier will just make them angry.

Certainly, I've always felt this way, which is why my house is full of ancient pieces I've picked up at antiques markets and little hidden-away shops over the years. However, the other day a man came round to value my collection for insurance purposes and it seems that a large, all-consuming fire would leave me out of pocket to the tune of £4.50.

He mooched from room to room, examining the various writing desks, grandfather clocks and oak linen chests, and not a single thing aroused even the slightest bit of interest. I live, it seems, in nothing more than a woodworm's larder.

Here's the problem. When you go into an antiques shop, the charming man with the wild white hair, the waistcoat and the eccentric spectacles looks like he knows his onions.

But secretly, deep down, you think that there have been 17 million furniture makers over the years and that no matter how wise the dealer looks, occasionally he's going to make a mistake. And accidentally sell you the Ark of the Covenant for £350.

Honestly, I always think this. I always think as I leave an antiques shop that I have done the deal of the century.

You only have to watch the *Antiques Roadshow* to know I'm right. All those old biddies with their surgical stockings and their crinkled-up mouths imagine their carriage clock was made by King Herod himself. But the expert, backed by a team of researchers, the internet and the British Library invariably finds some tiny little detail that proves it was actually made by an unemployed train driver who had the shakes – in 1964. And is therefore worth only 40p.

Oh they all try to look pleased with the valuation. But they're not. Inside, every single one of them is seething.

And that's because those of us who buy antiques do so for all the wrong reasons.

In our minds we are not spending money. We are investing in the well-being of our children. We always think that the umbrella stand we've just bought will turn out to have been made by Florence Nightingale, out of Lord Lucan's tongue. It never occurs to us that it's plywood and we were ripped off.

I am not suggesting that the antiques market is crooked. I'm sure that by and large it isn't. But the prices aren't based on fact. They're based, like British speed limits, on guesswork, on a vague assumption of what the market will stand.

I have therefore decided to burn all my old stuff, which is better than having eBay people coming round to my house with their smelly bottoms and their Nigerian banker's drafts, and I'm going to start buying modern.

This is only right and proper. The Victorians did not buy Georgian. The Edwardians did not buy Victorian. And the Heathites did not buy anything unless it was purple. I'm therefore going to get with it. I'm going to buy Brown.

Actually, it is all brown. And unbelievably expensive. I spent a morning touring the shops in Notting Hill and every single thing is £2,500. A kitchen chair that was covered with a peeled cow was £2,500. A coffee table, which was no such thing – it was a log – was £2,500. A rug, which came with the head of an animal still attached, was £2,500.

The sofas, however, were not £2,500. They were much more. And they all came with delivery dates some time in the middle of the next century. Why? A sofa is some nails, some wood, a bit of foam rubber and a sheet of brown Alcantara. Which, according to Wikipedia, is a composite material developed in Japan in the seventies. So that means it isn't, and it wasn't.

Whatever. Give me a hammer and some scissors and I could knock you up a sofa in an afternoon. Any size you like. Oh it wouldn't be very good, but I suspect the sofas I saw, behind the urban surfer, new edge design, aren't very good either.

Certainly, in a hundred years I doubt we will be seeing too many of them cropping up on the *Antiques Roadshow*.

The trouble is that all this stuff looks very good. It'll break the bank and it'll break your back, and because it's all designed by men in polo-neck jumpers, with needle-thin glasses, it'll be out of fashion long before you take delivery, but at least you know you're not buying an heirloom.

When it's valued at some point in the future and you're told it's worth less than a used carrier bag you won't be disappointed. Whereas if you buy an antique I can pretty much guarantee you will be.

This is important. Going to your grave broke is fine. Going to your grave disappointed – I can think of nothing so heartbreakingly sad.

Sunday 9 December 2007

Our poor bloody backroom boys

Well, that went well. Saddam Hussein has been executed with much dignity, the weapons of mass destruction have been made safe and Iraq is now in the hands of a well-organised government such as you would find in Sweden. So, seeing as everything is tickety-boo in downtown Basra, we can now turn our attention to Afghanistan.

To be honest, this isn't going very well at all. In fact, in the past 15 months our boys have fired 2.7 million bullets. That's 250 an hour. And still the Taliban keep coming in their flip-flops and Toyotas.

I popped over there for a couple of days last weekend and sadly I didn't get to the front line. Partly this was due to logistics. Mainly, though, it's because I am an extreme coward.

I suspect, however, that if I had gone the chaps would have been fine. Obviously, if I were in the army, I would volunteer for postal duties – in Scotland, preferably. But real army people like fighting. It's what they're trained to do, and loosing off 6,000 rounds a day, to them, is just a job.

My heart goes out instead to the thousands of backroom boys I met. Their life, far from the fighting, behind the blast-proof walls and the razor wire and the guard dogs and the sentries, is about as horrible as it's possible to imagine. Unless you work in the Nigerian sewers.

Some are based at Camp Bastion, in the middle of the desert. The view is grey. You look over a vast grey camp with grey buildings to the grey concrete walls and beyond to the grey desert that blends into the dust-choked grey sky. There is no green. There is no yellow. There is no relief.

And of course, this being the army, everything has to be done at o'crikey o'clock. You never hear anyone in the forces say: 'I thought we'd leave at 11ish.' Everything happens at three in the morning.

And at night it's cold. Bitterly, numbingly cold. So cold that even the Geordies roll their sleeves down.

Happily, the tents have heaters, which sounds lovely. But, annoyingly, the heaters in question have only two settings: 'off' and so 'on' you could bake a bloody potato in there.

If you're stationed at Kandahar you get a proper prefab building and the bedrooms have proper fan heaters that suck dust from the outside and shoot it into the room with such vigour that soon it sets off the smoke alarm.

Yup. Even though this is a full-on war, with Apache helicopter gunships and everything, you are not allowed to smoke indoors because it's bad for your health. Also, no vehicle is permitted to enter the battlefield – and I'm not joking – unless it meets EU emissions regulations.

I should mention at this point the lavatory doors, which someone erected four inches from the bowl. This is fine if you are Douglas Bader, but everyone else has to leave the door open. And, I'm sorry, but doing your number twos in plain view of everyone is only all right if you are a beast of the field.

Then you step into the showers, which are great. Except for one tiny detail. Water is in short supply so your allowance wouldn't be enough even to baptise a baby. It isn't anywhere near enough to wash a suicide bomber's spleen out of your hair.

At night there is nothing to do. There is no gym, no cinema, no bar, no pool, no tennis court. There is, however, a shop where you can buy orange juice and coffee. Beer? Nope. It's dry, even on Christmas Day.

So a typical day for the soldiers who keep the frontline troops fed, watered and armed is: get up. Chisel ice from your nose. Defecate in front of your mates. Shower your left foot. Walk to office. Do work. Walk to cookhouse. Walk to tent when tired. Repeat seven days a week.

And it's bloody hard work. Every day the planes and the trucks are bringing in kit and you've got to sort it while trying not to wonder why someone back in Britain has sent 200 office desks with no drawers, 20,000 pairs of chef's trousers and – get this – 2,000 jars of cockles. Any guns today? No. Just cockles.

The Royal Electrical and Mechanical Engineers, meanwhile, spend their days scurrying into the badlands to retrieve trucks and tanks that have been blown to smithereens by bombs. To judge by the sheer volume of wrecked machinery in their yard, they do this a lot, and it's not easy hauling stuff that weighs more than the moon over a desert while Johnny Taliban is taking pot shots all the time. Still, there's always the promise of some lovely cockles if you get back.

And it's not as if you're out there for a couple of weeks. The tour of duty is six months, broken only by 14 days' leave in Britain . . . theoretically. Sadly, the RAF has only three Tristars and they all date from the time of Montgolfier, which means they break down often.

That means you can spend the first five days of your leave sitting on the tarmac in Kandahar and then five hours at the baggage reclaim in Brize Norton waiting for someone to open the door to the hold. Which has got stuck. Again.

Still, there was some cheery news from Gordon Brown when he dropped in for a 40-minute pat on the back the other day. He said simply that the forces would be in Afghanistan for another 10 years. And then he got on a plane and went home.

Ooh they were pleased. Six months a year for 10 years. That's five years of their young lives in an alcohol-free sea of grey. This Christmas, then, spare them a thought.

Sunday 23 December 2007

Unhand my patio heater, archbishop

The Archbishop of Canterbury told the faithful on Christmas Day that unless human beings abandon our greed, we will be responsible for the death of the planet.

Hmmm. I'm not sure that I can take a lecture on greed from a man who heads one of the western world's richest institutions. As we huddle under a patio heater to stay warm while having a cigarette in the rain, his bishops are living in palatial splendour with banqueting halls, wondering where to invest the next billion.

And are the churches open at night as shelter for the homeless and the weak? No, they are locked lest someone should decide to redress the inequalities of western society by half-inching a candelabra and fencing it to buy Christmas presents for his kiddies.

Then we must ask how much old Rowan really understands about the implications and causes of global warming. He thinks that taking a holiday in Florida and driving a Range Rover caused the flooding in Tewkesbury this summer. But then he also believes it's possible for a man to walk on water and feed a crowd of 5,000 with nothing more than a couple of sardines.

Hmmm. Well, here are some facts that Rowan might like to chew on over his fair-trade breakfast cereal. The Alps are enjoying good snowfalls this year, in much the same way that the Alps in New South Wales enjoyed healthy snowfalls last summer.

The hurricane season finished a couple of weeks ago and, contrary to all the scaremongering from Al Gore's mates, the number of severe storms, for the second year in a row, was slightly below average.

Closer to home, Britain did not, as was predicted by the BBC's hysterical internet news site, bake this summer under record-breaking temperatures. It was wet and soggy, much like in all the summers of my youth. And the only reason Tewkesbury flooded is because we've all paved our drives and built houses on the flood plains so the rainwater had nowhere else to go apart from Mrs Miggins's front room.

In the light of all this, I would like Rowan Williams to come out from behind his eyebrows and tell us how many people have been killed by greed-induced global warming. Because even the most swivel-eyed lunatic would be hard pressed to claim it's more than a few dozen.

Meanwhile, I reckon the number of people killed over the years by religious wars is around 809 million. I tell you this, beardie. Many, many more people have died in the name of God than were killed in the name of Hitler.

Between 1096 and 1270, the Crusades killed about 1.5 million. Way more than have been killed by patio heaters and Range Rovers combined. Then there was the 30 years' war, which reduced Europe's population by about 7.5 million. And the slaughter is still going on today in Iraq and Afghanistan and Palestine and Pakistan. Benazir Bhutto was killed by a religious nut, not a homeless polar bear.

We have been told by those of a communist disposition that if we return to a life of sackcloth and potato soup (bishops excepted) and if we meet all the targets laid down by the great scientist John Prescott at Kyoto, then Britain will be a shining beacon to the world. Others will see what we have done and immediately lay down their 4x4s.

Rubbish. America and China and India will ignore our lunacy and our economic suicide and continue to embody the human spirit for self-improvement (or greed, as Rowan calls it).

No matter. Old Rowan will doubtless applaud the move. This is a man who was arrested in the anti-nuclear protests of the 1980s. Who refused to call the 9/11 terrorists evil and said they had serious moral goals. Who thinks that every single thing bought and sold is 'an act of aggression' on the developing world. Who campaigns for gay rights but wouldn't actually appoint a homosexual as a bishop. And who recently said in an interview that America was the bad guy and that Muslims in Britain were like the good Samaritans.

In other words, he's a full-on, five-star, paid-up member of the loony left, so anything that prevents the middle classes from having a Range Rover and a patio heater is bound to get his vote.

If, however, he really wants to bring peace and stability to the world, if he really believes Britain can be a force for good and a shining beacon in troubled times, then I urge him to close the Church of England.

If we can demonstrate that we can survive without a church – and when you note 750,000 more people went online shopping on Christmas Day than went to church, you could argue we already do – then, who knows, maybe the mullahs and the left-footers will follow suit.

Daft? Not as daft as expecting the government in Beijing to renounce electricity because everyone in Britain has swapped their Range Rover for a mangle.

But better? Well, yes. I genuinely believe we are born with a moral compass and we don't need it reset every Sunday morning by some weird-beard communist in a dress. I am, as you may have gathered, completely irreligious, but it doesn't stop me trying to be kind to others, and I'm never completely overwhelmed with a need to murder madmen in pulpits. Slightly overwhelmed sometimes, but never completely.

Morally, the world would be no worse if religion were abolished. Practically, it would be much, much better. And so, given the choice of which we should give up, God or the patio heater, the choice is simple.

Sunday 30 December 2007

JEREMY CLARKSON

MOTORWORLD

There are ways and means of getting about that don't involve four wheels, but in this book Jeremy Clarkson isn't interested in them.

Taking himself to twelve countries (okay, eleven – he goes to America twice), Clarkson delves deeply into the hows, whys and wherefores of different nationalities and their relationship to cars.

For instance, why is that Italians are more interested in looking good than looking where they are going? Why do Indians crash a lot? How can an Arab describe himself as 'not a rich man' with four of the world's most expensive cars in his drive? And why have the otherwise neutral Swiss declared war on the car?

From Cuba to Iceland, Australia to Vietnam, Japan to Texas, Jeremy Clarkson tells us of his adventures on and off four wheels as he seeks to discover just what it is that makes our motorworld tick over.

JEREMY CLARKSON

CLARKSON ON CARS

Jeremy Clarkson is the second best motoring writer in Britain. For twenty years he's been driving cars, writing about them and occasionally voicing his opinions on *Top Gear*.

No one on in the business is taller.

Here, he has collected his best car columns and stories in which he waxes lyrical on topics as useful and diverse as:

The perils of bicycle ownership

Why Australians – not Brits – need bull bars

Why soon only geriatrics will be driving BMWs

The difficulty of deciding on the best car for your wedding

Why Jesus's dad would have owned a Nissan Bluebird

… And why it is that bus lanes cause traffic jams

Irreverent, damn funny and offensive to almost everyone, this is writing with its foot to the floor, the brake lines cut and the speed limit smashed to smithereens. Sit back and enjoy the ride.

JEREMY CLARKSON

I KNOW YOU GOT SOUL

Some machines have it and others don't: Soul. They take your breath away, and your heart beats a little faster just knowing that they exist. They may not be the fastest, most efficient, even the best in their class – but they were designed and built by people who loved them, and we can't help but love them back.

For instance,

Zeppelin airships, whilst disastrously explosive in almost every case, were elegant and beautiful bubbles in the air.

The battleships were some of the least effective weapons of war ever built, but made the people who paid for them feel good.

Despite two tragic crashes, the *Space Shuttle* still leaves you with a rocket in your pocket.

Some might dismiss this list as simply being for boys and their toys, but, as Jeremy Clarkson shows, that is to miss the point of what makes the sweep of the Hoover Dam sexier than a supermodel's curves; why the *Princess* flying boat could give white elephants a good name; and why the *Flying Scotsman* beats the Bullet Train every time.

In *I Know You Got Soul*, Jeremy Clarkson celebrates, in his own inimitable style, the machines that matter to us, and tells the stories of the geniuses, boffins and crackpots who put the ghost in the machine.

JEREMY CLARKSON

THE WORLD ACCORDING TO CLARKSON

Jeremy Clarkson has seen rather more of the world than most. He has, as they say, been around a bit. And as a result, he's got one or two things to tell us about how it all works – and being Jeremy Clarkson he's not about to voice them quietly, humbly and without great dollops of humour.

With a strong dose of common sense that is rarely, if ever, found inside the M25, Clarkson hilariously attacks the pompous, the ridiculous, the absurd and the downright idiotic ideas, people and institutions that we all have to put up with at home and abroad, whilst also celebrating the eccentric, the clever and the sheer bloody brilliant.

'Hilarious ... it'll make you appreciate the ludicrousness of modern life and have you in stitches' *Sun*

JEREMY CLARKSON

AND ANOTHER THING . . . :
THE WORLD ACCORDING TO CLARKSON VOLUME 2

Everyone knows that Jeremy Clarkson finds the world a perplexing place – after all, he wrote a bestselling book about it. Yet despite the appearance of *The World According to Clarkson*, things don't seem to have improved much. However, Jeremy is not someone to give up easily and he's decided to have another go.

In *And Another Thing . . .*, our exasperated hero discovers that:

He inadvertently dropped a bomb on North Carolina

We're all going to explode at the age of 62

Russians look bad in Speedos. But not as bad as we do

No one should have to worry about being Bill Oddie's long lost sister

He should probably be nicer about David Beckham

Thigh-slappingly funny and – as ever – in your face, Jeremy Clarkson bursts the pointless little bubbles of idiots, while celebrating the special, the unique and the sheer bloody brilliant . . .

JEREMY CLARKSON

BORN TO BE RILED

Jeremy Clarkson, it has to be said, sometimes finds the world a maddening place. And nowhere more so than from the behind the wheel of a car, where you can see any number of people acting like lunatics while in control (or not) of a ton of metal.

In this collection of classic columns, first published in 1999, Jeremy takes a look at the world through his windscreen, shakes his head at what he sees – and then puts the boot in.

Among other things, he explains:

Why Surrey is worse than Wales

How crossing your legs in America can lead to arrest

The reason cable TV salesmen must be punched

That divorce can be blamed on the birth of Jesus.

Raving politicians, pointless celebrities, ridiculous 'personalities' and the Germans all get it in the neck, together with the stupid, the daft and the ludicrous, in a tour de force of comic writing guaranteed to have Jeremy's postman wheezing under sackfuls of letters from the easily offended.

JEREMY CLARKSON

DON'T STOP ME NOW

There's more to life than cars. Jeremy Clarkson knows this. There is, after all, a whole world out there just waiting to be discovered. So, before he gets on to torque steer and active suspension, he takes time to consider:

The madness of Galapagos tortoises

The similarities between Jeremy Paxman and AC/DC's bass guitarist

The problems and perils of being English

God's dumbest creation

Then there are the cars: whether it's the poxiest little runabout or an exotic, firebreathing supercar, no one does cars like Clarkson. Unmoved by mechanics' claims and unimpressed by press junkets, he approaches anything on four wheels without fear or favour. What emerges from the ashes is rarely pretty. But always very, very, very funny.

He just wanted a decent
book to read ...

Not too much to ask, is it? It was in 1935 when Allen Lane, Managing Director of Bodley Head Publishers, stood on a platform at Exeter railway station looking for something good to read on his journey back to London. His choice was limited to popular magazines and poor-quality paperbacks – the same choice faced every day by the vast majority of readers, few of whom could afford hardbacks. Lane's disappointment and subsequent anger at the range of books generally available led him to found a company – and change the world.

'We believed in the existence in this country of a vast reading public for intelligent books at a low price, and staked everything on it'
Sir Allen Lane, 1902–1970, founder of Penguin Books

The quality paperback had arrived – and not just in bookshops. Lane was adamant that his Penguins should appear in chain stores and tobacconists, and should cost no more than a packet of cigarettes.

Reading habits (and cigarette prices) have changed since 1935, but Penguin still believes in publishing the best books for everybody to enjoy. We still believe that good design costs no more than bad design, and we still believe that quality books published passionately and responsibly make the world a better place.

So wherever you see the little bird – whether it's on a piece of prize-winning literary fiction or a celebrity autobiography, political tour de force or historical masterpiece, a serial-killer thriller, reference book, world classic or a piece of pure escapism – you can bet that it represents the very best that the genre has to offer.

Whatever you like to read – trust Penguin.